D1599226

Swedish Foreign Policy during the
Second World War

# W. M. Carlgren

# Swedish Foreign Policy during the Second World War

Translated by
Arthur Spencer

St. Martin's Press
New York

Original Title: Wilhelm M. Carlgren,
*Svensk utrikespolitik 1939–1945*
Swedish edition published by
Allmänna Förlaget,
Stockholm 1973 for the
Royal Swedish Ministry for Foreign Affairs

English translation © Ernest Benn Limited, London, 1977

Printed litho in Great Britain
Library of Congress Catalog Card Number: 77 - 78681
ISBN: 0-312-78058-3
First published in the United States of America in 1977

# Contents

# List of illustrations

# List of maps

# Short biographies

Information about some prominent figures in Swedish foreign affairs 1939–1945 mentioned in the book. Other persons mentioned are listed in the Index

*Assarsson, Vilhelm*, born 1889, entered the Foreign Service 1916, counsellor in Washington 1923, in Moscow 1930, consul in Leningrad 1931, consul-general there 1933, envoy to Peru 1935, to Mexico 1938, to Soviet Union 1940–44, Deputy Secretary-General of Foreign Ministry 1944–53, †1974.

*Beck-Friis, Hans*, born 1893, entered the Foreign Service 1919, head of political department of Foreign Ministry 1931, chargé d'affaires in London 1938, envoy to Switzerland 1939, to Italy 1940, to Finland 1942, Secretary-General of Foreign Ministry 1947, ambassador to Denmark 1949–56.

*Boheman, Erik*, born 1895, entered the Foreign Service 1918, chief of political department of Foreign Ministry 1928, envoy to Turkey 1931, to Poland 1934, Secretary-General of Foreign Ministry 1938–45, envoy to France 1945–47, ambassador to Great Britain 1947–48, to United States 1948–58, MP 1959–70, Speaker of the Upper Chamber 1965–70.

*Boström, Wollmar*, born 1878, entered the Foreign Service 1905, counsellor in London 1913, Secretary-General of Foreign Ministry 1918, envoy to Spain 1923, to USA 1926–45, †1956.

*Gustaf V*, born 1858, King of Sweden 1907–†1950.

*Günther, Christian*, born 1886, author, various appointments in the civil service since 1916, private secretary to the Prime Minister 1924, head of commercial department of Foreign Ministry 1925, envoy to Argentina 1931, Secretary-General of Foreign Ministry 1934–37, envoy to Norway 1937–39, Foreign Minister 1939–45, envoy to Italy 1946–50, †1966.

*Hansson, Per Albin*, born 1885, working man, active in the Social Democratic party and political writer in leading party newspapers since 1905, member of party executive since 1911, MP 1918–46, Minister of Defence 1920, 1921–23, 1924–26, chairman of Social Democratic party 1925, party leader 1927–46, Prime Minister 1932–36, 1936–†1946.

*Hägglöf, Gunnar*, born 1904, entered the Foreign Service 1926, head of commercial department of Foreign Ministry 1939–44, Minister without Portfolio Oct.–Dec. 1939, envoy to Belgium 1944–46, to Soviet Union 1946–47, to United Nations 1947–48, ambassador to Great Britain 1948–67, to France 1967–71.

*von Post, Eric*, born 1899, entered the Foreign Service 1924, counsellor in Berlin 1939, head of political department of Foreign Ministry 1944–45, envoy to Turkey 1945–51, ambassador to Poland 1951–56, to Italy 1956–65.

*Prytz, Björn*, born 1887, managing director of AB Svenska Kullager-fabriken 1919–37, envoy to United Kingdom 1938–47, †1976.

*Richert, Arvid*, born 1887, entered the Foreign Service 1918, head of administrative department of Foreign Ministry 1928, of commercial department 1931, Permanent Under Secretary of State at Ministry of Commerce 1934, envoy to Germany 1937–45, Director-General, Board of Commerce, 1945–48, County Governor 1949–55.

*Sandler, Rickard*, born 1884, teacher, active in Social Democratic party, MP 1912–17, 1919–60, member of party governing board 1911–52, Minister without Portfolio 1920 and 1921–23, Minister of Commerce 1924–25, Prime Minister 1925–26, head of central bureau of statistics 1926–32, Foreign Minister 1932–36, 1936–39, County Governor 1941–50, †1964.

*Söderblom, Staffan*, born 1900, entered the Foreign Service 1921, head of political department of Foreign Ministry 1938–44, envoy to Soviet Union 1944–46, to Switzerland 1946–51, to China 1951–52.

*Thörnell, Olof*, born 1877, entered military service 1897, colonel 1928, major-general 1934, lieutenant-general and chief of defence staff 1937, Commander-in-Chief 1939–44.

*Undén, Östen*, born 1886, professor in civil law at Uppsala University 1917–37, Minister without Portfolio 1917–20, 1932–36, Minister of Justice 1920, Foreign Minister 1924–26, MP 1934–65, chancellor of Swedish universities 1937–51, legal adviser to Foreign Ministry 1920–24, 1926–32, 1936–45, Foreign Minister 1945–62, †1974.

*Wallenberg, Jacob*, born 1892, managing director of Stockholms Enskilda Bank 1927–46, Chairman of the Board 1950–69, member of the boards of various leading Swedish companies.

*Wallenberg, Marcus*, born 1899, vice managing director of Stockholms Enskilda Bank 1927–46, managing director 1946–58, Chairman of the Board 1969–71, Chairman of the Board of Skandinaviska Enskilda Banken 1972–76, member of the boards of various leading Swedish companies.

# Introduction

Geography plays a dominant role in the formulation of Swedish foreign policy. Sweden lies in the northern corner of Europe, separated from the European mainland by a large inland sea, the Baltic. Direct land communications with the Continent exist only in the desolate and sparsely populated districts along the north-eastern frontier with Finland. The Baltic separates Sweden from all land connections with the Great Powers. The Baltic has been at the centre of Sweden's policies since the Middle Ages.

During her period as a Great Power in the seventeenth century Sweden was also the dominant power in the Baltic. In the next century her possessions on the opposite shore of this sea, in the Baltic territories and Germany, were lost in various wars, and during the Napoleonic Wars at the beginning of the nineteenth century Russia conquered Finland, where Swedish rule had held sway since the early Middle Ages. Sweden thereby gained her present territorial limits. The basis of her foreign policy was further changed through her union with Norway, which was established in 1815 with the approval of the Great Powers of Europe. Norway entered the union as a junior partner, and it was expressly laid down that the union's foreign policy should be conducted from Stockholm.

1815 was a turning-point in Sweden's history. Sweden – apart from some transient exceptions – withdrew from Great Power politics. Whereas in earlier epochs the security of the realm had to a large extent been sought in alliances with, and subsidies from, Great Powers, now it became based on a policy of freedom from alliances, on efforts to avoid being drawn into Continental conflicts. Throughout the nineteenth century the international situation rendered this new course auspicious. On the European Continent there were no wars between Great Powers for half a century and, when they did come, they were short-lived. On

1

its periphery Britain and Russia balanced each other well. The interests and interventions of the Great Powers were to a significant degree concentrated on other parts of the world, and the Baltic region was much quieter than in previous centuries. The concert between the Great Powers of Europe, in spite of often basic differences of opinion and, on some occasions, open conflict, functioned as a factor for peace in numerous precarious situations. The belief that the development of international law could pave the way for a permanent peaceful coexistence between states grew ever stronger.

Total peace, however, had not yet arrived. On the southern shore of the Baltic three short wars saw the rise of Prussia as the leading Power of the German Reich; thereafter the new German Empire, with Prussia at its heart, became the most powerful state on the Continent. Rivalries between Britain, France, and Russia led to the Crimean War (1854–56), which involved Anglo-French naval operations in the Baltic. War between Britain and Russia was sometimes a threat in later years. Against such a background Sweden, on her own initiative, was several times near to launching warlike operations: against the Germanic Confederation in 1848; against Russia in 1856; and against Prussia-Austria in 1863. However, the final step to war was never taken and peace was maintained. Sweden's course thereafter became more cautious, not least thanks to a growing appreciation of her inadequate military resources compared with those of the Great Powers. Neutrality in war as a continuation of freedom from alliances in peace became for practical purposes self-evident. At the turn of the nineteenth century the main question was not Sweden's relationship with one or other of the Great Powers, but her relationship with Norway. Controversy over this bore at times a formalistic and moral stamp.

Norway abrogated the union in 1905. Its formal liquidation was achieved through negotiations between Sweden and Norway, without any intervention by the Great Powers. Swedish foreign policy got a new point of departure, and this in more unsettled circumstances than had obtained for many years. During Norway's first years as an independent state Stockholm at any rate judged the situation in the Scandinavian peninsula to be more unstable than formerly. At the same time relations between Germany, Russia, and Britain became more unsettled and more explosive. A war between Germany on the one side and Britain and Russia on the other must be expected to lead to large-scale operations right on Sweden's frontiers. (Finland at this date was a Russian grand duchy.) Pessimistic prophets foresaw the division of Scandinavia into three parts: Russia lording it in the north; Britain in the west; and Germany in the south. The liveliest discussion concerned the threat from the east; the building of railways in Finland, the harsher Russian rule there, Russian espionage in Sweden were seen by many as foreboding a Russian expansion westwards, through Sweden to the west coast of Norway. Protection against the Russian peril — which was also at the centre of spirited, often heated, disputes about defence and internal policy between Right and Left — was sought by some from a powerful Germany. But an alliance, or a more limited military agreement, for which cautious German soundings could open the way, was ruled out. Sweden's freedom from alliances and her adherence to neutrality in a war between the Great Powers were now too deeply rooted to be disturbed.

In 1914 Europe was hurled into war. After considerable successes for German arms, first in the West and then in the East, Berlin threw out repeated feelers to Stockholm for an alliance. In Germany's opinion, such a pact would bring attractive gains for Sweden at Russia's expense — the Åland Islands, a dominant position in Finland, and in the small countries south of the Gulf of Finland. The offer had advocates in Sweden, Queen Victoria (daughter of Grand Duke Frederick of Baden and Louise, daughter of Kaiser Wilhelm I), who actively worked on her husband, King Gustaf, and also some officials and academics. But the government, composed mainly of conservative officials, with Hjalmar Hammarskjöld, an eminent legal expert, as Prime Minister, and K. A. Wallenberg, a prominent banker, as Foreign Minister, resisted and refused. Moreover, intervention would not have been supported by the *Riksdag* or by public opinion. Sweden stood firm by the neutrality declared in August 1914.

True, during the first years of the war this neutrality leaned more towards Germany and her confederates than to their enemies. This state of affairs was connected with an inclination to favour Germany, a powerful neighbour extremely well equipped to wage offensive war. But Swedish foreign policy also aimed at enabling the government, with the help of international law, to preserve the greatest possible freedom of manoeuvre in trade policy against British and Allied blockade, and with it Sweden's trade with Germany. It soon became apparent, however, that the trade war waged by Britain had more significance than the law of nations. The Hammarskjöld government fell in March 1917, largely because of the Prime Minister's persistent wish to oppose British trade policy against Sweden. Succeeding wartime ministries, first the right-wing government of Swartz to October 1917, and then the Liberal-Social Democratic coalition under Edén and Branting, pursued a

3

more flexible policy of neutrality. It was not only the interests of the Great Powers which manifestly took precedence over the rule of law, but those of Sweden too. In 1918 the civil war in Finland, following the country's declaration of independence in December 1917, created difficulties for the Swedish government in both foreign and domestic affairs. Its attitude was often open to argument from the point of view of international law. All the same, Sweden stuck to her neutrality throughout the four years of war, outside a devastating Great Power conflict quite close to her own frontiers.

Neutrality thus gained a special glamour in Swedish eyes: a guarantee of escaping the havoc of a world war. But, intermittently at any rate, it had also been seen as something transcending Sweden's own interests; it had prepared the ground for Sweden's contribution to the service of a higher and more universal good. Hammarskjöld's declaration on the neutral's mission to safeguard for future generations essential rules of international law, won approval in many quarters. In fact Sweden, or, to put it more accurately, the Hammarskjöld government, could not live up to this declaration and was obliged, little by little, to put the country's survival before principles. Yet Hammarskjöld's attempt to hold the Great Powers to a system governed by the rules of international law makes him a forerunner of modern Swedish foreign policy. Neutrality had gained a moral dimension: the Great Powers, through their narrow nationalistic politics, had led their own and other peoples into a destructive war to protect their own interests; neutral Sweden had placed herself at the service of loftier ideals.

During the 1920s and 1930s different Swedish governments professed adherence to this latter aim – more or less consistently. And in the general haze of League of Nations illusions they departed – at least on the face of it – from Sweden's traditionally cautious foreign policy line and entered into far-reaching international commitments; in their political pronouncements solidarity between peoples was put forward as the aim of foreign policy and as a safeguard for smaller states. As tension grew between the Great Powers in the second half of the 1930s, however, a shift occurred. In step with the ever increasing fear of a fresh war between the Great Powers of Europe, international solidarity more and more became a side issue. Initiatives for a joint Nordic, or, more accurately, a Swedish-Finnish, defence policy also remained on paper. Once again, in the shadow of a threatening storm, neutrality became the guiding star for Sweden. The expectation – or, more correctly, the faith – that a policy of neutrality would enable Sweden to keep out of a second world war prevailed in the autumn of 1939 among politicians, officials, and the general public.

This faith was clearly of advantage to the government in its efforts to build a national unity around its foreign policy, which, according to a declaration issued on the first day of hostilities, aimed at complete neutrality. Suggestions that Sweden should of her own initiative join in the trial of strength between the Great Powers were from the outset doomed to discredit those who made them. The possibility of playing off the parties against one another, which the Great Powers had done to a certain extent in 1914–18, no longer existed. Unanimity on the need for Sweden to stay neutral thus prevailed. But on how to preserve neutrality in the various contingencies that might arise and on its judicial and moral significance and demands, there were conflicting opinions. Very soon, however, the concept became even more elastic than at any time during the First World War. 'It was widely and popularly believed', a minister stated in a crucial debate of June 1940, 'that a policy of neutrality was nothing beyond keeping out of the war. A declaration that the government intended to renounce this policy would be taken as signifying that the government wanted Sweden to opt for war'. The tradition of neutrality had bewitched men's minds. The term 'a policy of neutrality' covered all measures which served to keep Sweden out of war, whether or not they were consistent with the rules of neutrality in international law.

In June 1940, faith in neutrality as a means of keeping Sweden out of war was rather strained. Its empirical foundations – the fact that in previous wars and conflicts the Great Powers had not encroached on the territories of the Northern countries, even if they had made inroads on their rights – had been badly shaken during the months just passed. The North had been drawn directly into the military operations of the Great Powers, either because they themselves wanted bases on Nordic territory or because they wanted to keep their opponents from establishing them. Finland, Denmark, and Norway had been attacked for such reasons. Sweden had until now been left alone. But was she really less attractive to the Great Powers than the other Northern countries?

Throughout most of the war years Germany controlled not only Norway and Denmark, but also the entire Baltic east coast. Sweden was thus for long encircled by Germany, a fact reflected in Swedish foreign policy. The chances of extricating herself from this German grip obviously depended on the victory of Germany's opponents. In expectation of this – at first only in hope of it – the only reasonable Swedish course, and in this government and public opinion were of one mind, was to lie low, to take no unnecessary risks, and not to get tied up with any Great Power bloc. Differences of opinion arose time after time on what risks could be faced, but on the basic policy unity prevailed. In the final years of the war, when Germany's circumstances became ever more straitened and her ultimate defeat more certain, the government and public opinion sometimes drew further apart; the latter often wanted to adopt a more negative attitude to Germany than the government considered would serve Sweden's interests. But no demands to take part in the war were ever raised. Exactly as in 1914–18 the general feeling was that neutrality, the refusal to join Great Power blocs, was the line Sweden ought to follow for as long as possible.

In fact the Great Powers allowed Sweden to follow it. For none of them had Sweden a central strategic value. Germany's forward positions lay in Denmark, Norway, and Finland; if Sweden met German demands in the matter of exports and transit traffic and if Germany's opponents did not get a foothold there, no German occupation would be required. The Western Powers and the Soviet Union – except for some half-baked Anglo-French plans in winter 1940 – never saw the North as a decisive theatre of war; they let Germany hold on to Norway and Denmark to the last, they did not primarily seek to eliminate Finland as an opponent, and they never made any attempts to improve their positions in the North through operations against, or in concert with, Sweden (preliminary enquiries during the last week of the war about co-operation against the German troops in Norway excepted). Quite simply Sweden was not of sufficient interest to occasion military measures which would give a better return in other quarters, provided, of course, that she suitably met the demands and desires which the Great Powers from time to time considered appropriate.

Factors outside Sweden's control thus exerted a decisive influence on the success of Sweden's policy of neutrality in war. Her own determination to keep herself out of Great Power blocs and war was not by itself sufficient. It was also necessary that Sweden's resources or territory should not be judged by the Great Powers to be worth the price an attack would cost. This said, it must nevertheless be emphasized that during the war years, perhaps more than at any other time, a skilful foreign policy was required of Sweden, a policy which resolutely guarded her own interests without at the same time challenging the Great Powers, with possibly disastrous results. Their demands were often harsh and far-reaching. In 1940–41 and 1944–45, when the balance of power was upset, Sweden's room for manoeuvre was extremely limited. The veil which the rules of neutrality drew over various moves dictated by political reality was thin, sometimes indeed rent. Sweden's policy of neutrality, the Swedish Foreign Minister, Christian Günther, asserted in a speech of 1943, was shaped by world events. But it was solid at the core. Sweden, Günther clearly brought out, was determined to oppose by force of arms any attack and any attempt by one side or the other to drag her into the war. And this – to keep Sweden outside the war –

is indeed the aim of our policy of neutrality, and all problems concerning the application of such a policy, or which otherwise touch on neutrality, must be solved with this main goal before our eyes. And, it is from this viewpoint that Sweden's neutrality during the war of the Great Powers must be considered and judged.

The account that follows seeks to plot the course of Swedish foreign policy in the storm of the Second World War. Its central theme consists of diplomatic activity, since in the first instance it was precisely in this area that Sweden's contacts with the Great Powers took place. Defence policy has been touched on only incidentally. Foreign policy was throughout the first line of defence.

The book tries to cover the central events and lines of Swedish foreign policy during the period 1939–45, but does not aim to describe the development of Swedish-German, Swedish-British, etc., relations during the war years. Stockholm's role as a meeting-place for discussions between representatives of various foreign powers or as a convenient place for the gathering of intelligence about any country has not been investigated. First-hand reports of these activities are obviously not to be found in Swedish sources.

It has not been the intention to discuss disputed issues: the Scandinavian governments' foreknowledge of the German attack against Norway and Denmark in April 1940; the so-called 'abdication crisis' in Stockholm during midsummer 1941; or Swedish-Norwegian relations at the end of the war. Press and public opinion and debate have for reasons of space been only summarily treated.

This book is a shortened version of a larger work in Swedish, commissioned by the Swedish government and published in 1973. The account has been based first on documents in the archives of the Swedish Ministry for Foreign Affairs. Second, notes by different government members then active have been drawn upon. German and British sources have been used only to a limited extent, primarily to throw light on particularly interesting questions and on the Great Powers' general attitude towards Sweden.

The English version omits reports of Swedish government and *Riksdag* discussions. These were considered to be of less interest to a foreign reader than the factual account of the policy which Sweden followed. The character of the original text, as a description of specific positions adopted and their background, has nevertheless been retained, since in my view it reflects the conditions governing Swedish foreign policy during the war years. There has been some updating, especially with very recent works in mind. At the end of the book a summary of sources and relevant literature is given. For fuller and more detailed information the reader is referred to the Swedish edition.

I am indebted to Mr Arthur Spencer for all his work in rendering the Swedish draft of this book into English. I am grateful to Mr Gunnar Sandberg, formerly Legal Adviser, International Law, to the Swedish Foreign Ministry, who read the manuscript and gave me much valuable advice. Mr Allan Kastrup in New York has been kind enough to go through the typescript and has made many useful suggestions. Finally my special thanks to Mr John Collis of Ernest Benn for his kind interest and assistance in editing the typescript.

*Stockholm,*                                                      *W.M. Carlgren*
*March 1977*

# 1 The new balance of power in the Baltic and the war in Europe

## The war approaches

The inter-war period 1919–39 was, for the foreign policy of Sweden as for that of so many other countries, the era of illusions *par préférence*. Her leading politicians, in particular the Social Democrats Hjalmar Branting, Östen Undén, and Rickard Sandler, believed in the capacity of the League of Nations to lay a new and lasting foundation for peace. They worked assiduously to safeguard and to enlarge the League's potential for this. During these decades Swedish foreign policy was mostly conducted with its sights on Geneva, and its big questions were League issues: the Corfu incident, the Geneva protocol, disarmament, the Italo-Abyssinian conflict, and the failure of sanctions. Swedish politicians, representatives of a small country without significant resources in power politics and on the periphery of Europe, participated with enthusiasm, and sometimes not without success, in the deliberations and decisions of the Great Powers at Geneva. Concern for the maintenance of neutrality in the shifts and changes in the balance of power among those states, which in earlier times had dominated Swedish foreign policy, faded into the background. In the prevailing circumstances such concern appeared unnecessary or, at any rate, not pressing. After the peace treaties at Brest-Litovsk and Versailles, Russia and Germany had been reduced to second-rank countries, and the leading victorious powers, Britain and France, on the whole showed no great interest in Baltic affairs.

The course of events, however, gradually took a direction quite different from that envisaged in the illusions surrounding the League of Nations. This development had a sobering effect on Swedish foreign policy, which became obvious in the later 1930s. The League of Nations had not been able to prevent Japan from waging war in China, or Italy from conquering Abyssinia, or Germany from revising the Treaty of Versailles step by step. Nor had the League been able to

9

prevent the rivalries between these countries, on the one hand, and Britain and France, on the other, from assuming proportions which threatened the maintenance of peace. The disadvantage a small country then had to suffer as a member of the League of Nations, being compelled to follow its rules of solidarity in support of a member state under attack, became increasingly apparent. In 1936 Sweden, along with the other Northern countries, began a retreat from the policy of solidarity back to that of neutrality. Repeatedly and jointly they declared their intention not to be bound by provisions in the League covenant which involved obligations dangerous to their neutrality. The Northern countries stated time and again that as a uniform, closely interrelated group of states they wished to go their own way, avoiding any encroachment on the interests of the Great Powers. However, they seem never to have made deliberate efforts to establish a firm and extended co-operation. Certainly, at several meetings between Foreign Ministers and experts a joint policy in case of a Great Power war was discussed. During the Munich crisis in September 1938, when the danger of war in Europe was greater than at any time since 1914, the Foreign Ministers agreed that if war broke out, they would adjust their policies and hold consultations on how the common interest of remaining outside the conflict could best be served.

However, all manifestations of a common purpose notwithstanding, each of the four Northern countries assessed its position in regard to the surrounding Great Powers differently. Norway did not consider herself threatened. Denmark considered herself threatened by Germany; Finland by the Soviet Union. Sweden could not definitely decide whether danger threatened from the South or the East, from Germany or from the Soviet Union. Political co-operation between them, following the traditions of the war years of 1914–18 (then limited to Denmark, Norway, and Sweden) and of Geneva in the 1920s and 1930s, was of obvious value: it could give added weight to their views and arguments as well as prevent the Great Powers from dividing the Northern countries by playing off one against another. But there was little or no prospect that an undertaking of co-operation would be offered to another Northern country if that would involve accepting an increased risk of war. Only one attempt at genuine military and political collaboration was made in the face of the ever-growing threat of a Great Power war in Europe: the Swedish-Finnish Stockholm Plan of July 1938 for a joint defence of the Åland Islands and the adjacent sea-lanes into the Gulf of Bothnia (consequently to the harbour of Luleå, from which was exported the iron-ore so important for the economy and war industry of Germany).

Discussions on this matter between the Stockholm and Helsinki governments had begun in April 1938 under the impact of Austria's *Anschluss* to Germany and Hitler's entry into Vienna some weeks earlier. Despite many doubts in both government and *Riksdag* — Sweden had not entered into any military engagements in support of other countries since the mid-nineteenth century — the Foreign Minister, Rickard Sandler, succeeded in slowly pushing his plan forward. After a year, in April 1939, the Chiefs of the Swedish and Finnish Defence Staffs agreed on detailed plans for the joint defence of Åland and the adjoining shipping-lanes.

The Stockholm Plan, however, at any rate for Sweden, was not only a Swedish-Finnish question. Åland was, under the 1921 Åland Convention, a neutralized and demilitarized area. Some measures envisaged in the Plan entailed changes in the Convention, and the Swedish government considered it necessary to obtain for them the consent of the parties to the Convention and also of the Soviet Union, which had not signed it — a fact which in Stockholm had long been considered a serious disadvantage in attempts to keep the island group as well as Sweden and Finland out of international complications. The intention, once the parties to the Convention and the Soviet Union had agreed to the Stockholm Plan, was that the Council of the League of Nations — which under the Convention in certain circumstances was to decide on help to Finland to defend Åland against an aggressor — should give its final approval at a meeting in May 1939. In the preceding months, however, relations between the Great Powers, which had been relatively stable after the Munich Agreement, underwent fundamental changes. German troops marched into Prague on 15 March. Bohemia-Moravia became a German protectorate and Slovakia a German satellite state. On 31 March, Britain, with the aim of forestalling fresh German actions, gave Poland a guarantee that she would come to her aid if there was a clear threat to her independence. On 7 April Italy attacked Albania and rapidly conquered it. The Soviet Union, which at Munich had been kept out of the inner circle of great powers, had her international position strengthened; the Western Powers wanted her co-operation in their attempt to hold Hitler back, even if they did not see themselves obliged to pay a particularly high price for it.

The deterioration in the international situation called forth numerous precautionary measures in Stockholm. The *Riksdag* approved a number of defence appropriations. The Chief of the Defence Staff

presented the government with proposals for a comprehensive new
defence plan. The Secretary-General in the Ministry for Foreign
Affairs, with the approval of the Foreign Minister, submitted to the
government a draft of instructions to Swedish Heads of Mission as
guidance for their conversations. These instructions were never sent
out, most probably because the government would not commit itself
to any forecasts. But they do show most graphically what the Foreign
Ministry's assessment of Sweden's position in a war between the Great
Powers would be and merit reproducing in full:

In the field of foreign policy the situation has increasingly developed
to the point where two coalitions of great powers may be seen
opposed to each other. On the one side stand Germany and Italy, with
whom Japan, Spain, and Hungary maintain an at present ill-defined co-
operation; on the other Britain and France, to whom Poland now
appears to be bound by a defensive alliance. The latter coalition
furthermore appears to count on the support of the Soviet Union and
also of the United States. Certain lesser states particularly open to
pressure from Greater Germany conduct an undecided policy, others
appear to seek the support of the coalition of the Western Powers,
and others again have openly declared their intention of adopting a
neutral position in the event of a conflict.

Among these latter states are the Northern countries. The Swedish
government has on repeated occasions stated emphatically that its
intention is to declare itself neutral in a conflict between the Great
Powers of Europe. This policy is certainly embraced by an absolutely
overwhelming majority of the people of Sweden and by a virtually
unanimous *Riksdag*.

The neutrality envisaged on the Swedish side in the event of
conflict would in significant aspects be different from that upheld in
the World War of 1914–18. The situation has changed in very many
respects. The rules of international law which then, at any rate in the
earlier phase, contributed to making the maintenance of neutrality
easier, must to a large extent be considered to have become invalid,
and, all in all, in a new conflict regard for international law may be
expected to be very slight or non-existent. The military and political
situation has changed. The Baltic Sea may thus be expected in large
measure to be dominated by German naval forces, and the development of modern air forces has in quite a new way made Sweden
vulnerable from various quarters.

The prospects for the maintenance of neutrality must be
considered to lie in the fact that it will be to the interest of both coalitions involved in the conflict that Sweden should not be dragged into
the war; in the fact that the Swedish military establishment is of a

size sufficient to command respect; and, finally, in so strong an internal unity in Sweden that any foreign interference is ruled out.

For Germany no interest appears to be served by driving Sweden over to the coalition of Western Powers. In this way a further link would merely be added to the dreaded chain of encirclement. The striking-down of Sweden would certainly call for not insignificant military sacrifices, which can hardly be deemed acceptable provided that Germany is at the same time committed on the Western Front as well as in the East. A Sweden joined to Germany inside the ruthlessly applied blockade of the Western Powers would furthermore not reduce, but at an early date increase, the troubles Germany already has with her supplies.

Germany has an important interest in obtaining from Sweden certain raw materials, primarily perhaps iron-ore. No transit export to Germany, comparable to that carried on in the first year of the World War, can now be counted on by Germany, nor can Germany hope that Sweden would deprive herself of her own goods essential for the sustenance of the Swedish people.

Export of other raw materials can, however, be expected to take place to a certain extent. This must, apart from Sweden's own economic interests, be limited by the consideration that the possibilities of maintaining neutrality should not be put in jeopardy.

For the Western Powers as well the maintenance of neutrality appears to be of overwhelming interest. It would certainly be tempting to try to compel Sweden to join the encircling chain, but by doing so the Western Powers run the risk that Sweden would be subjugated and that Swedish raw materials, especially iron-ore, would fall into German hands. The appearance of, for example, .the fleets of the Western Powers in the Baltic can hardly be expected. The Western Powers should therefore now, as during the First World War, be open to persuasion that it would be better to have Sweden remain neutral and continue – admittedly to an extent conditioned and limited by the above-mentioned considerations – to maintain her trading ties with Germany than for Sweden to be dragged into the war.

It is evident that the policy of neutrality here outlined will be subjected to extremely strong pressures. To a certain extent neutrality must in its realization be 'negotiated', above all in the commercial sphere. But the political and strategic prerequisites for its maintenance by no means appear ruled out. At all events the Swedish government is firmly resolved to try to carry out such a policy in close co-operation with other Northern governments and under the greatest possible material and moral collaboration with them.

This guidance on Sweden's policy of neutrality has been communicated to Your Excellency to serve as background for your remarks in any forthcoming conversations you may see fit to hold. It is obviously important that there should on both sides be an understanding of Sweden's position and of the Swedish government's intentions in case a Great Power conflict of the sort mentioned does in fact break out.

The Foreign Ministry's assessment was thus that the expected struggle between the Great Powers would in essentials follow the same pattern as in 1914—18, even if weapons now had a longer range and were more effective, and even if less regard for the rules of international law could be expected. Sweden – and other Northern lands – should have the prospect of again staying out of a major war, although this time under even greater pressure than on the former occasion.

After Mussolini's *coup* against Albania a fresh period of comparative political calm ensued. But the Great Powers had entered upon more intensive diplomatic manoeuvres than before, and the Northern countries also were directly involved. In response to an appeal for peace and negotiations from President Roosevelt, Hitler at the end of April invited a number of European countries, among them the four Northern ones, to conclude non-aggression agreements. Intensive deliberations followed between the four governments, but no common approach could be established. Norway, Finland, and Sweden courteously declined with thanks, while Denmark, which lay nearest to Germany and could not risk ignoring the fact that Hitler might wish to move the frontier in Slesvig northwards to where it ran before 1919, accepted the invitation.

Further evidence of the limits to the co-operation of the Northern countries in regard to the Great Powers was forthcoming some weeks later when, at the end of May, the Soviet government in forthright and stern language refused to approve the Stockholm Plan, stating that the interest of the Soviet Union in the fortification of the Åland Islands was greater than that of Sweden. The Finnish government, even after this Soviet declaration – and even without the formal approval of the League of Nations, which Moscow's attitude ruled out – was willing to go ahead with the Plan; and at the beginning of June, the Finnish parliament voted funds for starting the fortification of the Åland Islands. The Swedish government, however, wavered and withdrew the bill which had already been placed before the *Riksdag*. The Swedish government thereby accorded to the Soviet Union a *de facto* veto in fortifying Åland. During the summer of 1939 Moscow was thus able to reject, quite unruffled, fresh Swedish and Finnish attempts to talk them into a more favourable attitude to the Stockholm Plan.

The *démarches* in Moscow were made under gloomy omens. Available information on the negotiations then going on between the

Western Powers and the Soviet Union concerning an alliance revealed that Moscow regarded Finland as a Soviet sphere of interest and sought to induce the Western Powers to accept that view. Finland tried in London, with cautious Swedish support, to gain understanding for her efforts to be allowed to continue her policy of Nordic orientation outside the Great Power blocs. Her representations met with a benevolent, but not entirely reassuring, response. During the summer's British-French-Russian negotiations in Moscow the Northern countries' prospects of pursuing a joint policy of neutrality in the event of a conflict between the Great Powers became more doubtful than before.

Against this darkening scene the Soviet-German non-aggression agreement, signed during Ribbentrop's visit to Moscow on 23 August, was almost welcome news in Stockholm. A war between Great Powers in the Baltic, which had broken out in August 1914 and had been feared both in September 1938 and April 1939, appeared no longer an immediate threat. On several points the agreement clearly left a door open for far-reaching collaboration between Berlin and Moscow in various fields. But there was hardly a sure basis for general concern about the consequences of such co-operation for the parties' neighbouring countries, Poland excepted – the secret additional protocol, in which, among other things, Germany acknowledged that Latvia, Estonia, and Finland belonged to the Soviet Union's sphere of interest, being still unknown. The overwhelming feeling was relief that the pressure which the negotiations between Britain, France, and the Soviet Union and the Soviet demands for guarantees had brought upon Finland, and thus to a lesser extent upon Sweden also, had now ended; and that German military action against Poland, which as the days passed was regarded as more and more inevitable, would not, as feared earlier, give rise to a Great Power war in the Baltic. Only a few people thought back as far as the Tilsit agreement of 1807 between Emperor Napoleon and Tsar Alexander, as part of which Finland was handed over to Russia.

Nor was the optimistic view that Sweden would be able to keep herself out of an approaching war between the Great Powers entirely without foundation. During the Munich crisis emphatic assurances had been given in Berlin that Germany had absolutely no offensive plans against Sweden in case of war, provided that Sweden observed neutrality and maintained her exports to Germany, especially of iron-ore. There was no indication that these assurances were not still valid. Britain (and France) could be expected, as in 1914–18, to carry out a policy of strict blockade, but hardly without first giving Sweden an

*Enlistment, autumn 1939*

opportunity to negotiate. The Soviet Union had shown negligible interest in Sweden's policy in a Great Power war. There was hardly any fear of more exacting demands from this quarter so long as Sweden could preserve her neutrality. And, as mentioned above, the prospects for this were, after the Moscow agreement in August 1939, rated better than for a long time.

Since the Swedish government did not see any immediate dangers threatening Sweden, the measures it took at the outset, 1–3 September, were comparatively limited. A declaration of neutrality was issued and corresponding action taken in regard to shipping-lanes, harbours, and so forth. The degree of readiness of the armed forces was raised; not more than 70,000 men, however, were called to the colours. A ban was promulgated on the export of certain items. On the whole, Sweden's policy of neutrality was adapted to a war footing without undue strain. 1914, said King Gustaf V to his ministers on 1 September, had been much worse than 1939; then, in the first days of the war perpetual conferences with foreign envoys had been held and the danger of Sweden becoming involved had been greater.

## The start of wartime trade policy

The dangers and difficulties which a doctrinaire and inflexible neutrality policy had inflicted on trade during the previous war had at all costs to be avoided. To reach long-term trade agreements with London and Berlin was therefore a matter of urgent priority in Stockholm. Since there was more trade to the west, an agreement with Britain was the first goal. But discussions with Britain implied a sort of double bargaining. For the Swedes freedom of action was considerably restricted by attention to German demands. These were at this time uncertain, but in the first instance must be assumed to involve an unchanged, or even increased, export of iron-ore. An agreement with Britain had to be reached in a very short time to clear the way for an agreement with Germany, which could not be put aside for too long. The obvious and basic premise in relation to both Britain and Germany was that, as far as humanly possible, normal trade and freedom of movement should be maintained. But the government was aware that some restrictions were unavoidable, and from the beginning took steps to prevent a sudden and excessive increase in trade with Germany similar to the one in 1914. An extensive ban on exports was promulgated on 8 September.

Swedish-British negotiations began in London at the end of September. Since Sweden was the first neutral country the British negotiated with and since, moreover, Swedish exports of iron-ore to Germany were one of the main targets of Britain's wartime trade policy, it took some time to reach an agreement. The texts were signed on 7 December. However, in all essentials they had been ready for some weeks. Both governments indicated in a short agreement their intention of trying to maintain the exchange of goods at the normal level; and the British government further undertook to practise its contraband control in such a way that it did not place undue restrictions on normal Swedish imports. A Joint Standing Commission would be established to handle matters of trade policy which required adjustment. In a unilateral declaration the Swedish government promised not to re-export certain specified goods (by and large Sweden's overseas imports), except in certain closely defined cases (including re-export of the above products to the Northern countries and export of finished products which did not contain more than 12½ per cent of the specified goods) and to maintain its total exports at the level of 1938 (with certain minor variations being allowed). The British government, also in a unilateral declaration, promised to ensure that re-export guarantees were not required for certain goods to Sweden and to speed up the contraband control procedure. Exchanges of letters contained modifications and reservations to the above texts and in addition separate agreements

17

were concluded on payments and shipping: thus the Swedish tonnage, which was not required for Sweden's trade with Britain or for her seaborne imports, would be chartered to the British. The whole arrangement – commonly described as the 1939 War Trade Agreement – was to come into force on 20 December; but in expectation of an equivalent Swedish-German settlement its existence was kept secret.

The 1939 agreement was a great success for Sweden's war trade policy and for its negotiators, above all for the Secretary-General at the Ministry for Foreign Affairs, Erik Boheman, and the banker, Marcus Wallenberg. Guarantees for continued trade to the West, with its seaborne imports so important for Sweden's survival, had been provided for without unduly protracted negotiations and without Sweden assuming unreasonable or hazardous obligations in return. The rapid and comprehensive Swedish ban on exports in September, the obvious desire to reach a quick, all-embracing settlement, had been appreciated by the British. Very soon, it is true, more critical comments were heard – the Swedes were altogether too anxious to earn money, altogether too afraid of running any risks with the Germans.

A quick settlement was desirable also to the British, both in order to gain control of such Swedish tonnage as Sweden herself did not need, and to limit the Swedish export of iron-ore to its pre-war level before the Germans could get it increased. The Swedish negotiators gave no explicit undertakings in respect of iron-ore exports apart from the general promise to maintain them at the 1938 level. The British obviously considered this level to be about 8 million tons (whereas, if exports to German-occupied Czechoslovakia and Poland were to be included, the estimate could be raised to over 10 million tons). The British also appear to have counted on an oral Swedish promise that there would be technical obstacles to exports of iron-ore, while the Swedish delegates, according to their interpretation, had said no more than that exports would be kept at the lowest level justified on technical grounds. The British also took for granted that the ore-carriers on their way south from Narvik had to navigate outside Norwegian territorial waters at some points, and then could be detained by British naval forces: the Swedes had not demurred. The policy of blockade played a dominant role in the British war effort. It also attached great importance to Sweden's iron-ore exports to Germany. When one takes into account too the advantage the British held in the negotiations, it must be acknowledged that the Swedish negotiators were remarkably successful.

Despite the favourable outcome of the London negotiations it was obvious that Sweden's imports from the West must become both more difficult and more expensive. Sweden was therefore obliged to rely more heavily on Germany for her needs, particularly in regard to coal and coke (since Poland had disappeared as a supplier and transport from Britain had become more difficult), steel products, chemical products (fertilizers), machinery, and instruments. Furthermore, the Swedes were extraordinarily anxious to start talks with the Germans about their methods of waging the trade war, partly because Swedish ships were being sunk on their way to England, partly because those bound for Holland, Belgium, and the United States were being detained for contraband inspection. (The Germans has as long a list of contraband as the British.) Moreover, in order to disrupt more effectively the sea trade between Baltic ports and Britain, and to deny the Baltic to British submarines, Germany wanted to extend her mining of Öresund inside the four-mile limit of Swedish territorial waters, a limit which Sweden had maintained for a century and a half, even though in the First World War no action had been taken to prevent German mine-laying inside it off Falsterbo. Here Sweden had a most important interest to protect. Because of the depth of the sea off Falsterbo a vessel drawing more than 5 metres could pass from the Baltic to the Kattegatt inside Swedish territorial waters only if these had a four-mile limit, and the most powerful ships in the Swedish navy, three small battleships, drew nearly 7 metres.

Against this background the Swedish negotiators, led by the Swedish Minister in Berlin, Arvid Richert, and banker Jacob Wallenberg, tried a low opening bid: 7 million tons of iron-ore for 1940. They wanted to get a German undertaking both to increase German deliveries and to promise a more considerate conduct of the war at sea. Swedish import requirements were treated by the German negotiators with great understanding. They refused, however, to discuss the war at sea. Nor did they accept the Swedish view about normal exports – i.e., that the 1933–38 average was normal but not that of 1937–38. This implied that the development of Swedish-German trade would be to Britain's advantage, and would thus be un-neutral. In these circumstances no agreement could be reached. In mid-November the discussions were adjourned. At the end of the month the Germans laid mines up to 3 miles off Falsterbo. The Swedish government protested sharply but bowed to the inevitable. Following the precedent of the First World War, orders were issued that rules of neutrality should not be enforced for more than 3 miles out to sea.

The German action shook the Swedish government, which had

expected more consideration for Sweden in Berlin. But the possibility of taking a strong line was slight. It was further diminished when, a few days later, the Soviet Union attacked Finland and Sweden's situation at once became much more serious than hitherto. Sweden had to support Finland against the Soviet Union and could not afford to challenge both Great Powers in the Baltic. She therefore had to be far more accommodating towards Germany.

This was the background of a thorough revision of Sweden's tactics in the negotiations. The question of the war at sea was divorced from the trade negotiations and whereas in November a figure no higher than 7 million tons of iron-ore a year had been mentioned, in the first week of December a hint of 10 million tons was given privately to the chief German negotiator. This figure was obtained by including the 1938 figures for Poland and Czechoslovakia, and thus was not contrary to the agreement with Britain. This offer immediately broke the ice. After some weeks of discussions in Berlin, on 22 December an agreement was concluded on the exchange of goods for 1940. It went far towards satisfying Sweden's extensive requirements for increased German exports to Sweden. Swedish exports to Germany would in general be based on the 1938 figures; there would be no decrease in wood-products and pulp, while for about thirty categories of goods (copper, rubber, lead, and so forth) Sweden's own stocks (as well as her undertaking to Britain) ruled out exports. The agreement also contained a general provision for fixing the prices of iron-ore in relation to those of coal, coke, and iron and steel products. For 1940 they would in principle be stabilized at their level before 1 September 1939.

Sweden's negotiating position towards Germany was in some respects stronger than towards Britain. The discussions were not about a war trade agreement for the whole of her Western trade for an unspecified period, but about the Swedish-German exchange of goods in 1940. It was not a question of a new venture, but of negotiating in a long-established framework where one had old contacts. The Germans needed Swedish iron-ore, of vital importance to their industry, and, to pay for it, they had to increase their exports to Sweden. At the same time, however, attention had to be given to political considerations, which required concessions to Germany's demands in order as far as possible to avoid mistrust and friction. During the autumn, leading German circles had clearly adopted a more severe attitude towards Sweden. The reason was primarily the attitude of the Swedish press. The German Foreign Ministry considered it spiteful and one-sided; and it was pointed out to the Swedish Minister in Berlin that Hitler and

Ribbentrop were kept continually informed of anti-German articles and remarks. Sweden, Richert summed up in November,

is regarded among the leaders of the German Reich as a country unfriendly to Germany, in which sympathy with Germany's enemies is unconcealed and commonly expressed, and the Swedish government is not considered to have done what, in the German view, it could have done to check anti-German utterances and activities.

The Soviet attack on Finland of 30 November added to Sweden's predicament; and her position deteriorated.

Further discussions took place in Stockholm during January 1940. Jacob Wallenberg negotiated skilfully and succeeded in getting agreement on iron-ore prices in relation to those of coal, etc., and arrived at figures advantageous to Sweden. By this settlement, known as the 'price-balance', prices for the major imports from Germany were stabilized, unlike the prices of goods coming from the West. As subsequently during the war years, there was only very little trade with the West, while trade with the continent of Europe increased proportionately, the fact that this 'price-balance' already existed became even more advantageous to Sweden than at its inception.

By Christmas 1939, the Swedish trade negotiations with Britain and Germany were safely home and dry. Very short communiqués were issued first on the German, then on the British, agreements. The press was privately requested to abstain from comment – statements in the press which could prompt the British and the Germans to pry too closely into Sweden's undertakings to the other party were obviously unwelcome. In this case developments in the war were helpful; for, at the turn of the year, Finland's struggle against the Soviet Union virtually monopolized the interest of the press and the general public.

The war at sea had been intensified in November by both sides. German mines were laid off the east coast of England, and, as mentioned above, the Germans also took steps to obstruct the approaches to the Baltic. Britain reacted by a decision to seize at sea all goods of German origin. Consequently the war at sea also hurt Swedish trade and shipping. Gradually, however, both with the British and the Germans arrangements were reached allowing Swedish vessels easier passage than in the first months of the war. The two trade agreements brought about a feeling of confidence in both Berlin and London that Sweden was determined to maintain normal trade and not to make exceptions for the benefit of one side or the other. Up to the German attack on Norway and Denmark on 9 April 1940 Sweden's trade and shipping were thus able to carry on in circumstances which were, even

21

though there was a war on, comparatively favourable. Goods essential for the sustenance of the Swedish people could be imported and not insignificant stocks built up.

Although nobody could predict how long the war would last, the agreements entered into in December 1939 with Britain and Germany could be assumed to guarantee supplies for the Swedish people and the Swedish economy for the forseeable future. Both belligerent camps had acknowledged Sweden's policy of neutrality and were willing to permit Swedish trade with the outside world. Nevertheless, they by no means recognized or accepted all Sweden's interests or policies. Germany refused to accept the four-mile limit for Swedish territorial waters and registered obvious dissatisfaction with Swedish public opinion and with the Swedish government's failure to guide it on the right path. Britain noted with disappointment what she considered to be Sweden's exaggerated regard for Germany and her interest in short-term gains. The danger that Sweden would be squeezed much harder by the belligerents was plainly there. Yet meanwhile the balance between Britain and Germany in matters of trade, which the Swedish government, on the basis of the experiences in 1914–18, judged to be the main problem in the present war too, had been well maintained. Sweden's trade policy had been successfully switched over from peacetime to wartime conditions.

## Sweden and the Finnish-Soviet negotiations before the Winter War

In a matter of weeks in September Britain and France had seen their ally Poland crushed without themselves taking the offensive against Germany. But they were certainly not prepared to make peace. If Hitler wanted to end the war, he had to seek a decision in the West by force of arms. In the late autumn he issued in instalments directives for a major offensive, but time after time for various reasons withheld the definite order to attack. As winter began, the Great Powers' armies on the continent had still not done battle with each other. Meanwhile the Soviet Union had begun to reap the profits of the August agreement in Moscow. From 17 September her troops had swept across the Polish frontier. On a second visit to Moscow by Ribbentrop a new German-Soviet agreement was reached on 26 September, which confirmed the fourth partition of Poland and, at the same time, put Lithuania in the Soviet sphere of interest. In return, Germany obtained a more favourable realignment of her new eastern frontier than in August.

At the end of September the Moscow regime opened negotiations with its small Baltic neighbours, all of which had now been acknowledged by Germany to belong to the Soviet sphere, with a demand to lease naval and air bases in their territories. Without support from Germany, Estonia, Latvia, and Lithuania had no other choice but to agree quickly. However, when, on 5 October, Finland's turn came, Stalin met vastly more intractable negotiators. The Finns refused to agree to the Soviet demands for a defence treaty, for frontier adjustments and – the most important point – for a base at Hanko at the entrance to the Gulf of Finland. Stalin wished to reach an agreement by negotiation and in three rounds of discussions made big reductions in his original demands, even finally about Hanko. But the Finnish government still considered the Soviet demands excessive: approval of them would jeopardize the continuation of its policy of neutrality. Nor did it consider Soviet military action likely either. When the final round of negotiations ended on 13 November, Finnish ministers believed that their resolute behaviour had, at any rate for a while, fended off any Soviet forward moves. But just as in the beginning Moscow misjudged Helsinki, so now Helsinki misjudged Moscow. Stalin had by no means abandoned his aims. On 30 November the Red Army attacked on a broad front across the Finnish frontier, not merely to enforce the demands he had made earlier in the negotiations but to incorporate Finland in the Soviet Union. In the frontier town of Terijoki, which the Finns had immediately evacuated, he installed a Finnish communist satellite regime under Otto Kuusinen and announced that he considered this, his own creation, to be the real government of Finland.

Helsinki had several times asked Stockholm for help and support during the negotiations and continued to do so during the subsequent war. At first, Finnish approaches were of a private nature and directed by the Finnish Foreign Minister, Eljas Erkko, personally to his Swedish colleague, Sandler. The latter had been the leading protagonist of the Stockholm Plan ever since the spring of 1938. He also envisaged the prospects of Swedish troops defending Åland, whether Finland went to war or not. He now proposed to the Swedish government undertakings to help Finland defend the Åland Islands and the shipping-lanes around them. The government was certainly prepared to go to war to defend Sweden against a foreign attacker. But it was not prepared to allow the Foreign Minister to saddle Sweden with undertakings towards Finland which, even if they did not go as far as those envisaged in the Stockholm Plan, could drag the country into war as a result of negotiations in Moscow which the government had no possibility of influenc-

23

ing. Sweden's aid to Finland was limited to deliveries of war material and to diplomatic support, and the Prime Minister, Per Albin Hansson, informed various members of the Finnish government both orally and in writing that Swedish military assistance should not be counted on. That Sweden, resources permitting, should afford diplomatic and material support to Finland was generally agreed within the government, in the *Riksdag*, and by public opinion.

Sweden's aid did not significantly improve Finland's negotiating position. True, the deliveries of war material were important for Finland, but because of Sweden's own shortage of arms were not particularly large in absolute terms. Diplomatic *démarches* made both in Moscow and in the capitals of other great powers were on the whole ineffectual. Moscow rejected what it considered Sweden's attempt to intervene in the Soviet Union's dealing with a former Russian possession in its own sphere of interest. The governments of other Great Powers naturally enough concentrated their efforts and resources on the hostilities already in train in Europe and showed slight interest in the fate of Finland. Nonetheless, Sweden's support for Finland was more determined and wholehearted than that of any other country. Furthermore, the Swedish public almost unanimously, and more openly than usual in Sweden, took the side of Finland against the Soviet Union. Consequently even Finnish inner circles gained the impression that Sweden's official attitude was above all tactical, aimed at encouraging Finland's willingness to negotiate. Hansson's negative reply to the request for armed help was not felt to be Sweden's last word. If the worst happened and the Soviet Union attacked Finland, Swedish public opinion would surely force a military intervention in Finland.

To what extent this interpretation influenced Helsinki's refusal to comply with Moscow's demands is a question which must here be left unanswered. But one may ask whether the Swedish government, in order to avoid all dangers of misunderstanding, could not have made its position clearer in Helsinki. It was obviously to Finland's advantage during the Moscow discussions that a veil had been drawn over Sweden's retreat from her Åland policy of 1938 and all its forward implications. Nevertheless, it would have been more honourable and more proper officially to make clear to the Finns that solidarity would stop at diplomatic support, deliveries of war material, and displays of public opinion. However, such a definite statement would have implied an open and directly humiliating negation of the previous Åland and Nordic co-operation policies and Sandler, their foremost champion, was personally not prepared to take such a step. Quite the contrary. He consistently increased Sweden's contribution to Finland as far as possible. But he was not really up to being Foreign Minister in wartime: his assessments and proposals on the policy Sweden should follow were inadequate; he spoke in private against the government's official line; in his relations with colleagues and foreign diplomats he was gauche and arrogant. When Russia's attack on Finland brought forth official Finnish requests that Swedish troops be sent to Åland and Sandler recommended a positive reply, his position was already undermined: the government refused to follow him and his pro-Finnish line was thereby wrecked. He offered his resignation on 2 December. Given the slight support he had among his colleagues – only one or two were prepared to back him – the acceptance of his offer was a foregone conclusion. This step provided an opening for negotiations between the four democratic parties – the Conservatives, the Liberals, the Agrarians, and the Social Democrats – with a view to forming a coalition government. There was a general understanding that the government in office, which was backed by the two latter parties and thus already had a majority in the *Riksdag*, should be more broadly based to enable the country the better to withstand future pressures.

During the talks about the new government's formation there was no disagreement on the basic points of future foreign policy. No party recommended falling in alongside Finland, although opinions were divided on how far one could bind oneself for the future and on the extent of the facilities which should be granted a Swedish volunteer movement. All were united in the view that Sweden should not make any declaration of neutrality in the war between the Soviet Union and Finland and thereby reduce her ability to help Finland. All were united on continued neutrality in the war between Germany and the Western Powers. Evidence of the parties' common foreign policy was their agreement on the appointment of a career diplomat as Foreign Minister, a rare occurrence in recent decades. The decisive influence in choosing this diplomat was Per Albin Hansson. As Prime Minister designate, leader of the country's biggest party, the Social Democrats, and a skilful politician, he completely dominated the formation of the government. After one refusal, he turned to the Swedish Minister in Oslo, the former Secretary-General at the Foreign Ministry, Christian Günther.

The Prime Minister's speech on the occasion of the new government's entry into office on 13 December 1939 was designed to underline first how little this event, and above all the replacement of the Foreign Minister, betokened a change in policy; and second how

25

firmly the new government would stand by its predecessor's principles: independence; neutrality; co-operation with alliance-free neutral states; Nordic collaboration. The reason for this speech seemed obvious. Confidence in the sincerity and the stability of Sweden's policy of neutrality must not be impaired either at home or abroad, and on no condition should the impression be given that Sandler had been sacrificed to German pressure: the Germans might then be encouraged to demonstrate their displeasure afresh, and the unity of Hansson's and Sandler's own party would be seriously jeopardized. Viewed with hindsight, it is obvious that there was no break in two vital aspects of foreign policy: keep the country out of war and afford Northern neighbours the utmost material and humanitarian assistance. All the same, Sandler's resignation was a more important event in the annals of Swedish foreign policy than Hansson in his public utterances at the time could, or would, admit.

His party colleague, the Defence Minister Per Edvin Sköld, was more

*Per Albin Hansson, Swedish Prime Minister*

frank when, on 5 December, he told the leading Social Democrats that the change of government must involve 'a shift in our policy to a more moderate, and a more modest, attitude than previously'. The description of the government's, particularly the Foreign Minister's, foreign policy up till then which this remark indirectly conveys should be noted. Sandler had been happy in the League of Nations at Geneva, where, to quote his more perspicacious predecessor, the Agrarian K. G. Westman, now Minister of Justice, he had 'enjoyed being in the front row of this formal play with the representatives of the Great Powers and being acknowledged for his skilful application of the rules of the game in all their subtlety'. But an honoured place at the League of Nations was, in the dire circumstances of the late 1930s, when the Great Powers threatened to end, or in several cases had ended, the existence of peaceful small countries, a completely valueless asset: the Soviet Union was voted out of the League some weeks after her attack on Finland, without Finland's position being in the least bit improved. The era of illusions was over. Sweden found herself in her gravest situation since the Napoleonic Wars at the beginning of the nineteenth century.

# 2 Sweden between the Finnish winter war in the East and the Great war in the West

## December 1939. Preliminary peace talks

The Soviet Union's attack on Finland had brutally dispelled all the hopes of the 1930s that in any future war between the Great Powers the neutrality of the Northern countries could be maintained on the pattern of 1914–18. As so often before, the military intervention of a Great Power in an area previously free of alliances and standing apart from Great Power combinations prompted other Great Powers to take note of, and to safeguard, their interests in that area. The Soviet Union wanted to improve its strategic position. The Western Powers wanted to exploit the war in Finland to interfere with Germany's supplies of iron-ore and to open a new front against Germany in the North. Germany, herself contemplating action against Norway, held back for the time being, but kept a wary eye on the plans of the Western Powers and permitted no doubts of her determination to meet by force of arms an armed intervention by them in the North. To a greater extent than at any time since the Napoleonic Wars, the Great Powers had involved the Northern countries in their wartime strategic and commercial rivalries.

The aim of Swedish foreign policy in this tense situation was the same as before: to keep Sweden out of warlike developments. It had two essential objectives: to prevent any fresh armed interventions by the Great Powers and to promote an end of the Russo-Finnish war, thereby restoring peace to the North and, to that extent, reducing the risks of Great Power intervention.

As far as aid for Finland was concerned, the Swedish government decided to allow volunteers to leave for the front and to afford as much material help as Sweden's own resources and requirements permitted. Since there had been no declaration of neutrality concerning the war in the East, the government had greater freedom of manoeuvre here than in the West. The Swedish volunteers arrived later and in less numbers than had been hoped in Finland. Nevertheless, Swedish deliveries of war material, especially during the first weeks of the war, were on a considerable scale, and thus contributed to the stabilization on all fronts, at Christmas, of the Finnish defences, which had at the start wavered in the face of the numerically far superior Soviet forces.

Optimism now increased in Helsinki. Early in December the Finnish government had tried, with Sweden as an intermediary — Sweden now looked after Finland's interests in the Soviet Union — to persuade the Russian government to agree to new negotiations. Molotov, however, had summarily rejected this request. His government, he declared, now recognized only the Kuusinen regime. A further Finnish attempt in mid-month to talk directly with Moscow had also proved fruitless. More confident that the turn of events would improve Finland's negotiating position, the Finnish government now postponed new attempts to establish contact with Moscow. The Finnish armies had won an indisputable defensive victory and had seriously damaged the Soviet Union's international prestige. Reports had come in that the Western Powers' Supreme War Council had in principle decided on military assistance to Finland. On the Swedish side the danger of Allied military intervention in support of Finland was perhaps underestimated. Information on the War Council's decision was slight and unclear. But Günther's assessment of the situation was quite clear. To avoid an Anglo-French invasion of the North, which would immediately bring a German attack in reply, Finland should make peace as soon as possible. An active intervention by the British and the French would certainly provoke German counter-measures which could bring the gravest danger to Finland and Sweden — this was the message he had sent to Finland's new Foreign Minister, Väinö Tanner. With extreme caution he sounded out of the Soviet Union's Minister in Stockholm, Madame Alexandra Kollontay, on the chances of Moscow still coming to terms with the Helsinki government. When he asked Tanner if he was interested in a Swedish *démarche* to this effect in Moscow, however, the latter showed slight interest. Günther then came up with a proposal for Swedish enquiries in Berlin whether Germany was willing to mediate. If so — as through a direct Swedish *démarche* in Moscow — the Swedes would be able to pass on information of Finnish concessions over and above what had been put forward when negotiations were broken off in November. But Tanner was not interested this time either. Soundings should not be taken too often, he replied, and, if a *démarche* was made, it should be made in such a way that a positive result was obtained. Finland preferred a joint *démarche* in Moscow led by the United States, and was now awaiting information on Washington's attitude to such a step.

Günther's attempt in the last week of December to interest the Finnish government in a Swedish peace initiative had failed. Tanner and his colleagues were obviously not anxious to have Sweden as a mediator. In fact, earlier in the year, Sweden had tried to put Finland's case in Moscow, but without success; and the help given Finland by Swedish volunteers and Swedish equipment and Swedish public opinion's overwhelming support could hardly have improved Sweden's standing in Moscow. Moreover, the idea that Finland should express her readiness to make concessions through Sweden, which had a selfish interest in bringing about an early peace to improve her own position, was hardly a source of satisfaction to the Finnish government. In existing circumstances the Finns, in a relatively favourable military position and with the Western Powers' promise of speedy and substantial assistance in mind, were not disposed to make any new concessions to their Eastern neighbours, and they saw in the United States and Germany more effective spokesmen in Moscow than Sweden.

## January 1940. Moscow agrees to Swedish mediation

Arvid Richert, Sweden's Minister in Berlin, wrote a long mid-December despatch on 'Sweden and Germany', to sum up for his old and good friend Günther his very grave view of German-Swedish relations. He did not exclude the possibility that the recent anti-Swedish press comments could be the opening for a German move against Sweden. Günther, at his first meeting with foreign envoys, spoke to the German Chargé d' Affaires, Carl von Below, who made him listen to a long enumeration of Sweden's misdemeanours, a rather unusual procedure. (The Minister, Prince Victor zu Wied, had been called home to report, a measure intended to express Berlin's displeasure with Stockholm.) Reports of critical comments by Göring and of Hitler's conspicuous annoyance at the Swedish government and the tone of Swedish newspapers underlined Richert's warning. Göring was one of Hitler's closest associates and his officially chosen successor. Through his first marriage to a Swedish lady, Carin Fock, he had ties of kinship and other connections in Sweden. He could speak Swedish and in a general sense was clearly well disposed. But there was obviously some uncertainty on the extent to which he could be expected to champion Sweden's interests against Hitler. His key position and the knowledge he had of Hitler's intentions, however, meant that his remarks and suggestions had to be given weight in Stockholm. It was a matter of some concern to keep channels to him open and they were often maintained unofficially through a

*Prince Victor zu Wied, German Minister in Stockholm*

Swedish industrialist, Birger Dahlerus.

In such a situation a newly appointed Swedish Foreign Minister must consider it exceptionally important to try to overcome Berlin's suspicion and distrust as far as possible. In an interview for Europa-Press in Frankfurt on 23 December, Günther emphasized that friendly relations with Germany were an essential component in Sweden's neutrality, that the Swedish government honestly wished to maintain and strengthen these friendly ties, that Sweden would adhere to a sincere policy of neutrality; and would oppose all efforts by other

31

powers to use her for their interests. He also drew attention to
Sweden's qualifications for the role of mediator. At home, he repeatedly
exhorted the Swedish press to observe caution and tact. In the early
days of 1940 he assured the German government through both Wied
and Richert that there had been no pressure whatever from the Western
Powers to draw the North into the war against Germany and that, for
its part, the Swedish government was firmly resolved to reject any
attempt to persuade Sweden to abandon her neutrality.

However, not only Germany had to be restrained. At the same time
as Günther was sending soothing assurances to Berlin, the Swedish
government replied to an Anglo-French *démarche* concerning help to
Finland. The Swedish government stressed that its aid to Finland had
played a decisive role on certain sectors of the Finnish front, just short
of military intervention. The government declared that it could best
serve Finland and the interests of Europe generally by resolutely maintaining its policy of neutrality. It would be willing to facilitate
deliveries of war material from other countries to Finland, but the
greatest caution and discretion must then be observed. Orally it was
added that no reason was seen to agree to discussions, as proposed at the
end of the Anglo-French *démarche*, on Western military assistance to
Sweden and Norway against the possible consequences to those
countries of giving assistance to Finland.

The eagerness of the Western Powers to interfere in the North was
not to be restrained so easily. The French government, not least for
reasons of internal politics, started the ball rolling. Early in the new
year London took the lead; the British government felt serious concern
over the continuing flow of Swedish iron-ore to Germany from Narvik,
during the winter closure of Luleå harbour. After the conclusion of
the War Trade Agreement with Sweden in December the British
had apparently reckoned on annual exports of 7 to 8 million tons, but
according to new information from Stockholm a figure of 10 million
was more correct. During the autumn trade negotiations the British side
had assumed (see p.18) that ore-carriers on their way south from Narvik
could not stay entirely within Norwegian territorial waters, but, at some
places, would have to move out to international waters where they
would be intercepted by British naval units. Gradually, however, the
British discovered that in order to seize the ships they had to operate
within Norwegian waters. A decision to do so was taken by the War
Cabinet early in January 1940 (pending measures somehow to get
direct control later on of the Lapland ore-fields themselves). In a long
memorandum to the Norwegian and Swedish governments on 6 January

1940, the British government stated that because of the sinking of ships by Germany in Norwegian territorial waters, it was reluctantly compelled to extend its own naval operations to those waters.

The Norwegian government, more directly concerned than the Swedish, immediately lodged the most emphatic protests. The Swedish government ordered its Minister in London, Björn Prytz, to place before the British Foreign Secretary, Lord Halifax, an urgent and serious request not to carry out the proposed naval measures. They could lead to immediate German counter-measures and the consequences could be limitless, not only for Sweden's trade and shipping connections with Britain and the Empire, but also for the Scandinavian states' position as neutrals. The unfavourable repercussions on public opinion were also stressed. In a conversation with the British Chargé d'Affaires in Stockholm, William Montagu-Pollock, Boheman, who often spoke with remarkable frankness to members of the British Legation, expressed himself more bluntly: the measures contemplated by the British would lead to German occupation of Denmark and, probably, to loss of independence for all the Scandinavian countries. 'I should have thought', he added, 'that the British government had the fate of a sufficient number of smaller states on their conscience as it is'.

In the face of the determinedly negative reaction of both Northern countries the British government drew back for a time. It certainly did not wish, by acting now against Norwegian and Swedish protests, to harm the prospects of direct intervention later on to get control of the iron-ore fields in Lapland. A few days later Prytz and his Norwegian colleague, Erik Colban, were quite convinced that the British plans for operations on the Norwegian coast had been abandoned for the time being. Indirect confirmation was obtained from a conversation between Halifax and Prytz on 18 January, when Halifax, rather than resort to the language of force, appealed for Swedish measures to cut down supplies of ore to Germany. He directed a similar appeal to the Norwegian government. Neither in Stockholm nor in Oslo did this request cause alarm. When the Norwegian Foreign Minister's chief assistant, Jens Bull, called on Günther and Boheman on 22 January, he spoke of laying a symbolic minefield or – probably more congenial – calmly waiting for whatever was going to happen.

Around the turn of the year Finnish arms had won important successes and on the Carelian Isthmus repeated large-scale Soviet attacks had been hurled back. Finland's urgent representations to Sweden in December for  instant deliveries of war material either Swedish or transported through Sweden, and for the immediate commitment of Swedish volunteers, had no exact counterpart in January. The Western Powers no longer insisted on discussions about their support in the event of Swedish intervention on the side of Finland. While the French press used help to Finland as an argument to persuade Sweden and Norway to enter the war against Germany on the side of the Western Powers — something which led to equally sharp comments in the opposite sense in German papers — official quarters expressed understanding of Sweden's position. The exchange of views with Britain was mainly concerned with ore-shipments from Narvik and gave no cause for alarm in Stockholm (see p.33). Germany, for her part, made no moves in Stockholm about the Finnish question; a cautious sounding by Richert in the German Foreign Ministry on the subject of mediation between Helsinki and Moscow could not encourage any Swedish activity in this direction.

As for relations with the Soviet Union, they were characterized by Molotov's remark to the Swedish Minister in Moscow, Wilhelm Winther, on 4 December that his government considered its relations with Sweden unchanged even after the beginning of the Russo-Finnish war. In the following weeks, when Sweden made her support for Finland exceptionally plain and when there were strong and wide stirrings of public opinion against the Soviet Union, nothing was heard officially from Moscow until just before Christmas. The Vice Commissar for Foreign Affairs, Lozovskij, summoned Winther to warn him in temperate language about 'the anti-Soviet propaganda in Sweden', which could lead to undesirable difficulties in Soviet-Swedish relations. A few weeks later the Soviet government felt it necessary to make sharper observations. On 6 January Madame Kollontay presented a note to Günther in which Swedish public opinion, the contributions to the Finnish war effort, and even the Swedish government's failure to react against behaviour which might be deemed incompatible with neutrality, were freely criticized. Günther's rejoinder of 10 January rejected all these accusations and, at the same time, emphasized the Swedish government's desire to avoid all complications between the two countries. The Soviet Union did not want any either and contented itself with publishing the exchange of notes accompanied by a brief commentary, moderate in tone.

At the opening of the 1940 *Riksdag* in Stockholm in mid-January the government again expressed its determination to provide Finland with all the material and humanitarian help which Sweden, having regard to her own position and capability, could give. Further, the government emphatically asserted Sweden's determination to stay out of the war between Germany and the Western Powers, and firmly rejected all speculations in foreign newspapers on Sweden's possible involvement.

A rather long memorandum, 'Sweden's neutrality. Sweden and the Russo-Finnish conflict. The question of Swedish iron-ore exports', dated 25 January, which Boheman wrote for Prytz's guidance in his talks in London and which was later sent to other Heads of Mission, throws light on the internal arguments behind this policy. Boheman strongly emphasized Germany's military domination of the Baltic and the risk of Stalin and Hitler collaborating against Finland-Sweden in the event of a Swedish intervention on the side of the Finns against the Soviet Union. From the German standpoint, he argued, Swedish measures in support of Finland could be tolerated only as long as they did not take on the character of international action under the aegis of the League of Nations, and only as long as the Allies' help to Finland did not become such that it assisted them, in one way or another, to acquire influence over, or bases inside, either Sweden or Finland. When the Western Powers offered to discuss military support for Sweden and Norway should the direct or indirect help these countries were giving to Finland expose them to difficulties, the offer had to be declined. Given the extensive espionage system then obtaining, such discussions could not be kept secret. Nor would they be consistent with Sweden's neutral status. It was perfectly obvious that this kind of policy — which London and Paris could perhaps interpret as hardly heroic and scarcely in keeping with the interests of the Western Powers — might be only temporarily possible. However, the Swedish viewpoint had been that,

with the help being given and likely to be given to Finland, Finnish resistance to Russian aggression will show itself to be such that, if the chance is given, a peaceful agreement between the Soviet Union and Finland will materialize.

Swedish foreign policy also tried to promote such a development. Thus on 25 January Günther discussed a Finnish-Soviet peace with Madame Kollontay. Sweden had some weeks earlier replied to the Soviet Union's note complaining of her help to Finland and Moscow had not reverted to the matter. Günther therefore considered that he could register anew Sweden's interest in a peace between Moscow and Helsinki. He took his cue from Madame Kollontay's statement during their previous talk of 27 December on the subject. Then she had declared 'a logical basis' must be sought for peace negotiations. Günther now asked whether such a basis was not directly to be found: if the Soviet government gave up their claim to Hanko and limited themselves instead to an agreement for the joint defence of the Gulf of Finland, or something similar — they had occupied all the territories they had originally demanded — a better logical basis could hardly be expected. If the war was allowed to continue and the Soviet armies thrust deeper into Finland, there was an increased risk that the Western Powers could achieve their desire of combining Finland's war with their own. For the present the pressure on the Northern countries from the Western Powers could be withstood, but, if Soviet troops advanced to the frontiers of Sweden and Norway, it must be foreseen that in Finland, Sweden, and Norway opinion would grow in favour of accepting help from the Western Powers. 'In other words: the greater the Russian success in Finland, the greater the risk of a French and British intervention against Russia'.

Four days later, on 29 January, Madame Kollontay returned with a written communication which she requested should be brought to the notice of the Finnish government: the Soviets would not in principle rule out an agreement with the Helsinki government, but must be informed before the beginning of negotiations what territorial concessions it was prepared to make.

In this approach, which implied a decision by Moscow to disregard the Terijoki government, Günther's warning to Madame Kollontay that hostilities both in the East and in the West could coalesce probably played a part. There was concern in Moscow over Britain's influence in Sweden, and intervention by the Western Powers in Finland with Sweden's co-operation would be extremely unwelcome: it would bring the Soviet Union into Germany's war against the Western Powers; it would prolong a war in Finland already costly in resources and prestige; and it could cause a German reaction, which would give Germany the opportunity to advance her position in the North. And this after the Soviet Union had gone to war with Finland precisely to be able to meet any future German attack away from her own frontiers. A sure move to start off such a development would be to involve Sweden in peace negotiations, the more so since the Swedish government could be expected to press determinedly in Helsinki for a Finnish-Soviet peace agreement, to reduce as soon as possible the serious risk of a war involving Sweden.

Finland was now fighting for her frontiers, but no longer for her survival. Finland's government and military command could register this as a most important gain. At the moment, however, the military

*Madame Alexandra Kollontay, Soviet Minister (later Ambassador) in Stockholm*

situation aroused no concern and immediate peace negotiations were not considered necessary. What Helsinki required from Stockholm in these circumstances was not mediation for peace but more military help to replenish her own strained resources. Prime Minister Ryti travelled to Stockholm on 1 February and, in a discussion with Per Albin Hansson, asked, in addition to war material, for 20,000 volunteers in self-contained units. Ryti and Tanner, however, wanted at the same time to keep open the contacts with Moscow which had been established by Günther. Through him as middleman they informed Madame Kollontay on 2 February that Finland had definitely decided to seek a peaceful solution and, with this aim and in exchange for certain

Soviet territories, was prepared to make various concessions beyond what had been asked for in November in Moscow. Some days later Tanner still sought direct contact with Madame Kollontay. Finland obviously still preferred not to have recourse to Swedish mediation.

## February 1940. Peace negotiations between Moscow and Helsinki get under way

The Swedish government stuck to its earlier line. Hansson adopted a completely negative attitude to the request for 20,000 men and warned that the appearance of Western troops in Finland would probably make the Germans take counter-action and that, in such an event, no regard would be paid to Finland. Günther thought it prudent not to show too much concern when Tanner called on him before his meeting with Madame Kollontay. But he let it be clearly understood that, in so far as the Finnish leaders wished to avail themselves of his services, he was obviously at their disposal.

Moscow left neither Günther nor Tanner in any doubt that they desired Swedish assistance. Molotov also showed manifest goodwill towards Swedish interests in Åland and held out the prospect that, should the Swedes want to bring up this question in Moscow, they would be accommodated. In negotiations on Åland the Soviet Union could obviously play off Sweden against Finland and thereby further weaken Finland's position. Günther did not swallow the bait; the Swedes, he said to Madame Kollontay, had no wish to advance their interests in such a way that there could be any question of their benefiting at Finland's expense.

While prospects for peace appeared a little brighter in the East, from the West came reports of an imminent intervention in the North. At a meeting of the Western Powers' Supreme War Council in Paris on 5 February a decision was taken to send an Allied military expedition to North Scandinavia. The expedition would nominally and to all appearances be mounted to help Finland, but was primarily envisaged as a mortal blow to Germany's supplies of iron-ore from the Lapland ore-fields, which would be occupied. During their visits to Stockholm on 1 and 5 February Ryti and Tanner had spoken only in general terms of the possibility of intervention by the Western Powers in the North; and the Swedish government never received any direct information about the War Council's decision on the above date. Three days later, however, on 8 February, warnings were received from the Swedish Legation in Paris. New information came from the same source the following week about preparations for an expedition. However, there were hopes in Stockholm that the war between Finland and the Soviet Union would be ended through Swedish good offices, before the Western Powers' expedition was ready to set out. 'Preliminary measures have been taken in Paris, but it appears that a Finnish initiative is required before further moves', explained the Prime Minister to the Parliamentary Foreign Policy Committee on 16 February.

The preliminary measures did not seem alarming either. Three landing ports had been mentioned: Murmansk, Petsamo, Narvik. An expedition to Murmansk or Petsamo would land well away from Sweden. An expedition to Narvik was a much more serious matter. However, the British government had not mentioned Narvik again after the determined Norwegian and Swedish reactions in January to the idea of encroaching on Norwegian territorial waters. After a visit of several weeks to Stockholm Prytz had seen Halifax at the beginning of February, explained the Swedish standpoint at greater length, and handed over detailed arguments. Halifax had not put forward any specific counter-arguments, but merely asked him to call again. Thus, in the face of energetic opposition, the Western Powers did not insist on forcing their will upon Sweden and Norway. Were they really more determined to go through with their intentions to get transit facilities for troops going to Finland – an even more crucial political question?

Finland's position was certainly difficult enough. From the beginning of February an uninterrupted Soviet offensive had been launched on the Carelian Isthmus. Little by little it breached the Finnish lines, tremendously inferior in men and equipment. Simultaneously with its military progress the Soviet Union stiffened its conditions for peace; in a statement which Madame Kollontay handed to Günther on 12 February, demands were made (in addition to Hanko, which the Finnish government had so far refused to cede) for the whole of the Carelian Isthmus and the area north of Lake Ladoga. The following day, 13 February, the main Finnish defence line of the Carelian Isthmus broke and Tanner, on a new visit to Stockholm, received yet another refusal from Per Albin Hansson when he repeated the Finnish request of 1 February for detachments of Swedish troops. Some days later, on 16 February, a Swedish newspaper reported that the Prime Minister had given a negative reply to the Finnish government's request for military support, and this announcement immediately prompted a communiqué from the Prime Minister which, in cold terms, confirmed the report.

Hansson addressed himself not only to his own country but also to Finland. He doubtless had in mind the events of the autumn, when the

Finns, in spite of his repeated statements to members of their government, had nevertheless not really wished to believe in his rejection of their enquiries about sending Swedish troops to Finland. He was therefore determined that there should be no uncertainty about his negative reply to Ryti and Tanner, even if that meant the refusal had to be expressed in brutally frank language. Hansson found some justification for his harsh tone on other grounds also. A large number of Finns in various recent public appearances in Sweden had asked — more or less directly, or indirectly — for Sweden's entry into the war. Hansson's intention was to deny the Finnish government the opportunity to incite Swedish public opinion in a direction favourable to intervention.

The Prime Minister's statement, however, did not at all impress public opinion in Sweden. He was criticized for being insufficiently sympathetic towards Finland, for being too unfeeling and too coldhearted, for shunning commitment to support the volunteer movement. In addition the government was accused of giving too little information to the *Riksdag* as well as to the general public. But, before any real crisis of confidence could arise, King Gustaf took a hand and made a pronouncement on 19 February. The King's statement in fact contained nothing more than the Prime Minister's communiqué three days earlier. But, at the same time as the King gave his approval of the government's policy of non-intervention and affirmed that no more than this could be demanded, even by Finland, he referred to Finland's plight with a degree of sympathy very different from that shown by the leader of his government. Most convincingly Gustaf V argued that his government's policy was quite simply dictated by circumstances and that there was no real alternative. He turned public opinion around and succeeded in establishing very wide support for the administration's foreign policy.

As a result of the 16 February communiqué Finland's negotiating position was obviously weakened. An attempt by Günther the following day to neutralize its effect by warning Madame Kollontay that events and the pressure of public opinion could force the government to review its non-intervention policy, if negotiations between Moscow and Helsinki were not started very soon, had little success. Madame Kollontay promised to report his statement back to her government, but, in a neat riposte, reminded Günther that, according to Moscow's interpretation, the obstacle to a speedy agreement was to be found in Helsinki; Günther should put pressure on the Finns for more effective concessions.

On 18 February Günther informed the Head of the Finnish Legation in Stockholm, ex-Foreign Minister Eljas Erkko, of this reply, and, at the same time, pointed out the inopportuneness of the propaganda for Sweden's entry into the war which was being carried on in Finnish circles. Günther's conversation with Erkko, conveying both a Soviet warning about delays and Swedish annoyance at Finnish propaganda, was – all the more so after Hansson's communiqué – an exhortation to the Finnish government to hurry up. The King's pronouncement the next day gave the statements of his Prime Minister and Foreign Minister increased emphasis. The effect in Helsinki was strengthened by the general deterioration of the military situation during the preceding days when the Soviet advance continued and the Finns retreated towards their rearmost positions on the Carelian Isthmus at Viipuri.

In this situation, on 20 February, Tanner requested Swedish good offices and let it be known that, if it became necessary, Hanko would be given up. After a war of nearly three months, Finland was prepared to make the concessions which Stalin had demanded at the final round of talks in Moscow at the beginning of November, and to accept Swedish mediation, which had not been sought before. It seemed that Günther had succeeded in the endeavours to which he had turned his attention immediately on taking up office: to get the belligerents together round the conference table.

But they were not there yet. Sweden's newly appointed Minister in Moscow, Vilhelm Assarsson, had to report after his first conversations with Molotov on 20 and 22 February that the Soviet Union had now raised its minimum demands to include the towns of Viipuri and Sordavala as well. What was asked for, as Molotov summarized it, to a large extent tallied with Peter the Great's frontier (from the Peace of Nystad in 1721).

On 23 February the Finnish government immediately replied to Günther's communication of these new demands of Molotov's with an official note requesting elucidation of the Swedish government's standpoint on Swedish assistance with men and material and on allowing troops from other countries to march through Sweden. Erkko asked for a speedy answer. To Günther's question why this *démarche* had been made just now he replied evasively, but let it be understood that Finland did not wish to take up her position *vis-à-vis* the new Soviet demands without having Sweden's attitude in black and white.

It was quite impossible that the Finnish government, after the conversations Ryti and Tanner had held with Hansson and Günther during their visits to Stockholm, and after Hansson's and Gustaf V's public

41

declarations on 16 and 19 February respectively, should have any doubts about the Swedish government's negative attitude to the two questions raised. What Tanner was after was obviously an official and precise written version of the oral replies which had earlier been given to Ryti and himself. This he could use as documentary support for his arguments in favour of peace negotiations. The formal answer was immediately given in a note on 24 February. The previous Swedish refusal was repeated in definite, yet moderate, terms.

Molotov's new conditions had not led to any reappraisal of Sweden's policy. Nor did the danger that, faced with stiff Soviet demands and with a written refusal from the Swedish government, the Finnish government might ask for help from the Western Powers. For the Swedish government, Günther declared on the same day before the Parliamentary Foreign Policy Committee that it was essential

there was now an offer for a peace, which entailed something much less than the annihilation of Finland. The Foreign Minister asked what Swedish government could assume the responsibility of so conducting its affairs that the Finns would be inclined to refuse the offer.

But Helsinki hesitated. The Soviet Union was demanding more than a tenth of Finland, a region with over 400,000 inhabitants, including Viipuri, Finland's second city, and with important economic resources. With Hanko and the Carelian Isthmus in Soviet hands, Finland's strategic position would be untenable. Finland was still unconquered, even if the front had been pulled back. Finnish public opinion was still not convinced that, despite all the sacrifices and losses, a victorious Soviet peace was unavoidable. At the same time the Western Powers raised the prospect of help more explicitly than before; about 20,000 troops would be able to sail on 15 March and would be available at the Finnish front on 15 April. A majority of the Finnish government was not, in these circumstances, willing to accept a peace concluded on the basis of the latest conditions laid down by Molotov. But, on the other hand, the government could not agree either on gambling on help from the Western Powers. So a decision was postponed and Tanner went again to Stockholm.

For the third time in a month Tanner, on 27 February, discussed with Hansson the three options: Swedish military help; Western intervention; the conclusion of peace. Hansson recapitulated the Swedish standpoint, and he now went further than before in his attempt to 'push the peace line' by saying, in contrast to his earlier conversations, that in his opinion peace was necessary even on harsh terms; a continuation of the war could involve the subjugation and occupation of Finland. Tanner raised the questions of help in reconstruction and of a defensive alliance. Hansson replied that, to the best of his belief, economic help from Sweden in the reconstruction of Finland could be counted on, and that he was prepared to discuss a defensive alliance without, however, being willing to commit himself on his final position.

All the same, Tanner was unable to induce his government to come to a decision on peace negotiations. On 1 March, Erkko delivered to Günther for transmission to Moscow a statement in which the Finnish government declared itself interested in negotiating, but also expressed a desire to have a more exact delineation of the new frontiers than hitherto. At the same time Erkko brought Günther a message from Tanner that, in view of the Soviet Union's stiff peace terms, the Finnish government was seriously considering an appeal to the Western Powers.

After having read Assarsson's reports, Günther must have considered it unlikely that the threat of intervention by the Western Powers in the North would induce Moscow to grant Finland more favourable peace terms than the latest communicated. Rather might the offensive in Finland be pressed forward to enable the Soviet Union to face any foreign expedition as far from its frontiers as possible. With such an outlook, and also in the conviction that an intervention by the Western Powers in the North would immediately provoke German counter-measures, Günther's reaction to Tanner's message could not reasonably be other than an attempt to get from the Finns a more accommodating reply to the Soviet Union — and immediately, since the Moscow government's deadline for a Finnish answer was that same day.

Günther thus immediately made it clear that he would not forward Erkko's text to Moscow. He warned Tanner against giving an answer which could be interpreted in Moscow as a rejection, with all the fateful consequences that this would entail, and against relying on any effective help from the Western Powers. Besides, when faced with an expected intervention by the West, Germany would step in and 'at best Germany and the Soviet Union would settle the Finnish problem exactly as they wanted'. He further suggested that in the text of the Finnish reply should be inserted a remark that 'the government of Finland is therefore prepared in principle to accept the Russian proposals'.

The Finnish reply was received some hours later, but was not an unqualified acceptance. The Finnish government sought shelter behind Sweden in an appeal to Stalin for better terms and, in addition, asked for a Swedish undertaking to enter into a military alliance with Finland.

Günther dismissed the second point – 'such a question cannot be settled off-hand and requires thorough handling' – but held out the prospect of 'a further attempt' in respect of the first.

Behind Moscow's markedly well-disposed attitude towards Sweden in recent weeks, Günther discerned an attempt to lessen her interest in Finland. He did not permit himself any excessive expectations that he could use it to gain concessions for Finland. On the evening of 1 March he nevertheless considered he had the occasion and the opportunity for 'a further attempt': in his talks with Madame Kollontay he had already repeatedly mentioned how difficult it was for Finland to accept the stiff, and ever stiffening, Soviet terms. He had in fact talked with her earlier in the day, and he must have been encouraged. She had delivered a message from Molotov to the effect that 'whatever was requested from the Finns should be reported to me'. Rumours that Kuusinen was to join the Finnish government were consequently without foundation. There was, moreover, Madame Kollontay continued, a very clear perception in Moscow of the extreme importance Sweden attached to Finland's internal freedom and a desire to pay all due regard to it, since the Soviet government was particularly anxious to stand on a good footing with Sweden. Finland's reply could accordingly be deferred for another two days, until 3 March. After this friendly message, which certainly indicated Molotov's desire for a peaceful settlement, Günther, during a new discussion with Madame Kollontay that same evening, thought it opportune to follow up Tanner's afternoon message. He asked her whether she could not still appeal to Moscow for milder terms, which would allow Finland to retain Viipuri. He pointed out the risk of the Western Powers becoming involved and promised to see to it that a Soviet offer of peace without Viipuri would be completely accepted by the Finns, provided their reply was on the whole positive (which he obviously could not guarantee). The very next day, 2 March, he asked Madame Kollontay for news about his proposal.

Speed was certainly called for. Immediately before putting this question to Madame Kollontay, Günther had been summoned to the King, to whom a message from the French Prime Minister, Daladier, had been transmitted through the Swedish Consul-General in Paris, Raoul Nordling. France proposed to send troops to Finland, in the first instance 50,000 men through Narvik. The despatch of these troops was part of a plan for a general offensive against the Soviet Union 'which, beginning on 15 March, would be set in motion against Baku and before then through Finland'. France did not want Sweden to be dragged into the war and would, in the event, let her soldiers travel without their arms, which would be sent separately. Immediately after Günther's conversations with Madame Kollontay, her British colleague, Victor Mallet, handed over a statement which had already been announced the night before. At greater length and in more flexible terms than Daladier's message, it presented the Western Powers' plans to help Finland. The British government declared its intention of requesting permission for troops to travel through Sweden to Finland. In the event of a strong German reaction, they would be willing to give Sweden and Norway extensive military assistance and were prepared to send officers for immediate staff discussions to that end. For the route planned for the envisaged expedition (Daladier's message had spoken of Narvik) Mallet's text gave no names at all.

The screws were now being turned harder than before on Sweden. In the East, the Soviet armies were advancing deeper into Finland, and thus nearer to the Swedish frontier. In the West, Britain and France proposed staff talks about Sweden's participation in the Western Powers' war against Germany. In the South, Germany's threat to repay in their own coin an intervention by the Western Powers in the North was substantially unchanged. So far the danger of such an intervention, with which Hansson and Günther made effective play in arguing for a policy of promoting peace between Finland and the Soviet Union, had not been imminent. Now it was. Now, at a stroke, the situation was more serious than at any previous time during the winter. Sweden, in the Foreign Minister's judgement, was in 'a race against catastrophe'.

## March 1940. Mediation in a race against catastrophe

Information on an approaching intervention by the Western Powers in the North had come in earlier to Stockholm. In recent weeks, however, in spite of the *Altmark* incident, when a British destroyer boarded a German auxiliary cruiser inside Norwegian territorial waters and freed several hundred captured British seamen, and in spite of the information this gave on the interests of the belligerent powers in Norwegian home waters and in the North in general, the reports from the Swedish Legations in London and Paris had occasioned no great alarm. There had also been indications of a Finnish request for help from the Western Powers, but no advance warning in Stockholm by the Western Powers of any very imminent demands.

The conclusion of peace between Finland and the Soviet Union would fundamentally alter the grounds for an intervention by the Western Powers in the North and (if it was persisted in) would make it directed openly at Sweden and Norway. It could no longer be camouflaged as help for Finland. To counter such a development the Western governments, and in particular Daladier, who badly needed a success to satisfy French public opinion, forced the pace. They held out in Helsinki the prospect of extensive and speedy military assistance, and they appealed in Stockholm and Oslo for passage for their troops and for staff talks.

Günther got several hours' advance notice when, on the night of 1 March, Mallet informed Boheman that instructions to make representations for passage of troops and for staff talks would be reaching him next morning. When Mallet handed over his *aide-mémoire*, Günther immediately counter-attacked. The measures not only comprised aid to Finland, but had also to be seen as a link in Britain's military operations against the Soviet Union and Germany and in her efforts to block Germany's supplies of iron-ore. Mallet's rejoinder that Britain's war was of vital interest to Sweden prompted the reply that the total defeat of Germany was not in Sweden's interest either, since the balance of power would then be altered unfavourably for Sweden. Günther promised to lay Mallet's declaration before the government, but said straightaway that there could be no question of foreign troops marching through Swedish territory. When he asked whether the Allied troops were to be expected even if Sweden refused, Mallet was unable to provide an answer. The official Swedish reply to these proposals, which confirmed Günther's preliminary negative response, was delivered to Mallet's French colleague, Roger Maugras, the same day, and to Mallet himself the next.

The arrival of troops of the Western Powers at the frontiers of Sweden would face her with the choice of acting in the interest of the Western Powers, if the troops were let through, or in the interest of Germany, if their way was barred. It was essential to avoid such a situation, and it followed that an official Finnish request for help from the Western Powers had to be prevented. In a long conversation with Erkko on the evening of 2 March, during which he spoke sharply, Günther pointed out that if Sweden were forced into the dangerous position which now appeared to threaten her, she would be compelled to pay more regard to her own military security, 'which must affect the continuation of deliveries to Finland'. It had also to be borne in mind, said Günther, that the Swedish government might be compelled to inform the *Riksdag* that the possibility of peace did exist, but that Finland was unwilling to seize it.

Faced with Günther's grave warning, receiving only uncertain information from the British and French Ministers in Helsinki on whether and when effective military assistance to Finland could be counted on, and, last but not least, threatened by even more serious Soviet territorial gains on the Carelian Isthmus, the Finnish government had no option but to negotiate on Soviet terms. A Finnish attempt on 3 March to save Viipuri resulted only in a fresh warning from Molotov that, if the Soviet government's terms were not accepted, they would be stiffened and a definitive agreement concluded with Kuusinen. The fact that the Soviet government had so far refrained from adopting this line was – like its willingness to wait a few more days for its conditions to be accepted once and for all by the Finns – due to its respect and esteem for the Swedish government, whose peaceful attitude was deeply appreciated, Molotov said (twice). As a result of these exchanges and the now critical developments at the front at Viipuri, the Finnish government decided on 5 March to accept the Moscow government's terms.

At the conference table the Soviet Union again stiffened its terms. In a telephone conversation with Günther on 9 March, Tanner referred to these tough terms and the Western Powers' announcement that Finland could call on them for help until 12 March. He asked whether Sweden's attitude to military support and the passage of foreign troops remained unaltered. Günther confirmed that it did. Tanner also asked for further Swedish representations in Moscow to get the terms softened.

Stockholm saw on the horizon the very obvious danger that any further delays in the conclusion of peace would bring the wars in the East and in the West together. The news of the negotiations in Moscow had on 8 and 9 March raised a storm of disappointment and bitterness in the French press; the British papers had behaved more calmly. What the French emphasized above all was that the Soviet Union would now be relieved of a military entanglement and thus be more free to help Hitler. German pressure in Stockholm was suspected to be behind Sweden's mediation. This in turn had led to Swedish pressure in Helsinki, aimed at getting Finland to make peace on Soviet terms. More or less open accusations against Sweden for running Hitler's errands could, in an atmosphere as highly charged as the French, bring sudden and far-reaching decisions by the Paris government. The more so as in recent weeks Daladier, whose position was generally considered rather weak, had come out as one of the most enthusiastic protagonists of an expedition by the Western Powers to the North. On 8 March Günther had told Mallet and Maugras that there had been no contacts between Sweden and Germany in connection with getting the peace negotiations started and that the rumours of Swedish pressure on Finland were untrue.

A quick conclusion of peace, which did not allow time for fresh Finnish doubts or new Anglo-French intervention moves, was more than ever a vital Swedish interest. By representations through both Madame Kollontay and Assarsson, Günther tried to get Moscow to abide by the terms which the Finnish government had accepted on 5 March. The danger, he explained, would be that public opinion in the Northern countries in favour of intervention could not be controlled after learning that the Soviet terms, in spite of promises to the contrary, went far beyond the agreed basis for the negotiations. But when Assarsson saw him in the evening of 11 March, Molotov would not budge. Foreign support for Finland, he declared, would have no effect on the Soviet Union, which wished only to secure its frontiers. He brushed aside hints of the possibility of a Swedish intervention and forcefully expressed the Soviet Union's desire for normal, indeed for friendly, relations with Sweden. Towards the Finns he was unyielding: nobody was compelling them to sign, but the next time the Soviet terms could be even stiffer.

A further attempt by Sweden to speak for Finland in Moscow had thus been fruitless. The Finnish delegation had by then decided to accept the Soviet Union's terms anyway and had requested from Helsinki plenary powers to sign the peace treaty. When Mallet in a note of 12 March formally sought the Swedish government's approval for the passage of British and French troops across Swedish territory and in support cited an appeal for help from the Finnish government to Britain and France, he was thus overtaken by events.

The Swedish government had successfully pursued its policy of keeping Sweden out of the war. No political grouping effective enough to push through a policy of intervention had ever been formed, even if an influential body of opinion, with strong support in different sections of the community, had urged the despatch of regular troops to Finland. Nor had the Western Powers' proposals on passage for their troops met with approval in any quarter during the final weeks of the war. There was criticism that not enough had been done for Finland or that unseemly pressure had been exerted on Finland to make peace, but there was complete agreement that Sweden must try to keep herself out of the war between Germany and the Western Powers.

In Britain and France there was general disillusionment with Sweden, so the government was informed, not unmixed with exasperation that she had rendered so little help to Finland. She had stood in the way of the Western Powers providing the help she herself would not give. She had advised, even exerted pressure on, Finland, and that under German direction, to comply with the Soviet Union's conditions. Suspicions that Sweden had acted as mediator under German influence in order to extricate Germany's ally, the Soviet Union, from a serious situation and to increase her ability to deliver in full those essential supplies she had agreed to send to Germany, must be expected to influence unfavourably the Western Powers' policy towards Sweden. The Swedish government in consequence strongly denied the reports of both German pressure in Stockholm and Swedish pressure in Helsinki. It was easier in London than in Paris to get these disavowals heeded. In a short House of Commons debate on 11 March on his government's Finnish policy Neville Chamberlain avoided discussing Sweden. Prytz, who thought the British government divided on whether an expedition should be sent or not, had the impression that there was a growing understanding of the Swedish standpoint in the Foreign Office. He believed that public opinion in Britain would adopt the same attitude. In Paris, however, Daladier made a most hostile speech against Sweden in the Chamber of Deputies on 12 March. He accused her, among other things, of exerting pressure in Helsinki. The formation of a new French government on 20 March, when Reynaud succeeded Daladier, pushed the North and Sweden more into the background, for the French press now directed its strategic speculations towards the Balkans. But the Swedish government's attempts to restrain the Great Powers from military intervention in the North certainly did not convince the French government. It continued to insist on military action there.

If, at the end of the Winter War, Sweden's relations with the Western Powers cooled or, with the Daladier administration, worsened appreciably, in Germany there was a calmer and more appreciative assessment of Swedish foreign policy and its conduct than at the beginning of the war. Exchanges of views on Finland between Berlin and Stockholm seem, however, to have been rather few. Apart from a warning from the German Legation in Stockholm at the beginning of February about Swedish activities in support of Finland, there were no German diplomatic moves. On the whole, during February and March Günther found Swedish-German relations better than when he had taken office in December – an improvement to which he himself had obviously contributed. It is fairly certain that this improvement would have borne the strain of even more substantial Swedish help to Finland than had been forthcoming. Swedish troops could possibly have been sent there by the same methods as Germany herself had used in Spain during the

49

Civil War: then the soldiers had travelled as private individuals and were provided with arms and assembled into units only on foreign territory. Günther, however, had manifestly not been anxious for more precise information on this. In fact it was better for him not to have it than to get limited concessions which might have been exploited to bursting-point by Helsinki and by the government's domestic critics. Quite logically therefore he avoided bringing any questions to a head and concentrated his arguments on the inevitable German intervention which the presence of Allied troops in Sweden would bring. The accuracy of this assessment was confirmed from the most reliable source of all when the famous explorer Sven Hedin visited Hitler, with whom he was *persona gratissima*, at the beginning of March and was able subsequently to report the Führer's comment: 'One thing you in Sweden must be quite clear about, and that is that the moment British or French troops set foot on Swedish soil, Germany will instantly intervene'.

Mediation brought blame in the West. In the East, however, it was appreciated. Because of it Moscow overlooked the volunteer movement, Swedish deliveries of war material, and anti-Soviet opinion. Again and again Moscow expressed appreciation of the Swedish government's policy. Several times it promised to meet Sweden's interests in the Åland question, should the Swedish government wish to take it up in negotiations. The Soviet government's consideration, however, did not stretch as far as heeding repeated Swedish appeals for more lenient peace terms for Finland. On the contrary, its conditions gradually stiffened, and this even after the Finnish delegation had arrived in Moscow and after Molotov had stated that no conditions which the Swedish government did not know of would be put forward. What more could possibly have been done on the Swedish side to soften the Soviet terms cannot readily be stated without more precise information on the Moscow government's motives in wanting peace. Stalin at all events cannot seriously have envisaged a Swedish intervention: if this had been so, Molotov and Madame Kollontay as well as the Soviet press would certainly have used a much sharper tone.

In the *Riksdag* on 13 March, Günther justified the Prime Minister's communiqué of 16 February, and the King's pronouncement of the 19th, by the need to

dispel the dangerous misconception of the Finnish people that adequate help would presumably arrive from either the Northern countries or the Western Powers, as soon as it was realized in Sweden and Norway how threatening the situation was for the whole of the North.

Finland, he maintained, could not be allowed to continue the war on false assumptions and in the hope of early rescue, which in reality was not even remotely possible. The reports of the Swedish Legation in Helsinki provided Günther with grounds for this argument beyond all doubt. They showed clearly that Finnish public opinion refused not only to end a just war into which the country had been forced in self-defence by allowing the aggressor to decide the conditions of peace, but also to embark on a rational consideration of how continued resistance to an opponent with such superior resources could produce better terms than those now available. Hansson's and Günther's statements to Tanner and Erkko in the final weeks of the war can be seen in the same context: as steps in the Swedish policy of sign-posting for Finland the road to peace with the Soviet Union, which under the existing circumstances was judged by Sweden to be incomparably the best solution, not only for Sweden but also for Finland. For this policy to succeed, determined plain speaking both to the Finnish public and to the Finnish government was obviously required.

The Swedish government's foreign policy during the Winter War had succeeded in preserving integrity and peace for the country. The government, and especially the Foreign Minister, had stood a severe test very well. Christian Günther had hitherto been considered a gifted but not especially prominent career diplomat. Now, all at once, he had shown himself capable of steering a steady and resourceful course under most difficult and strenuous circumstances. He had managed too to establish himself as a leading member of the government, listened to with respect both by his colleagues and in the *Riksdag*, as well as by the King.

Nevertheless, unlike other ministers, Günther had no party of his own behind him. He was consequently more vulnerable to attacks from adversaries and critics. All the more important for him were his excellent personal relations with the Prime Minister. Per Albin Hansson was not really interested in foreign affairs and content to leave them as much as possible to a person whose judgement and skill he relied upon. This close relationship may have had its strains at critical moments, but on the whole continued smoothly throughout the war, and much strengthened Günther's position, not least in the ranks of Hansson's own party. For Günther was often criticized by Social Democrats for his seeming readiness to give in to German demands.

The Winter War had taken place quite close to Sweden's frontiers. Swedish military forces had been mobilized, Swedish rearmament had proceeded at a new, hitherto unknown pace, even if the real efforts did not come until after 9 April 1940. Sweden had run obvious risks of getting involved in the Great War. The military leaders had, however, no influence on foreign policy. Sometimes they proposed more active support for the Finns, but their proposals were turned down every time. Only seldom were they called upon to present their views on Sweden's strategic situation at government meetings. Otherwise they were given no access to government discussions. This pattern was maintained throughout the war. Although Sweden's military position was most of the time precarious, and although Günther and his collaborators in the Foreign Ministry kept close contacts with General Thörnell and his leading officers, the military took no part in decisive foreign policy deliberations. On the other hand, in various questions their professional contacts, especially with German and Finnish colleagues, could influence the background conditions for government decisions.

All party leaders, except the communist, were in the government. After government discussions they were bound to follow collective decisions. These then bound their party colleagues in the Parliamentary Foreign Policy Committee, who could not oppose what their leaders had sanctioned without wrecking the unity upon which the government was built. Consequently Hansson and Günther usually had no great difficulty in getting the Committee to agree to the decisions they proposed. Moreover, there was not always enough time to call and hear the Committee before crucial decisions had to be taken, and information to Committee members could not in every case be complete for practical or security reasons. True, two prominent Social Democratic members of the Committee, Rickard Sandler and Östen Undén, often criticized Hansson's and Günther's proposals. Their comments, however, had no real political importance as the Prime Minister could as a rule reckon to have the rank and file of his party behind him. Thus, on the whole, the Committee had a certain importance for the government as a suitable body for reinsuring its policy among the leading members of the various parties. In foreign policy decisions, however, it had no primary role. Indeed, it would be difficult to show more than one or two cases where Committee standpoints altered ministerial decisions already agreed upon.

The *Riksdag* as a whole had still less of a chance to steer government decisions. Party leaders were in government and the most important questions had already been discussed by the Committee before they came before the *Riksdag*. True, the government called some secret sessions, but more to reinsure itself in certain crucial decisions than to leave these to the assembly. Moreover, individual parliamentarians might have difficulties in discussing with the Prime Minister or Foreign Minister big, complicated questions, about which they seldom knew very much. Some exceptions apart, especially during 1944—45, the government could reckon on sure *Riksdag* support for a cautious foreign policy.

Thus, during the first months of the Winter War, the pattern for the management of wartime Swedish foreign affairs was already set. The final decision lay with the Prime Minister and the Foreign Minister. When they agreed, as they nearly always did, they were usually able to enforce their opinion.

# 3 The war in Norway and the transit traffic to Norway

## Between the Soviet-Finnish treaty in Moscow and Allied and German actions against Scandinavia

As a sequel to the Winter War there was a short dialogue between Moscow and the Northern capitals on a Nordic defence union. During the frequent Finnish-Swedish talks in the final phase of the peace negotiations the Finns had time and again pleaded that Sweden, after the eventual conclusion of peace, should enter into a defence alliance with Finland. No binding Swedish commitments had ever been given. But unofficially the Swedes agreed to an investigation into the preconditions of such an alliance, certainly in the hope that this would help to smooth the way for a Finnish decision finally to accept the Moscow peace terms. On the day before peace was concluded, an official Finnish question was put to the Swedish and Norwegian governments: were they willing to explore with the Finnish government the possibilities of a defence alliance between Sweden, Finland, and Norway? Both immediately answered in the affirmative. Official news of this was published in the three Northern capitals on 14 March.

However, before any examination of the matter started, Moscow intervened. An alliance of the type now under discussion, Molotov asserted to Assarsson on 16 March, could only be directed against the Soviet Union and would conflict with the Swedish and Norwegian governments' policies of neutrality. The Soviet government wanted a free Finland and the best relations with the Scandinavian countries. What, he asked several times, would be the use of an alliance? Was it not advisable, he wondered, to calm down public opinion and, in the interests of future relations, to abstain for the present from plans for a defence alliance?

Energetic Swedish rebuttals ensued. The Swedish government maintained that it in no way intended to give up the policy of neutrality which it had so far strictly observed, and that an eventual defence alliance would be completely defensive in character and, moreover, was intended to strengthen Finland's ties with Scandinavia and inclinations towards peace. But Moscow was not to be moved. If Sweden's policy changed and the Swedish government gave up its policy of neutrality, then, Molotov declared to Assarsson on 25 March, the Soviet Union would also alter its policy towards Sweden. At the same time he emphasized that on the Soviet side they only wanted the best relations with Sweden. Molotov gave corresponding warnings to the Finnish and Norwegian Ministers in Moscow.

It would have been impossible, in the face of such a momentous veto for the Northern countries, and especially for Finland, after the Winter War, to gamble on a defence alliance without getting reassurances from some other Great Power. And, on the other hand, by seeking such support they would at a stroke abandon their attempts to keep the North out of Great Power entanglements. The position Moscow had taken led logically to the conclusion that all thought of a Nordic defence alliance must be put on ice. One should not, the new Finnish Foreign Minister, Rolf Witting, said to the Swedish Minister in Helsinki, Stig Sahlin, 'talk too loudly' about it just now; meanwhile each of the Northern countries should go to work to strengthen its own defences.

At the time this remark was uttered, rumours of a new armed intervention by the Western Powers in the North had begun to circulate in the Northern capitals. First came reports of impending action by the Allies in Norwegian territorial waters to frustrate German iron-ore imports from Narvik. Faced with a similar threat at the beginning of the year, Norway and Sweden had reacted strongly (see p.33) and had made energetic representations in London. The mood in Oslo and Stockholm was now less nervous, and this greater calm and confidence did not seem unreasonably optimistic. Allied plans for naval operations in Norwegian territorial waters and for an expedition to Finland or, to describe it more accurately, to Narvik and the ore-fields in Lapland, had hitherto revealed inadequate preparedness and vacillation rather than effective resources and determination. The importance of ore-shipments from Narvik was bound to diminish as the arrival of spring and the melting of the ice in the Baltic would soon open Luleå harbour. Taking into consideration the now diminished importance of the Narvik route and the certainty of strong German counter-moves, the Allies should, it was thought, hesitate to embark upon far-reaching operations in the North.

Oslo and Stockholm, however, underestimated the pressure for a conclusive demonstration of a vigorous and ruthless prosecution of the war, to which the complete wreck of their Finnish plans and the ensuing criticisms of inadequate strength of purpose subjected the governments in London and Paris. At a meeting in London on 28 March the Supreme War Council of the Western Powers decided on French initiative that, after a warning on 1 or 2 April to the Swedish and Norwegian governments, minefields would be laid in Norwegian waters on 5 April with the aim of forcing the ore-carriers on their way from Narvik to Germany out into international waters. Plans for disrupting the ore-traffic from Luleå later in the spring should also be prepared. Germany's reactions do not seem to have been discussed in any detail at this meeting. A study by the British Chiefs of Staff on 1 April, however, mentioned as one among other possibilities a German decision to counter the mining by the occupation of air and naval bases in Norway. In that event, in the opinion of the Chiefs of Staff, the Western Powers should send troops to occupy Narvik and the iron-ore railway as far as the Swedish frontier (with the wider objective of the ore-fields at Kiruna and Gällivare), as well as Stavanger, Bergen, and Trondheim: there should be no landings, however, if the Norwegians showed themselves hostile. Sweden was considered less open to German counter-measures than Norway, but, if Germany took action against Sweden, the Allies could do nothing for the present.

Differences of opinion between the British and French delayed the mining of Norwegian territorial waters by some days, but, on 5 April, advance warning was given in notes to the governments in Oslo and Stockholm, and on 8 April the mines were laid. The operation was carried out successfully, but by the next day the situation had already suffered a catastrophic reverse. On 9 April German troops simultaneously occupied the whole of Denmark and the larger cities in Norway, including all the four – Narvik, Trondheim, Bergen, and Stavanger – which the Western Powers had planned to occupy in the event of a German reaction against their mine-laying operations.

Reliable indications of likely German action in the North had reached Stockholm as March made way for April. However, as during the Winter War, the danger of German intervention in the North was regarded there as less than that of Anglo-French interference. If the Germans could be convinced that the Western Powers would leave the North alone, no German action seemed probable. On 1 April Richert was therefore instructed to explain in Berlin that, according to available information in Stockholm, no British breach of the North's neutrality need be feared. If such action did occur, then the Swedish government would – and could – repulse it. During the next few days new reports of impending German measures were received. But the Swedish govern-

*General Olof Thörnell, Swedish Commander-in-Chief*

ment did not find them particularly disturbing. Demobilization of troops from the frontier with Finland in the North had begun after the end of the Winter War and was continued. A proposal of 4 April by the Commander-in-Chief, General Olof Thörnell, to strengthen defences in the South was left unanswered for the time being. Nor did reports from a German officer opposed to Hitler (Colonel Hans Oster), of an impending German attack in the very near future on Denmark and Norway and on Holland, Belgium, and France, which reached Stockholm on 5 and 6 April, occasion much alarm. At the meeting of the Parliamentary Foreign Policy Committee on 6 April, Günther was asked whether the German naval and troop concentrations, which he had mentioned in his analysis, were not something new and disturbing. He answered that there was indeed something new, but that he couldn't decide whether it was disturbing. Günther thus did not think these German military concentrations particularly alarming. This becomes more obvious when one realizes that the main issue at the Committee's meeting was not to consider these German moves. It had, in fact, been convened to be informed of the notes which the Ministers of the Western Powers had delivered the previous day in Stockholm as well as in Oslo. These notes were not, any more than the reported German moves, thought likely to lead to any alarming worsening of the situation. No drastic measures were feared in the next few days.

On 8 April it was immediately clear that the danger of Great Power action in the North had been grossly underestimated. In the morning news was received of the Western Powers' mining of Norwegian territorial waters. Later in the day a stream of reports came in that a German armada with warships and transports was sailing north through Öresund and the Kattegat and that a long column of German troops was on its way north through Slesvig towards the southern frontier of Denmark. Although it could no longer reasonably be doubted that the Allies as well as Germany were now conducting their military operations on Nordic territory, the Swedish government was confident that these operations, at any rate for the present, would not touch Sweden. In general it underestimated Hitler's ruthlessness and the effectiveness of his armed forces. Only to a limited extent did it meet Thörnell's request for mobilization in the south. When on 9 April the Germans occupied Denmark and took control of the biggest towns in Norway, there were no forces to speak of at readiness in southern and western Sweden.

Contacts between the Swedish, Danish, and Norwegian Foreign Ministers in the days before 9 April were limited to a reciprocal exchange of information which they already had largely in common.

The question has been raised whether the flow of information on German activities from Stockholm to Copenhagen and Oslo was sufficiently exhaustive and conveyed strong enough warnings. The Swedes, however, had good reasons for considering that the ability of the Danes and Norwegians to acquire information was roughly equivalent to their own. Moreover, real Nordic collaboration was no longer possible. In the Great War the small and poorly armed Northern countries were merely pawns. It must have been obvious to Günther that, given the basic geographical, military, and political conditions, Norway would not oppose a British landing, nor Denmark a German invasion.

Neutrality, the Northern countries' traditional means of avoiding participation in Great Power conflicts, brought results so long as the Great Powers did not extend their fronts northwards. In 1939–40, however, their war machines were much more developed than in 1914–18, and they began their intense struggle at sea and over trade earlier than in the previous war. Churchill and Hitler put their trust in bold and unconventional operations and, because of their inadequate defence policies, the Northern countries provided for outsiders open and tempting doors for such actions. Behind the Soviet Union's attack on Finland was the desire to take control of certain parts of Finland, which it considered essential to its security. Behind Germany's attack on Denmark and Norway, behind the Allies' mining of Norwegian territorial waters and their plans for the subsequent occupation of four Norwegian harbours, lay the effort to intensify the war against the enemy. Sweden was – for the present at any rate – left aside essentially because her territory did not have the same importance as those of her neighbours for the strategy of the Great Powers.

## Operations in Norway and German pressure for railway transit

Germany's move against Norway and Denmark on 9 April 1940 left Sweden outside the sphere of operations; and Germany's primary interest in Sweden was to keep her to a continued policy of neutrality. In the morning of 9 April the German Minister in Stockholm, Wied, handed Günther a note which spelt out what Germany at present wanted from Sweden: the strictest neutrality ('Wahrung strengster Neutralität'); abstention from all measures directed against Germany's occupation of Denmark and Norway; in particular abstention from mobilization and concentration of troops;

continued deliveries of iron-ore. Oral assurances were given that Swedish interests would in no way be harmed through German actions against neighbouring countries.

That same afternoon the Swedish government handed over a written reply which accepted Germany's conditions but, nevertheless, reserved for Sweden complete freedom to take such steps as were necessary to safeguard and to defend her neutrality. It was added orally that, in certain circumstances, Swedish military preparedness could be increased, but that moves in this connection were not directed against German actions. In the next few days a general mobilization was carried out, although this was formally called an 'increased state of readiness'. On 9 April about 85,000 men were under arms, a week or so later over 320,000 — four times as many. It could not be doubted that Sweden intended to defend herself against a German attack.

On 11 April in Berlin, Ribbentrop summoned Richert and expressed his satisfaction with the Swedish reply to the German message two days earlier. He reiterated Wied's assurances that Sweden would be left out of the action undertaken against her neighbours, and repeatedly asserted that Germany desired to maintain the friendliest relations with Sweden. At the same time, however, he let Richert plainly understand

*Reading newspapers in Gothenburg on 9 April 1940. The headlines read: 'Germany attacks Norway' 'Denmark under German administration', 'Bergen and Trondheim occupied by German troops', 'Denmark surrenders without fighting'*

that Germany did not consider Sweden was entirely living up to the demands of the hour. He referred to what he considered incorrect and tendentious accounts of events in Norway in the Swedish papers and on the Swedish radio. He warned the Swedish government not to let the President of the Norwegian *Storting*, Carl J. Hambro, appear on Swedish radio. An even more serious warning came from Göring: Hitler, Göring declared, would consider such an appearance by Hambro a hostile act by Sweden.

In the prevailing circumstances the Swedish government found no scope at all for supporting Norway against Germany, as it had supported Finland against the Soviet Union during the Winter War. The legal obligations of neutrality had now to be respected. Hambro's appearance on the radio was cancelled. When the Norwegian Foreign Minister, Halvdan Koht, asked if King Haakon and Crown Prince Olav, who were fleeing from the Germans, could cross the Swedish frontier with guarantees for their return to Norway, he got the answer that they were welcome in Sweden, but that no such guarantee could be given. The government also gave the Western Powers to understand that no intervention by Sweden on their and Norway's side was to be counted on. Quite the contrary, every attempt to encroach on Swedish soil would be violently resisted. It seems that Günther obtained an undertaking from Britain that Allied troops would not cross the Norwegian-Swedish frontier, unless they were asked to do so by the Swedes.

A corresponding declaration was addressed to the Germans. A special delegation, headed by Admiral Fabian Tamm, visited Berlin on 15 and 16 April to convince Hitler that it was the set policy of the King, the government, and all Swedes to defend the country's frontiers against any invader. Their reception in Berlin was not unfriendly, but Göring, who said he personally had been entrusted by Hitler with the handling of Swedish affairs for the present, gave an emphatic warning of Hitler's patent annoyance at the Swedish press and of the mistrust many influential individuals in Berlin had of Sweden.

Developments in the Norwegian theatre could also rapidly lead to a crisis in Germany's relations with Sweden. Certainly, in the first week of that invasion the Allies' capacity for counter-action had showed itself more limited than expected. But, if their coming landings did meet with success, German counter-moves more or less affecting Sweden were to be feared; the safest lines of communication to the German forces in Norway were, in fact, overland through Sweden. Accordingly, Stockholm could not disregard reports or rumours from various quarters of German plans for an attack on Sweden. With the aim of fending off the Germans and to reinforce the assurances which had already been given in Berlin, King Gustaf on 19 April sent Hitler a personal message, in courteous but firm terms. Sweden would continue to maintain the strictest neutrality and, in consequence, would resist with all her forces every attempt to violate her frontiers from whichever side it came. An identical declaration, the King added, had been despatched to both Britain and France.

While a reply from Hitler was awaited, however, the storm-clouds darkened further. From various quarters rumours of an imminent German attack on Sweden flowed in steadily and of plans for German *coups* against Gotland and Åland. Overflights of German planes increased ominously. In a conversation with the Norwegian Minister in Stockholm, Johan Herman Wollebæk, on 24 April Günther indeed said that from one hour to the next he expected reports that German troops had advanced into Sweden.

On this occasion, however, the height of the crisis had passed. On 25 April a report was received from Richert of a reassuring conversation with Ribbentrop. The following day King Gustaf put before his government Hitler's reply, in which the Führer gave firm assurances that Germany in her turn would respect Sweden's neutrality. Clear evidence, Hitler wrote, had been found in Norwegian documents of Sweden's wish to remain neutral and of the correctness of Sweden's policy (equally of the Norwegian government's decision to join the Western Powers in their war against Germany in the event of a long-awaited Anglo-French landing). After mildly reproving the nervousness of the Swedes, which gave undue importance to each separate incident, Hitler ended his letter with an exhortation to pay particular attention to the New Order in the trade of the Baltic region. With this letter and similar statements in a public declaration by Ribbentrop on 27 April, the immediate danger of a German attack seemed to be over, even if it was apparent that no sure trust could at the time be placed in German undertakings.

For some weeks after 9 April, even in inner circles in Berlin, there was some uncertainty about Hitler's intentions and final decisions. This was reflected in the reports from the Swedish Legation in Berlin. Repeated assurances from senior German officers, led by Göring, that there were at present no plans to attack Sweden, mingled with repeated exhortations from Richert and his staff for Sweden to maintain the highest state of readiness and be on the alert. Both these themes seem, in retrospect, to have been correct and justified. An attack on Sweden was not envisaged, but because Hitler's attitude was so strongly affected by the situation at any given moment, it could not be ruled out. When Richert reflected on the reasons for the stabilization of Swedish-German relations, which took place towards the end of April, he attributed it to the visit of the Tamm delegation, the King's personal guarantee of Sweden's firm neutrality and of her will to resist every attack, Germany's concern with the Soviet Union, the increase in Sweden's military preparations, and Göring's benevolence. All these factors certainly contributed to the *détente*, which was reflected in Hitler's and Ribbentrop's statements during the last week of April. But one should perhaps stress more the German military successes in Norway as well as the increased attention Hitler began to pay to the long-delayed major offensive in the West, now on the point of being launched.

The Allied attempt to retake Trondheim began by landings well to the north and south of the town, at Namsos and Åndalsnes. The advances from these harbours ended in retreat and re-embarkation. When they thus evacuated central Norway on 2 May, the move caused both disillusion and sadness in Stockholm. Sweden was now more dependent than ever on Hitler's decisions, not least in matters of trade

*Arvid Richert,*
*Swedish Minister*
*in Berlin*

policy and supplies. She had expected that the British and French action would be more effectively launched and more adroitly planned. The general opinion held that too much emphasis had been placed on Narvik – by far the greater part of the iron-ore exports went through Luleå – and too little on Trondheim, which was clearly more vital strategically. All the same, the Western Powers still had troops outside Narvik. They had not given up their plan to retake the town, and after their expulsion from central Norway, must surely, for reasons of prestige, pursue it more urgently than before. As long as the German troops around Narvik were in direct danger, so was Sweden. She was, however, now militarily better prepared than before. Concentrations in the south and west had largely been completed as April ran out; there were a number of fortifications in the south, and in the west a speedy start had been made on the frontier defences.

Ever since the second week of the war in Norway, the Germans continually came back with requests for Swedish approval for the passage through Sweden of military supplies to their troops in Norway, in the first instance to the forces around Narvik. Pressure was further-more maintained through proposals for the delivery of Swedish war material, especially for the German troops at Narvik, at the Norwegian frontiers in the North in exchange for a generous amount of German weapons to be delivered in southern Sweden. The Germans were also discovered attempting to smuggle weapons in Red Cross transports. The Swedish government agreed that from the end of April civilian goods, on a scale consistent with normal peacetime requirements, could be sent in transit through Sweden. Meanwhile, shipments of war materials were constantly refused and proposals for barter arrangements and attempts at illegal transport rejected. The government stuck to its position even when Göring took it upon himself to present the German demands. On 6 May, he stressed to another Tamm delegation sent to Berlin Hitler's definite order that no means of avoiding defeat in Narvik should be left untried. Göring was annoyed at this repeated refusal and, in a fresh discussion with the delegation in Berlin on 11 May, warned of all kinds of adverse consequences for Sweden: *inter alia* limitations on freedom of movement in the Baltic and on imports, especially of war material, from Germany.

An even stronger argument for the Germans, however, was the general development of the war. Germany's long-anticipated offensive in the West had begun on 10 May and had met with tremendous initial successes: after a few days the Netherlands were occupied and Belgium going down to defeat. Nor did the Swedish government in any way underestimate the danger that victorious German arms might be turned against Sweden as well. Numerous detachments of troops were moved from Skåne, in the south, to the central region of Lake Vänern, which was considered to be one of the first German objectives. On the night of 14 May troops on the Norwegian frontier were put on full alert.

The Swedish government nevertheless maintained its refusal to agree to the passage of war material from Germany through Sweden to Norway. A request on 16 May from Ribbentrop — Göring, disappointed with Sweden's lack of understanding of Germany's needs, had given up his position as special *Schwedenreferent* — for transit to Narvik of one hundred railway-cars with military equipment and clothing for the German troops in north Norway was courteously, but firmly, refused. The Swedish government probably did not look on this new refusal as necessarily final; after his written assurances to King Gustaf, Hitler could reasonably be expected to issue an ultimatum before he attacked, and consequently the time and the opportunity for reconsidering the position would be found. But the government did not absolutely rule out a German attack without an ultimatum and, on the night of 18 May, at both the southern and western frontiers a state of full alert was ordered.

The Swedish government had not overplayed its hand. The Germans accepted this new refusal for the time being. But the Swedish Minister in Berlin warned that Hitler might return to the issue and would then not be content with anything less than complete satisfaction of his demands; if the government then still persisted in its refusal to permit the passage of war material, the consequences for Sweden could be catastrophic.

A small state on the edge of Europe, reviewing its policy in the last weeks of May 1940, could not possibly avoid taking into consideration the German army's overwhelming victories in the West and the prospect of an ultimate German victory. Brussels had surrendered on 17 May. The same day a new French government and a new French High Command had taken over. But the Allied reverses continued. On 20 May, German tank formations had reached the Channel coast and cut off the forces which had been rushed to the aid of Belgium, a week or so earlier. In the days that followed a counter-attack on the German salient from the south was repulsed. A week later, on 28 May, Leopold III and his army had capitulated, and the British army had begun the evacuation from Dunkirk. From Berlin and Rome came reports of Italy's imminent entry into the war. Hitler was well on the road to becoming the master of Europe.

Hitler was obviously disposed to leave Sweden in peace for the time being. Fears of a lightning German attack had lessened and, on 20 May, the Swedish forces at the frontiers were placed on lower readiness. But the general background was unchanged and grave. Germany's naval Commander-in-Chief, Grand-Admiral Raeder, who had just returned from a visit to Norway, on 22 May let his Chief-of-Staff inform the Swedish Naval Attaché in Berlin that nothing had changed in Germany's attitude to Sweden. But, the Chief-of-Staff emphasized at the same time, Berlin feared that the Allies had more far-reaching objectives in the North than the capture of Narvik, namely operations against the Swedish ore-fields, and Hitler was determined to press his operations at Narvik through to final German victory, utilizing roads through Sweden if necessary. The latter was not now an immediate issue, but the Swedes would be well advised to reflect on the situation.

As Hitler was not willing to accept a defeat at Narvik, he could be expected, after his victories in the West, to pay less regard to Sweden's point of view than ever before. On the other hand, it would be a very serious matter for the Swedish government to yield to a new German demand for transit of war materials. All earlier refusals had strong support in the *Riksdag*. Both in Berlin and in Stockholm consent could be taken as a sign that Sweden was yielding and ready to make even further concessions. The situation was in truth difficult and became even more disturbing when, on 28 May, Allied forces captured Narvik and the German troops retreated eastwards along the iron-ore railway towards the Swedish frontier. The respite Hitler had granted Sweden could very soon be at an end.

To extend this breathing-space and to have an alternative proposal to put forward in the event of a German ultimatum, Günther let Richert notify the *Auswärtiges Amt* privately of the 'Narvik Plan'. The Narvik Plan was less a plan worked out in detail than a lofty concept: both belligerent parties would evacuate the Narvik district, where Swedish troops would move in until the end of the war; south of this neutralized zone the German occupation forces would be in control, north of it the Norwegian government; no iron-ore would be exported through Narvik. Sweden's exceptionally difficult situation could justify even a shot in the dark, and this attempt in fact turned out to be favoured by events. The British and Norwegians rejected it to start with. But when, at the end of May and in early June, military developments on the Continent unfavourable to the Western Powers prompted a decision to withdraw to Britain the troops landed at Narvik, the Swedish proposition evoked approving interest. British consent was given on 31 May, Norwegian on

3 June, and, on the following day, Richert presented a formal Swedish proposal in Berlin.

However, if the plan became, in step with developments in the fighting, of increasing interest to Britain and Norway, so, conversely, it became the more superfluous for the Germans. To be sure, the German troops had evacuated Narvik on 28 May and withdrawn eastwards towards the Swedish frontier. But the Germans now anticipated an Allied evacuation and with it a final German victory in Norway. In this situation the German troops at Narvik had to hold out for only a short time and had no need to fear a further retreat eastwards before new Allied advances. Nor had they long to wait. In the evening of 8 June, through the good offices of the Swedes, a message from the Norwegian Commander-in-Chief reached the German Legation in Stockholm to the effect that King Haakon and his government had left Norway and, before doing so, had ordered him to cease hostilities. The war in Norway had ended, and therefore the problem of transit traffic for the German armed forces across Swedish territory was no longer pressing — at least for the moment.

No doubt the Swedish people, when in 1940 May gave way to June, felt that they lived under the threat of war. In retrospect too, these weeks are generally considered to have been the most critical for Sweden during the war years. How justified this view is cannot be discussed in greater detail here. It is a risky business to determine Hitler's real intentions; and even a preliminary assessment would require special research. But for Sweden's foreign policy at this time what was known of Hitler's plans was less relevant than what was thought possible. After Hitler's attack on Norway and Denmark on 9 April and on the Netherlands, Belgium, and Luxembourg a month later, his ruthlessness and the effectiveness of his armed might seemed boundless. Although written proposals with definite demands for the transit of military equipment were never received, much less an ultimatum, it could not be overlooked that five neutral countries had just been attacked without any preliminary warning. Berlin's displeasure with Sweden for her persistent refusal to allow transit of war materials and its far-reaching presumption on Sweden's help with the transit of provisions and hospital staff to, and wounded from, Narvik, transit visas, and rail traffic on the lines to Oslo and Trondheim amounted to a war of nerves. The on-and-off play of assurances that there were no plans to attack Sweden and of warnings that Hitler's interest and prestige were so deeply involved in Narvik that a continued Swedish refusal to allow the transit of war materials would not be tolerated,

could be interpreted as another move in the war of nerves. The unprecedented German military successes on the Continent made the signs on
the horizon more and more threatening.

The war in Norway lasted two months. It actually posed less complicated questions of foreign policy than the Finnish Winter War; since the
Soviet Union remained inactive, pressure from the Great Powers came,
not as in the Winter War from three, but only from two, directions,
and, as the fortunes of war turned against the Allies, from only one,
Germany. Consequently during the war in Norway, Swedish foreign
policy became more and more a balancing act between tolerable
Swedish-German relations and Swedish neutrality. This act was
performed with considerable success. Without doubt it involved risks.
Repeated German proposals for transit passage or other measures to
help the German troops at Narvik were rejected. And this happened
while the German armed forces went from victory to victory in the
North and West, while several European countries were subjected to
Hitler's domination, and while Sweden, little by little, slipped into a
German strategic encirclement.

The Norwegian government, like the British and French, found
certain Swedish concessions to German demands inconsistent with the
obligations of a strict neutrality. The rules of international law on
neutrality are inclined to be vague and controversial. Furthermore,
belligerents have a tendency to disregard even rules which they
recognize in theory, when the application of such rules would in their
view jeopardize the attainment of important military objectives. In
these circumstances it is hardly fair to blame a neutral state desperately
trying to stay out of the war, if it interprets or even stretches the law in
a way which conforms to its policy of balance and peace.

## The new European situation and the Swedish-German transit agreement

On 13 June the Prime Minister and Foreign Minister gave both Houses
of the *Riksdag* an account of the government's policy during the
Norwegian war. They concluded their speeches by maintaining that the
changed situation which had arisen after the departure of the Allied
forces from Norway and the Norwegian army's cessation of hostilities
involved a lessening of tension for Sweden inasmuch as the opportunities
for friction produced by the fighting around Narvik had diminished.
This, however, was not the whole truth, since at the same time German
pressure on Sweden was in fact increasing. On 16 June, Ribbentrop

received Richert in a castle in Belgium and made a new *démarche* on the question of transit traffic. He pointed out that war in Norway and fighting against Norwegians had ended. Thus the reasons repeatedly quoted by the Swedes for rejecting earlier demands for the transit of war materials had vanished. In such circumstances the government of the German Reich assumed that no difficulties would any longer be raised against the transport through Sweden to Norway of provisions and other kinds of goods, including weapons and ammunition, nor against the passage of German armed forces personnel in Norway, particularly when on leave. If any difficulties were to be raised on the Swedish side, Ribbentrop asserted several times, these would be interpreted as a downright unfriendly act. Conversely, compliance with the request would re-establish a good relationship and cancel out the earlier refusals. He urged Richert to emphasize to Günther the seriousness of the situation. He also expressed the hope of meeting his Swedish colleague later to discuss economic questions also. These were becoming of ever greater importance for both countries.

Richert ended his dispatch on his conversation with Ribbentrop with a warning against a negative reply, which, in his opinion, would 'be followed by the most far-reaching, perhaps catastrophic, consequences for our country and, in present circumstances, appears to me to be politically impossible'. This opinion also prevailed in Stockholm, all the more since at the same time a telegram had been received from the Swedish Minister in London implying that Britain was leaning towards a compromise peace. On 18 June therefore Günther informed Wied that Ribbentrop's request would receive a positive answer the next day.

Just how serious the danger of a German attack was in the event of a fresh Swedish refusal is obviously a matter for debate. But it cannot reasonably be contested that there was danger, and that at such a time the rejection of a major German demand would mean playing with fire. When the Germans resumed the offensive in the West on 5 June, they promptly smashed French resistance. Mussolini now felt that the situation guaranteed a short and victorious war and, on 10 June, he brought Italy into the war against Britain and France. On 14 June German troops marched into Paris. On 16 June the French Prime Minister, Paul Reynaud, resigned. His successor, Marshal Pétain, with Spain as an intermediary immediately requested an armistice. When, on 18 June, Ribbentrop's request for transit facilities came up for decision in Stockholm, the war on the Continent had thus resulted in an overwhelming German victory. Were Sweden now to go to war with Germany, she would do so in a militarily hopeless situation and with no prospect of help. And even if the challenge to Hitler, the master of Europe, which a negative reply to Ribbentrop must have implied from the German standpoint, should not lead to war, an omnipotent and ruthless dictator could resort to effective reprisals, for example through his trading and supply policies. Moreover, a danger of major political complications had arisen quite close to Sweden's own frontiers. Soviet troops had invaded Lithuania on 15 June and Estonia and Latvia on 17 June. Günther saw in this conquest of the Baltic States a prelude to a future trial of strength between Germany and the Soviet Union. With this in prospect, friction had to be avoided with both Great Powers if Sweden were to keep out of a future war between them.

After two weeks of negotiations there took place, on 8 July, an exchange of notes between Sweden and Germany on the transit traffic. The negotiations had been awkward. The Germans started with a formula which would place the Swedish rail network at their disposal; the Swedes tried to introduce as many restrictions as possible. On essential points the Swedish efforts were successful: according to the final texts transports were to be limited to what was technically feasible, soldiers on leave were to travel without their weapons, single travellers were to give prior notice, the leave traffic should be a pendulum traffic and must not be used to reinforce the German troops in Norway. Outside the agreement consent was given to transports of very limited numbers of troops between Trondheim and Narvik over Swedish railways, the so-called horseshoe traffic.

Günther himself took part in the negotiations with the German Legation and – in the closing stages – with envoy Karl Schnurre, a special negotiator from the German Foreign Ministry. Schnurre stood well with Ribbentrop and was thus worth cultivating, but with his overbearing manner, he was hardly welcome in Stockholm, where he frequently cropped up in succeeding years, mostly to put forward far-reaching German demands. That the Foreign Minister himself took part in the negotiations shows what great importance he attached to them; not least because of fears of a new Soviet advance in Finland, it must have been a matter of urgency to settle the transit questions with Germany by agreement.

The Swedish government must obviously have reckoned that the transit concessions now granted to the Germans would not be well received in Norway. But this awareness could not have weighed particularly heavily, when its refusal could have jeopardized Sweden's own existence. Furthermore, there were good reasons to expect that developments in Norway would move in the same direction as in Denmark, and that a comparatively moderate occupation regime would be established in Oslo on the same pattern as that in Copenhagen. After its flight from the country, the Norwegian government was held in low regard. The Praesidium of the *Storting* had recently asked King Haakon to abdicate. The Norwegians appeared willing to negotiate with the occupying power on the government of the country. In such circumstances the advantages which the Swedish concessions on transit traffic gave to Germany were not now, after the termination of hostilities, of significance when viewed against developments in Norway.

The settlement would obviously be unacceptable to the Western Allies. Neutrality could not encompass it, however widely its limits were stretched. Given the facts of German power, however, Britain could not take strong action. The British government on 20 July delivered a written protest and a warning against the continuation of a policy of yielding to Germany. Disillusionment and bitterness against Sweden were obvious in London, especially since the British plainly had an exaggerated conception of Swedish concessions. The Norwegian government's protest arrived a few days before the British, with a detailed exposition of international law. In its replies the Swedish government laid stress on its unaltered resolve to remain out of the war as a neutral and independent power. With the British government it contested the view that concessions to Germany in the present circumstances could be considered a breach of neutrality. To the Norwegian government it emphasized that a neutral state could not alone determine its policy of neutrality. Somewhat simplified, the argument was that a policy of neutrality, like all other policies, has to pay due regard to reality. Hitherto Swedish policy had been built on a certain balance of power between Germany and the Western Powers. When this definitely collapsed in June 1940 and a German hegemony over Europe replaced it, the outlook for Sweden's resistance to German pressure had become distinctly unpromising.

Britain, however, was still in the war, and, even if her troops had been expelled from the mainland of Europe, her navy still ruled the seas. Sweden was well aware of this too. Even in the situation which arose after Germany's attack on Denmark and Norway and Sweden's isolation from the West, she announced that she wished to adhere to the 1939 War Trade Agreement. A new shipping agreement was concluded; under it Swedish tonnage, which remained outside the Skagerrak barrier as the result of British or German measures connected with 9 April, was in part placed at the disposition of the Allies on time

71

charters, in part guaranteed free passage with bunkering rights and other concessions in British-controlled ports. These Swedish measures must probably have been seen in London as a sign that Stockholm did not by any means consider the outcome of the war decided or its end imminent. But they were quite unable to compensate for misgivings in Britain that Sweden was irresistibly falling under even stronger German influence. The Swedish government had had conclusive evidence of the strength of these misgivings even before London's reaction to the transit traffic agreement with Germany; at Thorshavn in the Faeroe Islands on 20 June a superior British naval force commandeered four Swedish destroyers, which had been bought in Italy and were now on their way home. After sharp Swedish protests the destroyers were soon handed back, and the British government later expressed its willingness to pay compensation for any damage which could be shown to be directly attributable to the confiscation of the vessels.

London was determined to show that Britain intended to continue the struggle against Germany ruthlessly. But Stockholm could not ignore the fact that Germany's recent victories had fundamentally altered the general conditions of Swedish foreign policy. In any policy reassessment which Stockholm would have to conduct, much less weight must be attached to Britain than a few months earlier.

# 1940–41

## 4    Between the German campaigns in the West and the East

### Swedish Mediation?

By midsummer 1940 an armistice was concluded between the Axis Powers and France. After Austria, Czechoslovakia, Poland, Denmark, Norway, the Netherlands, Belgium, Luxembourg, and now France, Europe's leading military power a few years earlier, had been struck down. After a campaign of six weeks in the West, Hitler dominated Europe as only Napoleon had done before him.

British troops had been hurriedly pulled out of Norway. In France and Belgium, after a few weeks' fighting, they had been pushed back to the Channel coast, whence most of them were evacuated through Dunkirk, at the cost of abandoning their arms. Neither the Fleet nor the Royal Air Force had been able to interfere with the German forces' spectacular success. The German war machine revealed itself as incomparably superior to the British; and Italy's entry into the war would further strain Britain's resources. Churchill had assumed power on 10 May. Chamberlain and Halifax, earlier supporters of an agreement with Hitler, remained in the Cabinet. In such circumstances indications of a British desire to negotiate with the enemy could not be dismissed as false. Were they not rather to be regarded as peace-feelers?

During the night of 17–18 June the Swedish Foreign Ministry received a telegram from London giving details of a conversation in the Foreign Office between Björn Prytz and R.A. Butler, Parliamentary Under-Secretary of State for Foreign Affairs. What Prytz reported was that the British desired to conclude peace on suitable terms: Halifax himself had let it be known through Butler to Prytz that 'commonsense not bravado would dictate the British Government's policy'. Other MPs, according to Prytz, expected Halifax to succeed Churchill as Prime Minister once the prospect of negotiations opened up.

For Günther it was a reasonable assumption that Halifax had leaked this information to Stockholm in order to have it passed on to Berlin.

73

True, on 18 June, Churchill made a great fighting speech in the Commons in which there was not the slightest sign of any will to give in. But in Stockholm this was not wholly irreconcilable with a wish to inform Berlin of a British desire to negotiate — the official position, Butler had said, would still be that the war must go on. Accordingly, on 19 June, Prytz was asked by Stockholm for his opinion whether 'the British attitude' (i.e., Halifax's and Butler's remarks) should be passed on.

Prytz promptly replied that what Butler and Halifax had said should be taken as reflecting their private opinion. It should not be passed on to Berlin because the British government's position had not yet been determined. Meanwhile Mallet had got hold of a summary of Butler's remarks to Prytz from a British correspondent in Stockholm: 'Britain would only continue to fight if certain of ultimate victory'. He duly reported this back to London and gave his source as a British correspondent in Stockholm who had his information from members of the Parliamentary Foreign Policy Committee. Mallet's report alarmed Butler, since to be suspected of defeatism at this time was no light matter. Prytz therefore authorized Butler to inform Mallet that the correspondent had got his facts wrong. Prytz then reported to Stockholm that in his judgement the matter was now closed. The incident, however, was to be regretted for its possible effect on the obtaining of information in the future. With this latest report Prytz had established that Butler's earlier remarks to him obviously did not represent the British government's position. On instructions from London, Mallet denied that there was any question of British feelers for negotiations.

Nevertheless, on 25 June, Mallet was informed through Marcus Wallenberg that the German Foreign Ministry was interested in finding out whether the British were inclined to negotiate, Halifax being considered a suitable negotiator. On his own initiative, Richert on 19 June had mentioned to State Secretary Weizsäcker, the official next in rank to Ribbentrop, that according to a telegram from Prytz which he had read in Stockholm 'a certain commonsense and desire to negotiate' were discernible in London. Weizsäcker returned to the subject on 22 June on the basis of a press report that Lloyd George was to set up a peace regime in Britain. Speculating on leaders who might be able and willing to adopt such a policy, he dismissed one name after the other, except Halifax, adding that he could see little sign of a desire to negotiate. Mallet remarked to Wallenberg that he himself did not believe that such a desire existed, but that he would pass on the information.

*Björn Prytz, Swedish Minister in London*

A more definitive investigation into what must have been the intentions behind Butler's remarks to Prytz on 17 June would obviously require thorough research into the British documents. What can be read from the Swedish documents is that Günther clearly judged the information Prytz forwarded as a signal to Berlin of a British willingness to negotiate. He was perhaps not unduly surprised that such a signal should be routed through Stockholm; in January 1940 Prytz had already reported a train of thought in the Foreign Office running on Swedish mediation between London and Berlin. However, he must soon have grasped that, whatever information Halifax and Butler wanted forwarded on 17 June, the search for a compromise peace was not the line Churchill had in mind to let his government follow.

Events in the following weeks, above all the British attack on French warships in Mers-el-Kebir at the beginning of July, left no doubt about Britain's determination to continue the fight. Yet Germany's interest in ending the war was confirmed in Hitler's long speech in the *Reichstag* on 19 July, when he called for common-sense in England. Halifax on behalf of the British government rejected this appeal in a speech some days later. Nevertheless, German hopes for peace were not yet wholly abandoned. In conversations with Dahlerus, his go-between in peace talks with the British government in 1939, on 26–28 July Göring underlined the paramount importance for all Europe of avoiding a prolonged war, adding that the only person of sufficient standing and trust to persuade Germany and Britain to start negotiations was the King of Sweden. Göring's remarks struck an answering chord in Stockholm. The conclusion of peace would open up the prospect of an easier situation for Sweden. Denmark and Norway could be free. Trade with the West could be resumed, the German transit traffic ended, and – not least – the Soviet Union could no longer exploit Germany's engagement in the West and her preparations for the invasion of England to advance the Soviet position in Finland.

King Gustaf V had several times before expressed his readiness to help in the preliminaries to negotiations for peace. But now the Swedish government pushed the matter more than the King. On 30 and 31 July instructions were sent to the Ministers in Berlin and London to convey to the Heads of State of Germany and the United Kingdom the King's compliments and to tender his good offices in arranging any contacts in case they might wish to explore the possibilities of peace. The Ministers were empowered to suggest that if both sides responded positively, negotiators could meet in Sweden in the strictest secrecy. Prytz too was instructed to inform Halifax that the King had acted wholly on his own initiative in order to spare Europe further bloodshed.

Both Hitler and King George VI turned down the offer. Hitler answered on 6 August that negotiations with the present British government were impossible and fruitless. Ten days later (after consulting the Commonwealth governments) King George replied (with Churchill's help) that before such a meeting could take place, Germany must give effective guarantees for the freedom of France, Poland, and other countries she had conquered and for the security of the British Empire. He did not thank King Gustaf for his intervention, which Hitler had done. In a conversation with Prytz, however, Halifax softened the tone of the British reply. Ribbentrop, in discussing the question with Richert, was friendly but restrained.

After Göring's remarks to Dahlerus, Stockholm did not expect such a negative reply from Hitler. Nor was the rebuke King George administered foreseen. Anyway, the war went on and Sweden had to adjust herself to a Europe which seemed to be dominated by Hitler's Germany for the forseeable future. But it was from the East, rather than the South, that the immediate danger threatened.

## A Swedish declaration of solidarity with Finland in Moscow?

On 25 April, without any preliminaries, Günther informed Erkko that the Swedish government had decided to take part in the defence of the Åland Islands and assumed that the Finnish government would agree. The Finns probably found this an impetuous move. Sweden had parried Finnish enquiries about sending Swedish troops to Åland in 1938–39 to forestall Soviet action against the islands. In 1940, however, when Stockholm feared a German occupation of Åland as part of an attack on Sweden, Finnish co-operation was taken for granted. Günther desired immediate military discussions, but these were refused. Marshal Gustaf Mannerheim, Finnish Commander-in-Chief, politely declined the despatch of Swedish troops to Åland, yet would not definitely confirm that his government would defend the islands if the Germans proposed their surrender. His answer was reported to Stockholm on 29 April, when Hitler's conciliatory reply of 24 April to King Gustaf's letter of some weeks earlier had lessened the tension. Nevertheless, Stockholm desired a more accommodating answer from Helsinki on the Åland question. The Finns were not inclined to give one. The Swedes got no more than assurances that the Finns would be glad to continue talks about the defence of Åland and to maintain the present situation in concert with Sweden. So, when new fears of German moves against Sweden started up at the end of May, the Finns had entered into no engagements with the Swedes. But what risks was Sweden ready to run for Finland?

Soviet troops completed their occupation of the Baltic States on 20 June and marched into the Romanian border provinces of Bessarabia and North Bukovina on the 28th. Simultaneously, on 27 June, the Soviet Union presented Finland with far-reaching demands. The Finns were offered the choice between withdrawal of their troops from the Åland Islands and joint Finnish-Soviet defence. Further, Moscow proposed either to take over the Anglo-Canadian concession in the nickel mines at Petsamo, or to set up a Finnish-Soviet company. The Soviet demands over Åland affected Sweden closely. Assarsson was instructed to seek elucidation of the Soviet attitude on Åland and on Sweden's particular interests there. Jarl Wasastjerna, Finnish Minister in Stockholm, had intimated that Finland had nothing against Swedish representations to Moscow on Åland. It was known in Stockholm, however, that the Finns were counting on neither Swedish nor German support for a stiffer attitude, and consequently intended to comply with the Soviet demands.

Molotov himself manifested Soviet favour for Sweden in April, when, among other things, he had expressed his satisfaction at the prospect of increased trade between the two countries. Swedish trade with the West had been cut off on 9 April. Thus it was clearly vital for Sweden to expand her trade with the Soviet Union, not least to offset her growing dependence on Germany. Negotiations were, however, long drawn out. Stockholm considered the Soviet demands excessive, Moscow pretended that the Swedes were dragging their feet. At the beginning of July, Boheman was sent to Moscow with new proposals. On 5 July he also got the chance to discuss the situation in the Baltic and particularly the Åland question with Molotov. Molotov was well disposed and stated that it was of prime interest for the Soviet Union 'that Sweden should maintain her neutrality and independence both at present and in the future. This view had been made clear elsewhere'. When Boheman asked whether he could take it that, after the latest changes, the situation in the Baltic had been stabilized, Molotov replied firmly that it was so. 'No further changes are to be expected and the Soviet Union's relations with Finland are good'. The Soviet Union was also interested in the return of independence to Norway and Denmark. As for the Åland Islands, it was in everybody's interest that they should revert to this pre-war status and be demilitarized. The Finnish government shared their view. Did not the Swedish also? In any case, he could give positive assurances that there were no surprises in store for Sweden over Åland.

The Swedish Legation in Helsinki had meanwhile reported cracks in the previously solid home front in Finland. The newspapers began to discuss more and more a crisis in the government. From Moscow, Assarsson reported that the Soviet press painted the situation in Finland in ever darker colours; and he concluded a despatch on Soviet foreign policy with the ominous speculation that, if Hitler's war against Britain continued for a long time, Stalin would eventually try to exploit the situation by assuming complete control of Finland.

About the middle of July, Stockholm received yet graver intelligence from the East. The Soviet Union had requested rail passage for troops and war material to Hanko, their base just outside Helsinki. Witting expressed alarm at the consequences for Finland of worsening Russo-German relations. On instructions from home, Wasastjerna emphasized to Per Albin Hansson, who was acting as Foreign Minister in Günther's absence, that his government was worried at the way its relations with the Soviet Union were developing. There was always a new demand from Russia and, in the Finnish government's view, the request for transit rights to Hanko 'could be interpreted as the beginning of the penetration of the whole of Finland'. The Finnish government expected no instant reaction from the Swedes, but wished to give them time to consider all eventualities.

On 19 July, Günther expressed the view to his colleagues that there was no immediate reason for the Finns' concern. But in general he shared their pessimistic view of possible developments. If Hitler attacked England, and Stalin then decided to act, the whole of Finland would be in danger. To hold the Soviet Union back he proposed that Moscow should be informed that Sweden would consider an attack on Finland as an attack on Sweden. At first, however, the Swedes should take soundings in Berlin to make sure that the Germans would not act against them in Moscow and deny them supplies in a war. If Germany's reply was negative, nothing could be done to help Finland, but nothing would be lost by asking. There was, however, no support for this scheme to aid Finland, the Social Democratic ministers being strongly opposed to it.

Meanwhile Finland's prospects of finding in Berlin reassurance against Moscow became dimmer and dimmer. In his victory speech in the *Reichstag* on 19 July, Hitler announced that relations between Germany and Russia had been definitively settled. He emphasized that neither party had encroached on the other's sphere of interest, as defined in their agreement of the previous year – which seemed to imply that Germany did not see herself as having any special interest in Finland. When Dahlerus, on instructions from Stockholm, asked Göring what Germany's attitude would be to 'possible Swedish action in a new conflict between Finland and Russia', the Reichsmarschall's reply was evasive; he preferred to discuss the prospects of Swedish mediation for peace between Berlin and London. Continued soundings by Richert indicated that Germany would allow Russia a free hand in Finland. As long as the war with Britain continued, Richert concluded on 8 August, Germany would permit the Soviet Union to work her will on Finland, without helping in the least to counter Soviet aggression, and would probably take a negative attitude to help from Sweden. With her maritime trade cut off, Germany could not, on economic grounds, afford to risk a break with Russia.

Nevertheless, to the Parliamentary Foreign Policy Committee on 13 August Günther proposed that a determined Swedish effort should be undertaken in Moscow to restrain the Soviet Union from acting against Finland. Recent intelligence reports had been alarming, he said. There was a real danger that the Russians were preparing to act against the whole of Finland. The Finnish Foreign Minister had recently appealed to him to emphasize in Moscow Sweden's solidarity with Finland. The risk of becoming involved in the war in the West was now less than during the Winter War. The Finns had argued that, if Sweden, without consulting the Germans, took resolute action in support of Finland, Germany would be likely in its own interest to back her up. Swedish soundings in Berlin, however, had been negative. Furthermore, Günther added, there was a definite risk that if a war in Finland went against Finland and Sweden, Germany would occupy Sweden for the sake of her own security.

The doubts most of the Committee already held on the advisability of intervening in Moscow must have been reinforced by Günther's information about Germany's attitude. The Prime Minister spoke out strongly against intervention. Nothing good had come of the approach to Moscow the previous year, and there was now no real basis for trying again. Günther accordingly let the matter of a declaration in Moscow drop, but after lengthy discussions, the government authorized him to underline Sweden's interest in a free Finland.

There were no Finnish attempts, comparable to those during the Winter War, to change Sweden's standpoint. Witting reiterated his view that the Swedes should make it clear that they would consider an attack on Finland an attack on Sweden. But in reality he was betting on Germany, not on Sweden. More reassuring information, however, began to come in. The Soviet Vice Commissar for Foreign Affairs, Lozovskij, assured Assarsson on 13 August that the Soviet troop concentrations were necessary to protect the borders and that there was no question of marching into Finland. Deliveries of German war material to Finland and a calmer political situation in Finland were reported soon afterwards. On 19 August, Molotov himself informed Boheman that the Soviet Union would be very patient with Finland. On 21 August a friendly speech by Ryti three days earlier was reported correctly and in full in the Soviet press. Finally, on 24 August, Madame

Kollontay informed Günther that 'according to reports from Moscow there has been an improvement in relations between Finland and the Soviet Union'. According to Assarsson several diplomats in Moscow had the same impression; they considered that this development was partly due to increased Russian interest in the Balkans.

Günther was obviously conscious of the opposition in the government and in the *Riksdag* to his proposal to intervene in Moscow in Finland's support. He must equally have been aware of the wide-ranging implications of his policy – the danger of war with the Soviet Union; a growing dependence on Germany; ever closer ties with Finland, a country with an exposed position, a foreign policy difficult to control, and a disturbing internal situation. He can hardly have forgotten that no Swedish declaration of military support was forthcoming during the Finnish-Soviet negotiations in the autumn of 1939, or that his predecessor fell from office because of a policy which threatened to bring Sweden into a war on Finland's side or, finally, that he himself during the Winter War had assiduously striven to avert such a danger. That he now played for such high stakes must have been due to his basic conviction that a new Soviet move against Finland would have the aim of subjugating her after a short war and incorporating her in the Soviet Union, not, as at the end of the Winter War, of obtaining a new and strategically more favourable frontier. By such a move Sweden's position would be completely transformed. Finland's downfall could bring Sweden down too, since a German occupation of Sweden to counter the Soviet approach to the Norwegian coast and the Swedish iron-mines could not be ruled out.

Günther's suspicions of future Soviet action against Finland were not without foundation. Stalin was perhaps not considering the liquidation of Finland just at that time, but his policy towards Finland had begun to resemble that towards the Baltic States – subversion from within, pressure from without. The ultimate goal seemed to be the same – complete capitulation.

But those responsible for Finland's foreign policy now began to count on a vastly stronger ally. Germany's policy towards Finland had changed. On 18 August, Göring's special emissary, Josef Veltjens, and Mannerheim concluded an agreement on deliveries of German arms to Finland, in return for the right to transport troops and war material from harbours in the Gulf of Bothnia to north Norway.

Germany dominated the Baltic. Relations with Germany were the primary concern of Sweden's foreign policy.

## Swedish-German relations

In Sweden, the Prime Minister, summing up recent developments in Europe in a speech on 7 July, said that it was impossible to disregard events which involved the total or partial occupation of seven European countries and the conclusion of an armistice by France. In the election campaign a few weeks later he elaborated this theme. 'Our attitude to foreign affairs', he said on 28 July, 'has not been, and is not, determined by regard to political ideologies .... Our position and the structure of our economic life make it a vital interest for us to keep roads open to South and West and East alike'. In the *Riksdag* on 16 August the Foreign Minister, directing his remarks both to Swedish and foreign listeners, notably those in Berlin, expounded the government's attitude to foreign affairs.

. . . it would be absurd to presume that our country could remain untouched by what happens in Europe. It is essential for us to follow developments vigilantly and to make our natural contribution to them, while preserving for ourselves a decisive hold upon our continued existence as a free nation.

The Swedish government wanted to make known, both at home and abroad, particularly in Berlin, Sweden's resolve to maintain neutrality and independence, and to that end conduct both a firm and a flexible policy.

The background for these statements was the abundant oratory in Berlin, after Germany's victories, about the New Order which could be created in Europe and include also the Northern countries. The most authoritative and, at the same time, the most disturbing, contribution was a long speech by Rosenberg, the Nazis' chief ideologist, on 9 July. The Nordic lands, he said, were now called upon to share the common destiny of Europe in a common political and economic front under German leadership. This alarming prospect was widely commented on in the Swedish press, Rosenberg's invitation to accept the patronage and protection of Germany being everywhere rejected. His call to the Northern lands to join the new community of Europe was repeated in leading German papers, but damped down and embroidered with allusions to the economic and cultural advantages small countries could expect.

Although they posed no immediate problems, Rosenberg's opinions were taken very seriously in Stockholm as representing the long-term aims of German foreign policy. Berlin, furthermore, was now displeased with Sweden, Göring emphasized in conversations with Dahlerus on

26 and 28 July. He complained of the objectionable, inexplicable, and tactless remarks appearing in the Swedish press about leading Germans as well as of the speculations in the papers on a coming Russo-German conflict. To prevent complications and to ensure amicable co-operation, he said, the community of interests between Germany and Sweden should be clarified in the very near future. He insisted that to this purpose the Swedish government should establish clear guidelines for foreign policy and in military and commercial matters, because otherwise 'pressure from Germany with a request for an answer in a very short time' was to be feared.

Nevertheless, the concrete demands in respect of foreign, commercial, and military policies which Göring said were to be expected if Sweden did not comply, were not presented. There were obviously men in the German Foreign Ministry and in Party circles who had grandiose plans for the reorganization of the European economy. On the pattern of German trade with the Balkans, the foreign trade of the small countries of Europe was to be centred on Germany. The Northern countries were not to be cut off from their transoceanic trade, but the mainspring of their commerce would be the new, planned economy of Europe. Such was their vision of the future. Fortunately the German commission for Swedish-German trade was largely staffed by professionals with many years' experience of negotiating with Sweden and an understanding of Sweden's attitude and requirements. During this difficult spring and summer the Swedish commission led by Gunnar Hägglöf, then head of the trade department of the Foreign Ministry, and Jacob Wallenberg, the banker, accordingly succeeded in concentrating the negotiations more and more on topical issues concerning the goods to be exchanged and their prices. The extraordinary deterioration in Sweden's bargaining position was reflected in retreats from standpoints which had been successfully maintained at the turn of the previous year; the figures then agreed upon for Swedish exports in 1940 (not to exceed the level of 1938 and in the case of iron-ore specifically, not to exceed 10 million tons) were now cancelled by German request. For the Swedes this involved a departure from the Anglo-Swedish War Trade Agreement. This, however, was more a matter of principle than of practical importance; the long winter, the demolition of Narvik harbour, and the late resumption of sailings from Luleå could be expected to keep the iron-ore exports to the previously agreed level. On the whole, few concessions were in fact made, and a new freight agreement, although it served German interests better than that of the previous winter, was of value also to

Swedish ships which after 9 April were shut up in the Baltic by the minefields across the Skagerrak and could now be used for Baltic trade. Efforts to reach agreement on a limited amount of oceanic trade to and from Sweden fared worse, the conditions the Germans sought to impose being unacceptable.

On the political side the Germans did not raise any major questions for a long time after the conclusion of the transit agreement on 8 July. This, however, they immediately found unsatisfactory. Demands for extra single transit journeys as well as for extensions of transport facilities already agreed were made one after another. As a rule these German requests were accepted. Thus the 'horseshoe traffic' involving transport of German troops from Trondheim to Narvik was allowed to continue after the number of journeys agreed on in July had been completed in September — and this without laying down precisely what this extension involved. A supplementary agreement of 14 September doubled the normal leave traffic. Extra journeys were allowed for the transit of some special groups, and even of an SS battalion. On the other hand, a request for passage for 15,000 troops to north Norway in October was refused, reference being made to the departure from neutrality which the transit of troops involved and to repercussions in Britain and the United States. On an average, 1,800 German soldiers travelled through Sweden each day in October and November and by the turn of the year about 260,000 had passed through.

In Berlin, German-Swedish military contacts were considered very satisfactory — particularly after Hitler in August invited a Swedish military delegation to study the situation in the lands he had conquered in the West. After the end of the war in Norway, there was no longer any suspicion in Berlin that Swedish arms would be turned against Germany. Conversely there was in Stockholm no longer any direct fear of German action against Sweden. Germany's strategic aim was the defeat of Great Britain, and the conquest of Sweden had no part in it. Defence arrangements in Sweden were made accordingly; in April over 400,000 men had been under arms, in October 1940 there were about 200,000. Work on fortifications and training could now be directed towards more long-term efforts.

Pressures to the point of an ultimatum, which Göring had warned Dahlerus about, did not occur whether in trade, foreign, or military policies. German activity over Swedish press policy was, however, lively. In the two months of July and August 1940, twenty-five German representations about the Swedish press and radio, from *notes verbales* with the 'sharpest protests', to discreet, spoken interventions, were recorded against forty during the whole war to that date. The complaints ranged over a wide field — the repetitions of scandalous British comments on Hitler, slurs on the German army, the preference of the Swedish Telegram Bureau and broadcasting services for the 'enemy's' news, the *Göteborgs Handelstidning*'s *(G.H.T.)* 'hate campaign' against Germany, and so on. Berlin's patent displeasure with the Swedish press worried Stockholm exceedingly. By circulars, conferences, and personal contacts the authorities appealed to the newspapers' sense of responsibility. And Günther stated in the *Riksdag* on 16 August that it would be to the country's advantage if the press took a more objective and realistic line towards general political developments.

The press, however, remained the big issue in Swedish-German relations. On 13 September the German Legation, on instructions from Berlin, presented a sharply worded note declaring that the Germans could no longer tolerate the *G.H.T.*'s 'Greuelmeldungen' and demanding resolute action to end it. The overwhelming success of the Social Democrats in the elections to the Lower House a few days later, which the Germans might construe as support for a party unfriendly to themselves, prompted the government to act against *G.H.T.*, 'to show', in Günther's words, 'that the government was not unfriendly to the Germans'. Accordingly, on 16 September the issues of *G.H.T.* for 13, 14, and 16 September were confiscated; issues of several left-wing papers had already suffered. More issues of *G.H.T.* were confiscated in October. The German protests were noticeably fewer in subsequent months. The tone of the Swedish press, however, though now perhaps more subdued than before, was basically no more friendly towards Germany. One must therefore conclude that the main reason for the German leaders' displeasure was the fact that a small Northern neighbour refused to bow to Europe's new masters. When the Swedish government did make a suitable gesture, German protestations were toned down.

It is probable that those responsible for Germany's foreign policy felt all the more entitled to insist on such an action since they never put forward any specific proposals for Swedish co-operation in the New Order in Europe. In confidential and personal discussions they showed surprise at Sweden's obstinate failure to adjust herself to events, coupling this with more or less threatening predictions on what the future held for her. Göring (like the German Minister in Stockholm in the First War, Franz von Reichenau) spoke of a Great Germany, in which Sweden would have a position like that of Bavaria. Werner von Grundherr, head of the Northern Department in *Auswärtiges Amt*, was a bit more generous, being prepared to allow Sweden a place like Hungary and Slovakia. Hints were dropped that Sweden should of her own initiative offer suitable suggestions — but not too late, or they would be considered a purely opportunistic move. But the fact remains that, officially at least, no German proposals were ever made. Nor, for that matter, was Sweden's adherence to the Three Power Pact concluded in September between Germany, Italy, and Japan ever discussed. Indeed, when Hitler spoke to Sven Hedin on 5 December he categorically declared — for what it was worth — that the Swedish people should retain their freedom for ever and their national identity unimpaired.

## Swedish-Finnish co-operation in foreign and defence policies?

By the transit agreement with Finland, Germany again advanced her position in the North. Norway and Denmark lay under German occupation. Through Sweden and now also through Finland, Germany transported considerable forces and supplies. In certain respects the Finnish-German agreement was more far-reaching than the Swedish-German; it provided whole new formations to the occupation forces in Norway and envisaged a not insignificant German logistical organization on Finnish soil. Hitler, however, avoided any engagement to Finland in her negotiations over Åland and Petsamo in Moscow. He gave no guarantee whatsoever of German support against increased Soviet pressure or military action. Obviously he wished to avoid coming into conflict with Stalin over Finland. But the Finns knew, of course, that, with German troops in the country, they were better able to resist Soviet pressure; and in all quarters directly concerned, in Berlin and Moscow, in Helsinki and Stockholm, a growing Finnish orientation towards Germany had to be envisaged as a possible, not to say a certain, development.

On 20 September, Wasastjerna mentioned to Günther that in many quarters in Finland it was feared that her drawing closer to Germany would be at the expense of links with Sweden. Wasastjerna hinted that Sweden should take the initiative to deepen and widen Swedish-Finnish relations; even a union might be possible. Next, on 30 September, the Finns reported that Molotov had told Juho Kusti Paasikivi, Finnish Minister in Moscow, that he was aware of a secret treaty between

Sweden and Finland directed against the Soviet Union. On Paasikivi's immediate denial, Molotov had stuck to his story and asserted that he could produce documentary evidence of it. Wasastjerna stated that the Finns would appreciate Sweden's categorical denial in Moscow, provided that this explanation was qualified by a statement that 'obviously Sweden could not say in advance how she would conduct herself in the event of a conflict'. Without this qualification, the Finns did not want the Swedes to bring up the matter in Moscow at all.

On 5 October, Günther rendered an account of Finnish affairs in the Parliamentary Foreign Policy Committee. The Swedish government should not, in his view, turn its back on Finland but try to find ways of persuading the Finns from continuing on the pro-German course they had now set. Several members of the Committee recommended a more active Swedish policy towards Finland than to date.

However, it might be doubted that the prerequisites of such a policy actually existed in Helsinki. About the scope of the Finnish-German transit agreement, its importance in Finland's general policy, and the Finnish government's share in its creation Günther had no precise intelligence. He was without definite official information on the Finnish attitude to ideas of a far-reaching *rapprochement* between Finland and Sweden. Witting told Marcus Wallenberg (on a visit to Helsinki) that he did not rule out 'the sudden conclusion of an alliance with Germany', although, he said, he also toyed with the idea of close Finnish-Swedish co-operation. Ryti in his talk with Wallenberg put more stress than Witting on Finland's freedom of action *vis-à-vis* Germany, her desire for neutrality, and her readiness to try to dispel Soviet suspicion. But he did not elaborate on closer connections between Finland and Sweden. In a discussion with Günther in mid-October, Wasastjerna proposed that Sweden should make a declaration of support for Finland in Moscow in the event of a new Soviet attack. Günther refused forthwith; Sweden would not encourage Finnish plans for revenge or bind herself to Finland's foreign policy, which Sweden had no means of controlling. He was, however, prepared to discuss, on a personal basis and without obligations, the possibilities of a closer relationship between Sweden and Finland, subject to the understanding that the foreign policies of both countries were run by Stockholm and that Finland abandoned all thoughts of revenge against the Soviet Union. This was, however, also conditional on suitable preliminary soundings showing that neither the Russians nor the Germans had insuperable objections.

On 26 October, Wasastjerna informed Günther that the Finnish government had approved the proposals in principle. A few days later

Madame Kollontay called on Günther to give him the most definite assurances that the Soviet Union would not violate Sweden's neutrality and independence — which, she added, implied that the Soviet Union had no plans for aggression against Finland. She gave as her private opinion that an agreement between Sweden, Finland, and the Soviet Union to maintain the *status quo* should be pursued. Günther pointed out the danger of an adverse reaction from Germany and put forward the idea of an agreement between Sweden and Finland only. Madame Kollontay did not reject the suggestion outright, but remarked that it required careful soundings in Moscow where any proceedings to which the Soviet government was not a party aroused concern and suspicion.

In fact, Günther had already instructed Assarsson to take cautious soundings about Moscow's reasons for concern at Swedish-Finnish collaboration, with the aim of promoting Soviet understanding of such plans. On 11 October, Assarsson, in discussions with Molotov, expressed the view that collaboration between Sweden and Finland could restrain Finland from embarking upon adventurous policies. Molotov did not react and only emphasized his distrust of certain elements in the Finnish government which did not follow the same course as Paasikivi. Despite such an unpromising start, Günther deemed Sweden's position in Moscow to be strong enough to continue the effort. Relations between the countries had in fact been smooth in recent months. After Boheman's talk with Molotov in July about the Soviet demand for the demilitarization of the Åland Islands, Sweden had not pressed the matter. In August she had given *de facto* recognition to Russia's annexation of the Baltic States. Trade negotiations had ended successfully in September; in discussing them at the end of August, Madame Kollontay had said to Günther that the conclusion of an agreement 'would be important for the consolidation of Russo-Finnish ties and would on the whole result in a readiness in Moscow to lend an ear to Swedish wishes and Sweden's viewpoint'. On various occasions Molotov had given an impression of Soviet goodwill and a desire for good relations.

Günther surveyed Swedish-Finnish relations for his government colleagues on 30 October. He emphasized the influence of Germany in Finland, which could possibly prevent closer Finnish collaboration with Sweden, and the doubtful attitude of Moscow, where Molotov's suspicions of certain circles in Finland were clear enough. Two days later he returned to the question. If Sweden did nothing to encourage the Finns, Finland would come increasingly under German protection. A peaceful solution of the differences between Germany and the Soviet

Union was now most unlikely. If Finland became a German vassal, Sweden could not in the long term remain neutral in a Russo-German conflict and ran the risk of coming under German control. Something had to be done to meet what he chose to call the Finns' request for negotiations. After lengthy arguments the government on 4 November approved the text of a reply which, however, did not yet agree to negotiations, but proposed explorations, first in Helsinki, then in Berlin and Moscow, to see whether a basis for negotiations could be found.

But on 5 November, the day after this decision, things came to a head. Madame Kollontay requested an urgent meeting with Günther. From Finnish sources, she said, she had learnt that Sweden and Finland were planning a closer co-operation; although she had no instructions from Moscow, she most emphatically begged the Swedes to refrain from taking such a step. A *rapprochement* between Sweden and Finland would be viewed with the strongest suspicion in Moscow and would undoubtedly be interpreted as a German intrigue. Indeed, it would be construed as an unfriendly act. From Berlin, Richert had also reported from a good source that any Swedish attempts to woo Finland from Germany would seriously disturb Germany's relations with Sweden. Hansson and Günther now decided to let the matter rest for the present; and the Finns, the Russians, and the Germans were so informed. The Finnish government took the same view as the Swedish.

Finland was one of the chief topics in Hitler's discussions with Molotov in Berlin on 12–13 November. Molotov persistently tried to gain Hitler's agreement to the Soviet Union having a free hand in Finland. Hitler accepted that Finland was in the Soviet sphere of influence, but repeatedly declared that Germany was resolutely opposed to any conflict in the Baltic region. Sweden's continued integrity and neutrality they both recognized as being in both countries' best interests.

The information about these talks, mainly from German sources, which reached Stockholm in succeeding weeks gave no accurate account of the sharp disagreement about Finland, even if Göring said straight out that Molotov's aim had been to get a free hand for the occupation of Finland and North Scandinavia — which had been firmly refused. Günther reported to the Parliamentary Foreign Policy Committee on 3 December that 'everything pointed to the North having been discussed only as a side issue during Molotov's visit', while there was good reason to believe that the main talks were on economic matters.

In the circumstances Günther considered there was a possibility of Sweden and Finland together withdrawing from the rivalries of the Great Powers and with their permission forming a neutral Nordic bloc. Through cautious soundings he therefore set out to gain both German and Russian sympathy for such a move. Closer collaboration between Sweden and Finland, he told Grundherr on 21 November during his visit to Stockholm, was very much in Germany's interest, and the Soviet Union's objections to it could conceivably be overcome. He would not be averse to hearing, quite informally, Germany's views on this. In several discussions with Madame Kollontay a few days later he touched on Swedish-Finnish co-operation, emphasizing on 4 December that one great advantage of this would be 'that Swedish foreign policy would be dominant and not that of another power'.

The Soviet Union, however, would not allow any other power to dominate Finnish foreign policy. On 6 December, Molotov summoned Paasikivi to transmit a sharp warning to the Finnish government that, if an agreement was reached between Sweden and Finland which subordinated Finland's foreign policy to Stockholm, Moscow would consider the peace treaty of 12 March abrogated. Just to underline in whose sphere of interest the Soviet Union considered Finland to be, he also said that, while the Soviet Union did not wish to interfere in Finnish affairs, it followed closely the preliminaries for the Presidential elections. 'It was obvious', he remarked, 'that if somebody like Tanner, Kivimäki, Mannerheim, or Svinhufvud were to be elected President, we would conclude that Finland did not desire to fulfil her obligations under the Peace Treaty with the Soviet Union'.

The Finnish government now proposed a joint declaration to Molotov by Assarsson and Paasikivi. The Swedes were not ready for this, but made a statement of their own in which they took responsibility for initiating the discussions on Swedish-Finnish collaboration, and guaranteed that any resulting joint policy would be well disposed to the Soviet Union. No definite action would be taken without ascertaining that a positive attitude existed in both Moscow and Berlin. Molotov was not to be moved. When Assarsson put the above points to him at a meeting on 14 December, he merely repeated the remarks he had made to Paasikivi the previous week and asked whether a secret treaty had not already been concluded between Sweden and Finland — which Assarsson denied. Günther proffered the same denial to Madame Kollontay after he received Assarsson's telegram describing his talk with Molotov. The Russians never raised the matter again. About suggestions of closer collaboration between Sweden and Finland,

Molotov's declaration of 6 December was their final word.

A similar veto came from Berlin about the same time. Hitler himself was behind it. On 5 December he received Sven Hedin (see p.86), who had been carefully briefed by Richert with Günther's approval. Referring to his previous conversation with Hitler in March, Hedin inquired what the Führer's present attitude was to the situation in the North. The situation, answered Hitler, had completely changed. England's and France's plans had miscarried, and Sweden need no longer be concerned for Finland. Certainly, during his visit to Berlin, Molotov had made it clear that the Soviet Union wanted to occupy the whole of Finland, but after the answer he got, this was now ruled out. Asked about his attitude to Swedish intervention in the event of a Soviet attack on Finland, Hitler said that he had given Molotov to understand that Germany would not tolerate such a move. Nor would he approve of a union, or some similar agreement in secret, between Sweden and Finland: it would be a breach of the Moscow treaty and a provocation to the Soviet Union. Finland should pursue a cautious and shrewd policy and not give Moscow cause for fresh misunderstandings or unpleasantness.

In arguing against Swedish-Finnish co-operation Hitler stressed the interests of the Soviet Union. His true reason was different. Only a few hours after Sven Hedin had left, he received the Commander-in-Chief of the Army, Field-Marshal von Brauchitsch, and the Chief of the Army General Staff, Colonel-General Halder, who presented their plan for a major offensive against the Soviet Union the next year. Hitler decided that the Finns and the Romanians should take part in it. Finland was now definitely earmarked as an ally and a Swedish-Finnish union would disturb Hitler's plans.

For Günther it was essential to allay German suspicions that Sweden was carrying out an anti-German policy in Finland. He consequently let Richert tell Weizsäcker what had happened with regard to the plans for Swedish-Finnish collaboration. Richert was further instructed to state that in the prevailing circumstances Sweden would make no further moves in this direction. The German reaction was to issue a warning through normal diplomatic channels — Hitler had not given Sven Hedin permission to report his remarks to anybody apart from King Gustaf. When Wied called on him to transmit his government's view, Günther formally confirmed that the advice it offered was already being followed, remarking that, at any rate, Moscow was now more aware of Sweden's lively interest in Finland's fate.

Ryti's election to the Presidency in December was immediately followed by a new government in Finland with Johan Rangell, a banker, as Prime Minister, while Witting remained Foreign Minister. On behalf of this new administration Wasastjerna stated in mid-January that the Finnish government was still interested in the concept of a union, but this must be left in abeyance, since pertinent initiatives in foreign policy were not at present a practical proposition. Finland had noted with satisfaction the Swedish intimation to Moscow that an independent Finland was a major concern of Sweden. Could Sweden, at a suitable opportunity, also make it clear in Moscow that she could not stand idly by in the event of Finland's territorial integrity being violated? This question was again answered in the negative – as the Finnish government must have known it would be. A proposal originating with Mannerheim for collaboration between the military staffs of the two countries was also turned down.

Shortly after these exchanges Assarsson reported that, according to reliable Finnish sources, Hitler, about the turn of the year, had let a Finnish emissary in Berlin be informed that he would not permit any challenge to Finland's integrity and that future developments could be looked forward to with equanimity in Helsinki. This had greatly lessened the tension in leading Finnish circles and apparently caused them to abandon the thought of a *rapprochement* between Sweden and Finland for the time being.

Conversations between Stockholm and Helsinki on closer Swedish-Finnish co-operation, possibly leading to a union between the two countries, virtually ended after Madame Kollontay's warning of 5 November. Her intervention thus freed both from the awkward duty of defining just how far they were really prepared to go. Despite the absence of any binding commitments by either the Swedish or the Finnish government, Günther persisted in smoothing the way for the idea in both Moscow and Berlin. Possibly he thought that the concept could have some value for both Stalin and Hitler since, if Sweden and Finland could be maintained as a neutral zone between them, their strategic plans would be simplified. But neither Stalin nor Hitler was prepared to allow the two Nordic countries to co-operate politically in order to stand aside in a conflict between Germany and the Soviet Union. Consequently there was no basis for such a policy.

Later judgements on these events speak of the shipwreck of plans for a union. This is incorrect. The Swedish and Finnish governments had not reached the point of putting forward any such plan. They were only at the stage of agreeing to investigate whether the preconditions for it existed. It is extremely doubtful that they did exist. Those who directed foreign policy in Finland at the time were more eager for reassurances in Berlin than in Stockholm. As for Sweden, neither unconditional support for the Finns against the Soviet Union, nor acceptance by the public of complete political and military co-operation with Finland, could be taken for granted.

## Balance-sheet for 1940 – Hitler's great year

The events of 9 April cut Sweden's links with the West. After the Allies' retreat from Norway, Sweden was strategically surrounded by Germany. Relations with Britain had diminished as they had never done since the Napoleonic Wars. To be sure, Britain soon began to climb up from the nadir of her fortunes in the summer of 1940. The expected German invasion did not materialize. Italy's attack on Greece started disastrously for Mussolini. The British fleet scored several important successes against the Italian. The British army pushed the Italians back along the Libyan coast. America provided Britain with more and more resources. The British tried to bring the Soviet Union in on their side. But all this, even assuming an ultimate British victory, was of little help to Sweden in resisting German pressure. Indeed, as Boheman told Mallet at the beginning of October, Britain showed far too little understanding of Sweden's difficult position *vis-à-vis* Germany and was far too ready to criticize without giving any sign of encouragement or help. On the contrary, the Foreign Office's arguments relied on threats to influence Swedish policy.

Britain's control of Sweden's sea communications with, and imports from, the West was obviously her chief means of applying pressure. Both the conviction that Sweden was powerless to withstand strong coercion from Germany and the desire to tidy up things argued for a stiff trade policy towards Sweden; the system would be greatly simplified if Sweden were to be included in the total blockade of the rest of Europe. After 9 April, in spite of persistent Swedish approaches, the British permitted no Swedish trade by sea except a very limited one through the Finnish Arctic port of Petsamo, and this was obviously to facilitate the purchase through the United States of Swedish metal products important for Britain's war industry. When the Germans put a stop to all Swedish and Finnish trade through Petsamo in September, the British immediately withdrew their permission for it. However, after continual efforts by Sweden to revive regular traffic to and from Swedish ports, the British agreed in November to let four ships a month sail into Gothenburg and four ships out to various transoceanic destinations. This was construed in Stockholm as a sign of London's confidence in Sweden's ability to maintain her position. Still, Germany's consent to the traffic had to be obtained.

In Swedish· eyes Britain's displeasure at what was considered Sweden's too lenient attitude towards Germany was not unconnected with the Norwegian government's dissatisfaction with Swedish policies. For example, out of regard for Germany the Swedish government refused to accept the then Norwegian Chargé d'Affaires in Stockholm as Minister. But annoyance at Sweden was also felt inside Norway, where many false rumours circulated. Günther referred to these in a long survey he gave to the Parliamentary Foreign Policy Committee on 3 December. He pointed out that relations with all the Great Powers were reasonably satisfactory — Roosevelt, Mussolini, Butler, and Molotov had all made friendly references in recent speeches — and that Sweden's position was, in the circumstances, good.

Sweden in fact had come through all the events of 1940 remarkably well. After the upheavals of spring and early summer a provisional state of balance had been established in the Baltic, and Sweden's position, even if it had deteriorated, had at least been stabilized. Her relations with the Soviet Union and the West were good and with Germany at any rate much better at the end, than at the beginning, of the year. There were no German attempts to influence Swedish policies directly.

This fortunate state of affairs quite simply depended on Hitler not paying too much attention to Sweden. Sweden allowed German traffic on her railways, kept up deliveries of iron-ore, did not meddle in Germany's Finnish and Soviet policies, and showed Hitler proper respect. That sufficed for the present. For the future Hitler probably never seriously intended to invade Britain, but used air raids and the threat of an attack to try to bring the British to the conference table. He had his hands full elsewhere — particularly after Mussolini's attack on Greece at the end of October and the success of the British in North Africa. The British blockade meanwhile gnawed away implacably at Germany's resources. The rearming of the United States was speeded up after Roosevelt was elected President for the third time in November 1940 and could be foreseen to impose serious limitations on Germany's freedom of manoeuvre by the summer of 1942. Faced with this prospect, Hitler finally decided in December 1940 to attack the Soviet Union. A new *blitzkrieg* would crush the Soviet Union, like Poland and France before it. Britain's last conceivable ally in Europe would be eliminated. The threat to Japan's rear would be removed, leaving her free to go over to the offensive against the Anglo-Saxon Powers. German conquests in the East would provide the basis for a continental empire and fortify Germany's position as a world power. In this context Sweden played a very minor role.

Hitler's difficulties were not unknown in Stockholm. The Swedish Legation in Berlin had excellent connections who provided inside information on his problems, whatever public claims were made that Germany had already won the war. The fact remained, however, that Sweden was both economically dependent on, and strategically surrounded by, Germany. Swedish policy was bound to reflect this predicament in the second half of 1940, and so transit rights were granted to the Germans and action taken against newspapers critical of Germany. A cautious attitude had to be maintained. For the moment, indeed for the immediate future, the unpredictable Hitler, quick to take offence and with enormous power to vent his wrath on lands and peoples which annoyed him, was the master of Europe.

## Transit traffic through Sweden and deployment for Operation Barbarossa

Hitler's directive of 18 December 1940 for the following year's campaign in the East — 'Operation Barbarossa', so named from Emperor Frederick Barbarossa's crusade in 1189–90 — required all necessary preparations to be completed by 15 May and troop concentrations to begin eight weeks before the attack was to be launched. Although in these plans Sweden had only a minor role, that of a transit area in the far North, relations between Sweden and Germany inevitably came to be affected by them.

The first disturbing information of actions by the Great Powers directly concerning Sweden was received in March, shortly after a British Commando raid on 4 March against Svolvaer, in the Lofoten Islands (north Norway), which obviously irritated the Germans.

Swedish relations with Germany in general were at the time fairly good. In February Swedish negotiators had obtained her agreement to send four Swedish ships a month in and out of Gothenburg; the corresponding British consent had been given three months previously (p.93). German annoyance at the critical attitude of the Swedish press remained, however: outspoken comments on the sentencing to death of ten Norwegians for spying and on the taking-over by force of eight Danish torpedo-boats brought the irritation to the surface early in

March. There was, moreover, a growing discrepancy between the number of German soldiers travelling through Sweden on leave from Norway and the number of those said to be returning.

The Swedes kept careful track of this traffic. At the end of February and the beginning of March the figures showed a striking excess of journeys to Norway. The Germans were clearly sending in many more soldiers than they were withdrawing. When Günther took this up with Wied, he was told that it was a temporary irregularity due to difficulties with ice, and so forth, and that, from 10 March, the traffic would be normal. There was also no question of altering the current agreement. Günther was willing to accept a certain flexibility in its application. The surplus of troops going north rose, however, steadily: on 9 March it was more than 4,200. The next day Günther and Wied again discussed the leave traffic. Günther at first insisted that either the agreed limits should be respected or else the transit traffic should be stopped until further notice. Subsequently he took a more accommodating line and admitted that about 15,000 soldiers could be transported to Norway as an exceptional and unrepeatable concession to close the matter.

On 14 March, the Counsellor of the German Legation, Karl Geffcken (Wied having been called home), on instructions from Berlin, handed Günther a note which purported to explain the abnormal leave traffic. An unusually large number of German troops in Norway, Günther now read, had had to be sent home, some on health grounds, some for further training. This was done a long time ago, mainly by sea or over Finland. Since these routes were at present ruled out by ice, their replacements were being sent by rail through Sweden. Accordingly, if there had been an excess of soldiers going north, the figures were within the total permitted by the current agreement. There had also been other factors involved — a reduction of leave for troops in Norway and, due to ice, a temporary stop on return journeys. The increased traffic to Norway would be continued for a time, since about 76,000 soldiers and several thousand replacements were waiting for transport. When presenting this note, Geffcken told Günther that the Germans would soon request further discussions about a new agreement on transit traffic.

Possibly 80,000 men in all — more than 5 divisions — a quite unprecedented increase! Günther refused forthwith. Only the earlier figure of 15,000 could be considered. He put forward, however, the prospect of troops being transported by sea in Swedish territorial waters, which, in contrast to rail transport, a neutral state could permit under international law. He also expressed willingness to enter into discussions on a new agreement. Nevertheless, considering repeated German warnings about unseemly scribbling in the Swedish press, and Günther's insistence that the Germans should observe the transit agreement, Geffcken's note was disturbing. Did Hitler plan to invade England with troops from Norway? Or to attack the Soviet Union? Or was he strengthening his grip on the North with the probable aim of taking control of Sweden?

On the advice of the Commander-in-Chief, the government had already, before Günther's discussion with Geffcken, decided to increase the armed forces' state of readiness by calling up about 80,000 more men. Geffcken's utterances evidently intensified the call-ups. But the next day, 15 March, tension eased. The German Legation stated that the true figure was not 76,000 troops going back from leave, but 16,000. There had been a mistake in a telegram. Not least to clear the decks for the projected revision of the transit agreement, Günther immediately informed the Germans that there would be no difficulty in providing transport for that number. At the same time he requested more precise details. He was still awaiting these when the Swedish Legation in Berlin reported that they had been told that in a few weeks, as soon as the agreed number of surplus transports had gone north, fresh demands would be made for larger contingents to be moved; and Sweden would be well advised to comply with them. The reinforcement of the forces in Norway, it was emphasized, was not directed against Sweden. Indeed the Germans were grateful for the transport facilities provided up till now.

This report made Günther even more anxious to dispose of matters in hand before entering into talks with the Germans on a new transit agreement. Geffcken was told that the previously mentioned figure of 15,000 men would be reached by 22—23 March. The matter would then be closed. Richert was at the same time instructed to inform the German Foreign Ministry discreetly that his government wished to regulate the actual excess number, but that afterwards no further concessions could be considered. Public feeling would not allow the government to agree to the transit of troops to Norway. It was also inconsistent with Sweden's neutrality, the maintenance of which, according to the exchange of letters between Gustaf V and Hitler in the spring of 1940, was the basis of relations between the two countries.

The problem was not to be solved so easily. On 21 March, Geffcken announced that, in addition to the 15,000 soldiers returning from leave, the Germans wanted to send 10,000 reinforcements through Sweden before the end of April. Günther refused permission, saying that, as notified, the last date for such one-way movements was 23 March. However, transports could go by sea in Swedish territorial waters, the ships flying the merchant flag. Meanwhile there was considerable argument about a further German request, supported by ingenious but dubious arguments, to move three rail guns to Norway as 'ordinary military supplies' under the terms of the transit agreement. The guns were allowed through, but at different times and by normal goods trains.

Günther thus maintained limitations on Swedish concessions to German demands. He insisted that the Germans should in principle respect the previous year's agreement, but, by 25 March, almost 20,000 more soldiers had gone north than had come south. He refused permission for 10,000 reinforcements to travel by rail, but offered a protected route by sea in Swedish waters. For the time being, this policy of limited concessions succeeded in reducing tension over transit traffic. The Germans did not press too hard on their side. They gave and fulfilled a promise to reduce leave traffic from the end of March. They agreed to ship troops through Swedish waters.

The overall situation, on the other hand, seemed to worsen, as both Hansson and Defence Minister Per Edvin Sköld pointed out in speeches at the end of March. It was because of this general danger rather than to face any specific threat to Sweden, the ministers explained, that extra men had recently been called up — also to test how efficiently the call-up system functioned. Much more effective in allaying fears of moves against Sweden, however, was the Germans' attack on Yugoslavia and Greece on 6 April, an enterprise which was obviously going to preoccupy them for some time.

As indicated above (see p.95), in Hitler's directive of December 1940, Sweden had been allotted only a peripheral role as a transit area for deployment of the Northern Army Group in Finland. In subsequent months the Germans made discreet soundings in Stockholm about Sweden's readiness to play this role, but to no effect. The British raid on Svolvaer on 4 March forced Hitler to take stock of the strategic situation in the North. He must have noted the negative results of the soundings and also Günther's determined efforts to keep transit traffic within the limits agreed upon the previous year. At a conference concerning the defence of Norway on 12 March he decreed that alternative routes for transporting the Northern Army Group to its concentration area should be explored. A little later he told Halder that he ought not to rely on Swedish permission to use the railways.

Hitler had left Sweden out of his plans for Operation Barbarossa.

The German Foreign Ministry did not initiate the negotiations on a new transit agreement which had been notified in the middle of March. The Germans accepted (see p.98) the Swedish refusal to move by rail the reinforcements necessary to bring their forces in Norway up to strength and agreed to transport them by sea instead. This restraint cannot be adequately explained from the information available. The basic reason appears to be that, compared with the need to keep the situation in the North as stable as possible during the next few months up to the Russian campaign and the need to preserve the security of the coming operations against the Soviet Union, the transit traffic was not important enough to warrant pressing Sweden too hard. Reports from Richert tended in any case to show that for the time being the situation was not alarming, although Göring, as usual, complained of Sweden's negative attitude. There was also a growing tendency in Berlin to equate a refusal to make concessions on this traffic with a growth of anti-German feeling in Sweden.

When Wied, on his return to Stockholm, called on Günther on 3 April to bring him up to date on Germany's view of Sweden's policies, he adopted a reproachful, though friendly, attitude. Günther took the opportunity of dispelling German misgivings. It was not true, he said, that British pressure was behind Sweden's attitude to the transit traffic. He also strongly (but falsely) denied that the call-ups in March had any connection with Swedish-German relations; a strengthening of Sweden's defences had in fact been planned long ago. When Richert repeated these arguments to Grundherr, the latter remarked that this was what Wied had reported, and that otherwise there was nothing particular to discuss about relations between their two countries. He then launched into an attack on the policies of the Yugoslav regime. In fact, everyone in Berlin was now concentrating on developments in South-east Europe and had no time to spare for Sweden.

The campaign against Yugoslavia and Greece ended in German victory. The conquest of Yugoslavia was accomplished by 17 April, of Greece by 30 April. This diversion delayed the Russian campaign by several weeks, at first from 15 May to 15 June, then to 22 June. But the renewed demonstration of German power made a profound impression on those small European states which still survived.

## Finland slides towards Germany. Swedish concern for smooth relations with Germany

At New Year 1941 the Soviet press and radio sharpened its tone towards Finland. The Soviet government's attitude on the Petsamo nickel-mines hardened. The Finns had put them off the previous summer and autumn on various pretexts. But, at the end of 1940, the Russians put forward a firm demand for an agreement which would give them 51 per cent of the capital of a new concern to be created, control over its board, and Soviet management of the mines. Although they tried as long as possible to avoid entering into negotiations, the Finns were compelled to do so at the end of January 1941. They were determined, however, to do everything possible to retain control of both the nickel-mines and Petsamo itself.

What could Sweden do for Finland in such a situation? Any intervention in the negotiations about the mines was ruled out. Larger deliveries of food to sustain Finland's economy seemed the best solution. Yet Sweden's own scanty reserves limited this possibility; and even if such supplies buttressed the Finnish government against the agitation and dissatisfaction fostered from Moscow, they obviously would not provide sufficient support against actual Soviet pressure.

More effective aid could be expected by Finland from Germany. Berlin had given clear intimations that after Hitler's discussion with Molotov in Berlin in the autumn, renewed Soviet military action against Finland need not be feared. The Petsamo mines were Germany's chief suppliers of the nickel so vital for her war industry. Consequently Witting relied on Berlin for backing in his stubborn refusal to meet Soviet demands over Petsamo. At first the Germans showed great restraint in dealing with the Russians, although continually urging the Finns to hold fast. Then gradually they made their interest in the nickel-mines clearer and clearer in Moscow. Germany's position had now been definitely decided, Weizsäcker assured Toivo Kivimäki, the Finnish Minister in Berlin, early in March, and the Finns could now face any surprises, even in the matter of the nickel-mines, with complete confidence. Witting had stood his ground all the time and the negotiations were broken off in March without Moscow getting what it wanted. Molotov and other Soviet spokesmen had resorted to threats and sharp words. Paasikivi had asked to be relieved of his post as Finnish envoy in Moscow on the ground that his conciliatory advice was ignored in Helsinki. Yet no serious action ever followed the Soviet warnings.

Stockholm had direct information about some forms of German intervention in Moscow on behalf of Finland. Kivimäki told Richert in mid-February of a conversation with Ribbentrop a little while earlier. He had been assured that the Germans had impressed on the Soviet government that a fresh move against Finland would conflict with their interests. It was further known that Moscow recognized the existence of serious divergences between Soviet and German interests. Madame Kollontay explained to Boheman on 15 February that the Russians saw clearly that a conflict with Finland could not be limited, but would involve the Soviet Union in a major war. She stated categorically that the Soviet Union wished for nothing but peace in the North and had no plans to attack Finland. She pressed this view also at a dinner she gave for senior Swedish officers and officials, including Thörnell and Boheman, a week or two later. To Boheman she further developed the theme that for the present the Soviet Union was concentrating its attention on the Balkans. It had vetoed a German march through Bulgaria, and did not wish anything similar to occur in Yugoslavia. She was taken aback when Boheman sceptically asked what would happen if the Germans nevertheless took such action. It might not mean war, she answered, but the Soviet Union would certainly take economic counter-measures.

There had long been speculation in Stockholm on a rupture between the two allies of 1939, Hitler and Stalin; and in the early summer of 1940 Günther had foreseen war between them (see p.70). There was thus nothing surprising in the prospect Madame Kollontay's remarks opened up, but it was nevertheless astonishing that she revealed so openly how serious and how deep-rooted were the divergencies between the Soviet Union and Germany. For Swedish foreign policy-makers the grave long-term prospects were driven home by a letter they received at this time from Richert: rumours in various quarters pointed not to an invasion of England as the spring's great event, but to war between Germany and the Soviet Union. The same story soon circulated in Moscow as well as in Berlin. And Soviet alarm at Germany's military and political penetration of the Balkans became even more obvious. From Moscow, Assarsson reported that according to United States State Department information, the Germans were preparing to attack the Soviet Union. From Berlin, Richert relayed the remarks of the Soviet Military Attaché there that his country was arming at full speed and had confidence in its armed strength. Swedes in Warsaw told of very heavy troop traffic bound for the East.

This was the background of the meeting in Stockholm on 20–21 March of the Foreign Ministers of Sweden and Finland. For Günther the key questions were the frequent contacts between the Finns and the Germans, the recent intensification (with an increasingly anti-Swedish bias) of German propaganda in Finland, the statements by

Kivimäki to Richert that the Germans would not look kindly on closer collaboration between Finland and Sweden, and finally the visits by German generals to Finland during the winter. Nevertheless, Witting sought to allay Günther's fears that the Finns were veering towards Germany. In his notes on the discussion Günther stated

Witting affirmed that the Finnish government was firmly resolved to try to maintain Finland's neutrality even in the event of a war between Germany and the Soviet Union. The Finnish government saw Germany's present attitude as support for Finland. No promises had, however, been given by Germany, and Finland had no intention formally to join the Axis Powers.

Full agreement was recorded on all matters of common interest to the Swedish and Finnish governments. This included an understanding to hold back at present on further co-operation in military and political matters in view of the growing mistrust between Germany and the Soviet Union. It is worth noting that the discussions between the two Foreign Ministers did not lead to any genuine *rapprochement*. As Richert commented a few days later, Berlin, not Stockholm, was the target of the Finns' present foreign policy.

The accuracy of this comment was verified by the first impressions received by the new Swedish Minister in Helsinki, Karl Ivan Westman. Both the attitude of Finnish leaders and the influence of intensive German propaganda confirmed the trend. More disturbing yet were the military reports.

In mid-April the Swedish Military Attaché in Helsinki reported that the Finnish and German General Staffs were now collaborating on the technical level and that expectations were growing that, if Germany attacked the Soviet Union, the Finns would regain without serious fighting the territory lost by the Peace of Moscow and would thereafter be given the chance of establishing a more satisfactory frontier. It was well known that senior officers on the active list played a leading part in recruiting for a Finnish Volunteer Battalion to fight for Germany – more of a political than a military manifestation, it was true, but one which the Finnish government, though inwardly dubious, did nothing to oppose in public. The Chief of the General Staff, General Erik Heinrichs, had discussions at the end of April with Colonel Carlos Adlercreutz, Chief of Intelligence in the Swedish Defence Staff: Finland, he intimated, was going to embark on a new course of action. About this time the German Military Attaché in Helsinki told his Swedish colleague flatly that a German attack on the

Soviet Union would be made either at the beginning or in the middle of June; and that the Finns would come in at a later stage to benefit from German successes. They would operate independently and against the targets which the Finns themselves had chosen. In the North the Germans would send two divisions against Murmansk and two against Kandalaksha. They might have to ask at that moment for transit rights on Swedish railways, but perhaps, in return for this — and with Finnish consent — the Åland Islands would be offered to Sweden. But there was no question of Germany asking Sweden to join the Axis Powers or to intervene in the war.

The Swedish Legation in Moscow also referred more and more to a possible German attack on the Soviet Union and Finland's part in it. Stalin, in Assarsson's view, after the latest demonstration of German military strength in her Balkan campaign, could be expected to make relatively large concessions to preserve himself and his regime from the trials of war, involving at least an initially inevitable loss of territory. A report in *Pravda* on 30 April — immediately denied in Helsinki — that 12,000 German troops had landed at Turku could in this context be taken as a hint to both the Finns and the Germans that Moscow was keeping a close watch on events in Finland. The Finns, in Assarsson's opinion, did not try hard enough to dispel British, American, and Soviet impressions that Finland had given up her neutrality. Yet when on 6–7 May Günther went to Helsinki to return Witting's visit to Stockholm, he was given the most definite assurances of the Finnish leaders' desire to keep their country out of a war between the Great Powers.

Swedish-German negotiations on matters of trade and shipping in the spring of 1941 led to results not altogether satisfactory for Sweden. At the end of March the Germans withdrew their permission for the safe-conduct traffic to and from Gothenburg, asserting that the Swedes had provided misleading information on the courses of the ships involved. In addition, German exports to Sweden, especially coal, coke, and steel goods, dropped to well below the prescribed figures. Swedish efforts to change the German attitude in these matters failed. Only for a time had annoyance with Sweden been pushed aside for total concentration on Balkan affairs. The displeasure of Hitler and his government with the Swedish press was obvious and could, it was feared, conceivably flare up to an alarming extent. The strengthening of forces in southern Sweden in March and Sweden's negative attitude to German requests for extra transit facilities were not forgotten and were looked upon as evidence of anti-German sentiment. In mid-April, Admiral Raeder's

Chief of Staff warned the Swedish Naval Attaché in Berlin that 'there were limits to what this country and this government can tolerate'.

Günther tried to tone down Swedish press comments by painting a black picture of the situation at a press conference on 24 April. The same day Richert wrote one of his warning despatches from Berlin on the same topic. He had seldom seen Swedish-German relations so bad. Sweden's stubbornness over transit traffic was regarded as petty, disobliging, and formalistic. Swedish ties with Britain were viewed with suspicion, notably by German Naval Headquarters in connection with the sailings from Gothenburg. More important perhaps was the annoyance at the partiality, in German eyes, of the Swedish press and public for Germany's enemies and the government's supposed failure to lead opinion in the right direction. Such feelings were gaining ground in Party and ministerial quarters and, in fluid circumstances like the present, could lead to the most serious consequences for Sweden. It was imperative to restrain the press in the interests of the country's future.

There were similarities with the winter of 1939–40 when Swedish-German relations were also extremely strained. But Sweden was now in a vastly weaker position after Germany's overwhelming victories. In a speech on 1 May, Hansson was moved to criticize Swedish press statements as being felt by many to be inconsistent with the country's desire for good and friendly relations with other peoples and other lands. It was essential to make clear to people both inside and outside Sweden that such utterances represented neither the policy of the Swedish government nor the attitude of the Swedish people. Sweden was well aware she was part of Europe. She sought to play a role consistent with her power and 'in the future also would on a voluntary and independent basis offer her co-operation to other peoples working in the same area'. Two days later Günther broadcast on the theme 'a more disciplined intellectual life'. He called for self-discipline in commenting on questions of foreign policy and asked that attitudes which conflicted with the country's interests should be avoided. He pointed out the mutual advantages of good relations between Sweden and Germany. Both these statements were well received in Berlin; and, as the British Legation quickly noticed, during April and May the Swedish press contented itself with a comparatively colourless treatment of foreign affairs. The introduction in June of a stiffer law on the freedom of the press also pleased the Germans. Things were nonetheless precarious and required the greatest circumspection. Above all, it was to be assumed that Hitler – *so oder so* – would certainly stop any

Swedish attempt to work against Finland's growing dependence on Germany.

Although Sweden's position in an eventual Russo-German conflict must often have been discussed in the spring of 1941 by the Prime Minister and his leading colleagues, it appears to have come up first in a full government session only on 21 April. The occasion was a request by Thörnell for instructions in the event of a war between Germany and the Soviet Union. Much lively debate followed, but he had to wait for his orders. Early in May he was informed that, on the basis of the 'Government pact' of December 1939, which precluded Sweden taking any aggressive action whatsoever, he should prepare to defend the country's neutrality in every conceivable emergency.

The possibilities of acting against German interests were clearly limited, and Berlin's prevailing distrust of Sweden made them even more so. It was particularly important to tread warily in Helsinki. Before he left for Helsinki to return Witting's March visit to Stockholm, Günther gave firm assurances to Berlin that he had no intention of trying to separate Finland from Germany.

In his talks in Helsinki on 6–7 May, Günther was thus not prepared to give any specific advice to the Finns. Yet even to give a discreet warning that they should keep out of a Russo-German conflict must have appeared superfluous when President Ryti, Foreign Minister Witting, and Defence Minister Rudolf Walden unanimously assured him of their firm desire to keep Finland out of war between the Great Powers. Ryti did not think there would be a war between Germany and the Soviet Union that year. Walden, who ought to have been well aware of all the Finnish-German military contacts, was convinced – 'it was a matter of arithmetic' – that no such conflict would break out in the coming months. The President reaffirmed his government's wish to maintain close connections with the Swedish government and undertook 'to inform us immediately of any important development in Finland's position *vis-à-vis* Germany'. Witting was less communicative on the subject. When Günther raised the question of the Åland Islands, he said that the Finns expected that, in a Soviet-German war, there would be a contest for them between the belligerents.

What the President and leading ministers told Günther did not tally with reports from the Swedish Legation in Helsinki. Nor did it correspond with Günther's general impression of the mood in Finland. He had, however, been told in Helsinki what he had wanted to hear: according to leading Finns, there was no immediate danger of a Soviet-German conflict or of Finland adopting any policy except neutrality.

In his account of his visit to his colleagues he raised no doubts and avoided discussion which would have raised many awkward questions for him.

Partly as a sequel to this visit relations between Sweden and Germany were better in the middle of May than a month earlier. The Germans had heard from the Finns that what Günther had told them of his purpose in Helsinki was true. The German Military Attaché in Helsinki had meanwhile produced a far-fetched report of Swedish intentions, including an offer to Finland of a defensive alliance. But Berlin disregarded this report and chose not to discuss the question further.

For the Swedes it was a matter of striking a cautious balance. With a war between Germany and the Soviet Union in sight they could not concede too much in advance, lest their freedom of manoeuvre should be unacceptably restricted. On the other hand, they could not be too negative, or the Germans might react too strongly. So some German wishes on the transit traffic were granted. But when Ribbentrop's trusted envoy Paul Karl Schmidt was in Stockholm on 13 May, the Swedes argued that it was undesirable to try to conclude a formal agreement between the two countries. This would cause Swedish apprehensions of far-reaching German aspirations and revive distrust and polemics against Germany. Even difficult questions could most probably be solved, one by one, in a mutually satisfactory manner without any general treaty.

Altogether the Swedes sought through discussions with the German Legation in Stockholm and with visiting Germans to convince the Reich's leaders that good relations were an essential part of Swedish policy. The fact that the Swedes had broken the German code and could thus continuously read the telegrams between Berlin and Stockholm was of considerable help. Hansson and Günther also addressed suitable messages to Berlin, when the German envoy Karl Schnurre, known for the trust both Hitler and Ribbentrop placed in him, visited Stockholm on 24 May on his way back from Helsinki. He had obtained from the Finnish leaders their agreement to co-ordinate military measures with the Germans to counter any Soviet attack on Finland. He had also asked for a list of matters the Finns wished the Germans to include in the agenda of possible forthcoming talks with the Russians; the list was sent to Berlin after his return there. The Finns, incidentally, never gave Günther any account of these important talks.

In Stockholm, Schnurre contented himself with lesser matters, such as Swedish deliveries of grain to Finland. He avoided any discussion of

Sweden's policy in a war between Germany and the Soviet Union, explaining to Günther that such a development was highly unlikely in the immediate future. For the rest he stuck to the broad issues of future Swedish-German relations. When he had informed Hitler that he intended to visit Sweden, he said, Hitler's comment in reply had been to express dissatisfaction with the Swedish press. 'By and large', reads Günther's note of these discussions, 'Schnurre regretted that at the highest level Germany was not well disposed towards Sweden'. However, for the present Germany would not make any political or military proposals to Sweden; but Schnurre at any rate hoped some form of treaty of friendship in the political field might eventually be concluded. Hitler, seeing himself as the champion of Europe, could never accept a Swedish attitude which involved a refusal to support him. For Hansson, Schnurre varied his theme. He did not mention any treaty of friendship, but spoke instead of Germany's hopes of 'a more positive attitude on the Swedish side towards co-operation with Germany and co-operation within the New Europe'.

Günther passed over Schnurre's remarks about a treaty of friendship, his essential contribution to the discussion being to repeat an earlier statement to Wied that Sweden appreciated Germany's protecting hand over Finland and had no wish to disturb Finnish-German relations. Hansson replied to Schnurre's comments on closer future co-operation by affirming that 'Sweden had always been, and still was, prepared for international co-operation on a voluntary and independent basis'. He had opened the discussion with a declaration of principle which stressed the desire of both Swedish government and people for trusting and friendly links with the German Reich and a continuance of the mutual understanding which had solved difficulties between them in the past and would do so again in the future. This statement could obviously be interpreted as a guarantee of Swedish concessions in the future on the pattern of the past. In any event, the German Legation informed the Swedish Foreign Ministry a few days later that Schnurre had been particularly pleased with this discussion and would give Ribbentrop, and probably Hitler, a favourable report on his Stockholm impressions.

Swedish policy in May had in various small ways succeeded in softening the displeasure in Berlin. If a crisis came, relations between Sweden and Germany would be under less strain than a month earlier.

## Waiting for Germany's attack on the Soviet Union

During the spring of 1941 reports and speculations on a coming

German-Soviet conflict flowed in to the Swedish Ministry for Foreign Affairs. But no definite conclusions could be reached.

Spokesmen for the German Legation in Stockholm and prominent Germans on visits, such as the envoys Schmidt and Schnurre, obedient to their instructions, stated as their belief that there would be no war between Germany and the Soviet Union in the near future. Although German feelers relating to new demands for transit traffic in the event of a German attack on the Soviet Union were often put out in Stockholm, these did not effectively contradict the assurances given by the German diplomats. On the other hand, reports which continued to come in confirmed beyond all possible doubt a gigantic German concentration of forces in the East. Even the most extensive preparations of war, however, need not necessarily lead to open hostilities. They might aim in the first place at exerting pressure on the Soviet Union and getting Stalin to comply with whatever demands Hitler produced.

In the course of this tremendous German military deployment, relations with Germany came more than ever to dominate Swedish foreign policy. Relations with Britain sunk more and more into the background, while at the same time confidence in Britain's military capacity was again lessened under the impact of her catastrophic expedition to Greece which ended in the German conquest of Crete through airborne landings in the last ten days of May. Distrust and suspicion were to be found on both sides – in London over Sweden's submissiveness to Germany, in Stockholm over the exaggerated attention paid by the British to criticisms of the government's foreign policy in Swedish newspapers, in particular by Torgny Segerstedt's *Göteborgs Handelstidning–(G.H.T.)*. Mallet's reporting, behind which often lay Boheman's sometimes surprisingly frank information, did not always succeed in its attempts to convey to London an understanding of the extremely limited space for manoeuvre open to Sweden's foreign policy.

Such understanding was probably greater in Moscow. The Soviet Union in any case found it appropriate to signify its interest in Sweden and the continuation of her policy of neutrality. Madame Kollontay was instructed to sound out Boheman in the middle of May on the Swedish government's attitude to upgrading the diplomatic missions in Stockholm and Moscow to embassies. Boheman stressed his pleasure at this evidence of the Moscow government's appreciation of the work of its envoy in Stockholm and at its sympathetic attitude to Sweden. He pointed out, however, that the suggestion would be extraordinarily difficult to implement, having regard to Sweden's standing refusal to have ambassadors and to the fact that such an exchange with the Soviet Union would be interpreted as having a special political importance hardly appropriate in the present situation. On the Soviet side this negative reply could well have been expected, and the question was never raised again, but the gesture had at any rate been made. On the Swedish side Günther noted 'an apparently deliberate Soviet friendliness, well suited to general developments'.

At the beginning of June intelligence reports were received that German-Soviet relations had further deteriorated and were entering a critical phase. Intercepted and deciphered telegrams, together with other information, revealed that a German battle group of about 40,000 men would be stationed in north Finland east of Rovaniemi; the operation would be given the appearance of an exchange of troops by the arrival of detachments from the north (north Norway), and from the south (Finnish Baltic harbours), at approximately the same time. German troopships were sighted off the coasts of Bohuslän, Skåne, and Gotland. From Berlin it was reported that large-scale and intensive troop embarkations were taking place in Stettin. German-Soviet negotiations were allegedly going on in Berlin, where a Soviet emissary with extensive plenipotentiary powers was expected any day; it was anticipated that the negotiations would result in an agreement by the middle of the month.

Finnish territory was now a German deployment area. The first information of this from the Finnish government — Ryti had promised Günther 'to inform us immediately of any important development in Finland's position *vis-à-vis* Germany' — was received very late. A week after the German troop concentrations in the Rovaniemi area were known in Stockholm, Wasastjerna presented himself to Boheman with instructions to inform the Foreign Ministry.

It was still not possible in Stockholm to be certain that a war between Germany-Finland and the Soviet Union was inevitable. But the likelihood that the outcome would be war was very high. Assarsson was advised on 7 June to burn the Moscow Legation's political papers. The same day Mallet reported to London that, in the judgement of the Swedes, Germany would push matters to a 'show-down' around 15 June and that Boheman thought the prospects for war or peace were even. On 9 June (a Monday) Assarsson was told that during this week, according to reliable information, German-Soviet relations would enter a critical phase. The reports, however, did not lead to any great intensification of Swedish military activity. The state of readiness on Gotland was increased. Some 5–6,000 men in Norrbotten, who would otherwise have gone home on leave, were kept back, and preparations were made to move more troops there. Sweden's line was to lie low. The press was urged to exercise restraint in its reports and speculations on a future German-Soviet conflict and in its criticisms of Finland's policy.

Witting's tactics of defending Finland's attitude by putting Sweden forward as the country which gave a lead in meeting German demands for transit facilities – and stating that many more Germans had passed through Sweden than through Finland – were not welcome in Stockholm. He used this argument in a telephone conversation with the Finnish Minister in Washington, which he said would be listened to by the whole world. It was listened to anyhow in Stockholm. Günther sent for Wasastjerna on 13 June and told him that Sweden would do everything possible to avoid damaging Finland's position, but most certainly disassociated herself from these inaccurate comparisons: no concentration of German troops had taken place in Sweden. Günther further insisted that President Ryti should be made aware of his statement and that, to the extent that Finnish representatives abroad had been informed of the comparisons, they must be put right. Sweden was obviously anxious to avoid being compared by the world at large to Finland as an ally of Germany.

During the weeks before midsummer 1941 relations between Sweden and Germany were freer of friction and less troubled than for a long time. Hardly any official representations were made. Even personal exchanges of opinion and private conversations were remarkably few. No specific complaints were brought up, no feelers put out about easing transit restrictions or in some way getting closer to Germany. Sweden should continue to give favourable replies to Germany's requests, and should not use the term 'neutral' to describe her political position, the German Military Attaché in Stockholm suggested, but this remark could hardly occasion alarm. On 15 June, Göring expressed himself on Sweden without sharp criticisms and stated that, to his satisfaction and pleasant surprise, he had noticed that the Swedish press had not written a word about the transport of German troops to Finland. Only on 19 June, Grundherr – making it clear that he was putting forward 'purely personal and non-committal speculations relating to a completely hypothetical event' – referred to German representations to Sweden on transit traffic, over-flying, mining, and the internment of Soviet submarines in the event of a war between Germany and the Soviet Union. Also on 19 June the Swedish Naval Attaché in Berlin was informed of Germany's request for regular information on the movements and exercises of Swedish naval and air forces in the Baltic to avoid mistaking them for Soviet units. At the same time information came in that the German concentration in Finland had been completed, that the Finns were mobilizing, that enormous numbers of troops were being continuously moved towards the eastern frontier of Germany, and that hurried preparations for war were being made in Romania. Reports that the Soviet Union was feverishly strengthening its defences, yet on the whole wished to avoid a conflict with a Germany whose military might commanded such respect, were very persistent. From London came news of Eden saying he had reliable information that Stalin was prepared to lease the Ukraine to Germany; from Moscow the opinion of Count Friedrich Werner von der Schulenburg, the German Ambassador, that Stalin had made plain his willingness to grant far-reaching concessions to Germany by, among other things, promising 20,000 tons of grain to Finland. Assarsson read into a Tass denial of rumours of an imminent war between Germany and the Soviet Union feelings of anxiety and weakness in Moscow in the face of the German threat.

The only thing that is certain is that either we are now standing before an armed settlement of world historic importance between the Third Reich and the Soviet Empire, or we are going to witness the biggest blackmail in the history of the world,

Richert summed up the situation on 21 June.

It is impossible to reconstruct from the papers in the Swedish Ministry for Foreign Affairs the picture Sweden's foreign policy-makers had before them in the critical weeks before Germany's attack on the Soviet Union on 22 June. Oral comments by diplomats, military men, sailors, and travellers, news reports on the radio and in newspapers, both at home and abroad, deciphered telegrams, intercepted telephone conversations, and other snippets must also have contributed to the stream of information flowing in, which little by little provided the foundation for the overall assessment. In general it can be said that, the more time that elapsed, the more definitely the information-barometer indicated war. Those responsible for foreign policy were probably more convinced of this than they would admit in letters and statements. The fact that German ciphers and telephone conversations were continuously intercepted and broken had of course to be kept secret from the outside world. More or less certain knowledge that Germany had definitely decided on an offensive in the East and of its timing did not, however, influence the course Swedish policy followed while the storm-clouds around the Baltic became ever denser and ever darker. Sweden lay low all the while to stay clear of war. Efforts not to get in Germany's way,

111

not to irritate Germany, efforts to put the most favourable interpretation possible on Swedish-German relations, which came through so
strongly about the end of April and, at the end of May, culminated in
Hansson's and Günther's statements to Schnurre, were and remained
during the following weeks the guiding lines for Swedish foreign policy.
One should note that these matters met with greater understanding
than hitherto in the Swedish press.

Per Albin Hansson, in his Malmö speech on The Day of the Swedish
Flag, 6 June, set as the goal for Swedish exertions the preservation of a
good and friendly attitude to other lands and peoples and the maintenance of peace, freedom, and independence. He avoided the words
'neutral' and 'neutrality'. At press conferences and by private conversations with leading journalists the week after, the Foreign Minister
urged caution in news items and commentaries dealing with movements
of German troops to Finland and Finland's foreign policy, as well as in
speculations on German-Soviet differences. Swedish press restraint,
noted with gratification by the Germans, showed that these representations were not ineffective.

According to available sources no deliberations took place inside the
government on Sweden's policy in the event of a German-Soviet
conflict. Since the Germans said nothing, there was for the time being
no need to take concrete decisions. When the Parliamentary Foreign
Policy Committee met on 17 June, Günther reported on the situation.
He emphasized that no decisive information had been received as to
whether German-Soviet relations would end in war or not, but that the
crisis could not last much longer. Yet there was no discussion on
Sweden's policy in the event of either outcome.

In the weeks before midsummer 1941, Stockholm thus foresaw the
possibility of an armed conflict between Germany and the Soviet
Union. In the autumn of 1938 the same prospect, in conjunction with
the Munich negotiations, had led to considerable alarm and frequent
contacts with Finland on how Sweden's and Finland's neutrality
could best be safeguarded during a Baltic war. In 1938 peace was
preserved; and in 1939 when the Great War inevitably came, it was not
a repetition of 1914. Berlin and Moscow chose a political, not a
military, solution. Now, at midsummer 1941, the preconditions for
Sweden remaining aloof from a German-Soviet trial of strength were in
many respects more favourable than three years before: national unity
behind a government of several parties had long been established;
military resources were much greater; the economy had been put on a
war footing; the press and public opinion were accustomed to wartime

and the restrictions it could set on peacetime liberties; the foreign policy-makers had gained experience. It was, however, self-evident that Sweden's position depended in the last analysis on the Powers' intentions.

Britain, in spite of growing American support, had serious difficulty in holding her position in the Mediterranean region, where of late one military setback had followed another. No major British enterprises against the North could now be considered likely. In relations with Britain, Sweden ought to have considerable room for manoeuvre.

The Soviet Union was clearly on the defensive. Moscow itself was prepared to make concessions to German demands in order to avoid a war, and ought to assume the same attitude in Stockholm. As for the Soviet Union, Swedish foreign policy ought for the time being to have some freedom of movement.

Germany was the world's foremost military power and dominated Europe. Militarily, and on the whole also politically and economically, Sweden was dependent on her goodwill. Yet the demands which Berlin raised in Stockholm were, from the German standpoint, fairly slight and Sweden could sometimes refuse them. Greater indignation and displeasure were aroused by the criticism in Swedish newspapers of Germany's leaders, armed forces, policies, political system, and so forth and, probably above all, by the failure, real or supposed, of the Swedish government to take steps against such 'criminal' statements. But Sweden now knew that she, in contrast to Finland, had been left out of the enormous deployment in the East. If German policies continued to follow this pattern, Sweden's prospects of staying out of Germany's war should not be any worse than before.

# 5 Neutrality and the fortunes of war. Sweden's relations with Germany and the Western Powers

## Sweden and the beginning of the Eastern Campaign

The plan for Operation Barbarossa envisaged in all essentials a German campaign. Hitler requested no help from Italy and Japan, his Great Power allies. Finland and Romania were called in as allies, but were initiated into German plans at a late date and were not entrusted with any vital tasks. Berlin did not consider any Swedish contribution required. Victory was already certain. When, on the morning of 22 June, Ribbentrop asked Richert to call on him, he did not raise any precise German demands on Sweden in respect of the war that had just begun. He confined himself to expressing hopes of understanding for Germany in the Swedish press and of a friendly attitude, on the part of the Swedish government, to any problems that might arise. He stressed that the struggle which Germany had now taken up against the Soviet Union was in fact consistent with Sweden's old traditions and that its outcome would benefit Sweden too, especially by keeping Finland independent.

For all that, the requests which the German special negotiator, Schnurre, presented to Günther on the morning of 22 June were, from the Swedish standpoint, serious and extensive enough. The first point on Schnurre's list was the transit passage on Swedish railways for about one division of troops from the Oslo district to Finland. He further demanded that single German aircraft should be allowed to fly over Swedish territory; that air-crews who made emergency landings should not be interned nor their aircraft impounded; that certain minefields should be laid in concert with the German naval authorities; that, as far as possible, German traffic inside Swedish territorial waters should proceed under Swedish protection; and that German naval units, which sought shelter inside Swedish territorial waters or in Swedish harbours, should not be interned, even if they stayed there longer than permitted under international law; transports for war supplies to Finland were also required.

Günther tried cautiously to avoid according transit facilities by railway in the same way that he had used with success in March – by drawing attention to the possibility of using sea transport. Schnurre immediately rebuffed this attempt: transport by sea had been thoroughly investigated and shown to be unacceptable. Günther asked how a Swedish refusal would be received. Schnurre gave a very emphatic warning; in the German view it would be putting it too mildly to describe a rejection as an unfriendly act. At the same time he intimated that the transit passage he was asking for would be a one-time measure. Sweden, Schnurre further remarked, was not exposed to the threat of war, and there was no question of keeping German troops or German bases on Swedish soil. But, without actually entering the war, Sweden should interpret her neutrality to Germany's advantage.

Günther had probably feared much more extensive German demands – there were fears in Stockholm that the Germans would ask to occupy Gotland – and seems from the beginning to have decided to satisfy the demands now put forward; the commentary on Schnurre's list, which Boheman dictated the same day as guidance for the government in reaching a decision, is clearly in favour of approval. The decisive factor for the recommendation in Boheman's reasoning was less fear of Hitler's immediate retaliation than concern that a refusal would subsequently lead to the liquidation of Sweden, or, at any rate, of the present Swedish government. Germany's new campaign was expected to become the same victorious *blitzkrieg* as in the East in 1939, in the North and West in 1940, and in the South in 1941. Boheman also pointed out that a refusal could result in Sweden and Finland ending up on opposing sides in the war between the Great Powers. This would be too absurd for large sectors of the Swedish public to contemplate, and must, in any event, have serious consequences for future Swedish-Finnish relations. An acceptance, on the other hand, would not decisively worsen relations with the Western Powers. Boheman did not go into the possible consequences for Swedish-Soviet relations.

In the evening of 22 June, Wasastjerna called on Günther with an eight-point list of Finland's requirements. Some were identical with those already presented by the Germans. Some went further and assumed the same desire in Sweden to help Finland against the Soviet Union which had existed during the Winter War.

The German and Finnish demands led to intensive consultations in government and *Riksdag*, the question of the passage of the German division completely dominating the debates. Opposition was deep-rooted and serious, and in the discussions there was talk both of the

115

King's abdication and a government crisis. The Foreign Minister proposed acceptance of the demands. The Prime Minister, who also obviously considered approval necessary, even if he did not wish to say so directly, and who in general manoeuvred extremely shrewdly, finally succeeded in getting the government and the *Riksdag* to agree. In the afternoon of 25 June the formal decision was taken and a communiqué issued. Sweden, it was announced, would, in the war that had now broken out between Germany and the Soviet Union, steadfastly maintain her efforts to preserve her independence and to keep herself outside warlike conflicts. (The word 'neutrality' was not to be found in this text any more than in Hansson's and Günther's speeches of recent weeks.) However, the communiqué stated, a new situation had arisen. The government had had to clarify its position on Finnish and German demands that it approve the transport from Norway to Finland of a body of troops limited to one division. After taking the *Riksdag*'s opinion the government had agreed to the transfer taking place in a manner which safeguarded Swedish sovereignty. The 'Engelbrecht Division' – so named from its commander, Lieutenant-General Engelbrecht – immediately began its journey across Sweden on the night of 25–26 June.

Discussion about whether the King really had threatened to abdicate if the German demands, especially over transit, were not met, started soon afterwards. It was soon hushed by the noise of war. After the war, however, it started again. The question later gave rise to much debate in various newspapers and learned journals. Even now it seems impossible to state with certainty the King's exact words. However, the old monarch often used to say that he would not be a party to this or that decision which he did not like. After further deliberation and some persuasion from the ministers concerned, he usually gave way. Whether he had decided to insist that he would abdicate on just this crucial matter, must remain an open question. But what seems to be fairly certain is that the Prime Minister deftly used the King's utterance as a threat in order to get his reluctant Social Democratic colleagues in government and the *Riksdag* to accept a repugnant but, in the circumstances, realistic decision. There has also been discussion on how determined the opponents within his party really were, and how peremptory were the methods the Prime Minister resorted to. At any rate, it has to be acknowledged in retrospect that he acted wisely. Had the government split, a new administration without Social Democrat support would have had less strength to resist German demands. The Germans and the Allies would have been quick to exploit growing

*King Gustaf V*

disunity between the parties. As both the German invasion of the Soviet Union and Finland's involvement in a new war sharpened political feelings, there would have been a considerable risk of dissension aided from abroad, with foreign powers playing Swedish politicians off against one another. On the whole Hansson's attitude during these troubled midsummer days must be regarded as an essential contribution to the successful outcome of Swedish wartime policy.

Schnurre was delighted and expressed his readiness to arrange a favourable echo in the German press. He and his principals were after political gains as well as concrete concessions. Günther, however, gave him a warning; the German press had better not draw too many conclusions, partly because the Swedish press would react unfavourably, partly because it would not be correct to see in the government's decision a change of course in Swedish foreign policy. Schnurre did not press the point. He limited himself to expressing, on instructions from Ribbentrop, the German government's gratitude and satisfaction at the understanding attitude of the Swedish government.

Attention thereafter turned to concluding the negotiations on the other points on Schnurre's list. A week or so into July it was all settled. On the whole the German demands were accepted. Thus the carriage by rail of supplies to German troops in Finland was conceded to the extent that Sweden's own transport needs allowed. A new minefield was laid off Öland. Orders were promulgated that German and Finnish aircraft (which were assumed to be flying over Sweden only in case of need) should not be fired at, but turned away with warning shots. Courier-traffic by air between Germany and Finland and between Norway and Finland over Swedish territory was approved. However, no definite undertakings were given about forced landings of aircraft or warships and their crews seeking protection.

As an early response to these Swedish concessions, negotiations in Berlin during 4–9 July resulted in the German navy's consent to Swedish ships on the Gothenburg run following a course via the Faeroe Islands. This approval enabled the safe-conduct traffic to be resumed within a short time. It had, with a few exceptions, been virtually broken off since the end of March, when the Germans had extended the area of their operations around Britain and opposed a course for Swedish vessels via the Faeroes as being within their operational area.

All in all, the Swedish services which Schnurre on behalf of the German armed forces asked for and obtained in the first weeks of the new war were far from unimportant. Sweden's position in the German-Soviet conflict was not impartial. The minefield laid south of Öland completed a German minefield across the Baltic, which began at the Lithuanian coast. Orders not to fire in earnest on German and Finnish aircraft, and agreements on air-courier-lines and on the transit of war supplies to Finland indisputably served Germany's interests; moreover, they continued to do so until further notice and, unlike the passage of the Engelbrecht Division, were not a one-off event. It is obvious also that the Germans counted on a great deal of future sympathy from Swedish military authorities who would handle regular contacts, forced landings, internments, and other matters.

Schnurre's reports on these negotiations show that sometimes the staffs in Berlin did not promptly supply him with instructions and information – a further proof that only secondary importance was ascribed to Sweden in Berlin. What real significance the concessions granted by Sweden had for the German military achievements can be ascertained only by special research. It must be remembered, though, that these negotiations were held during the days when not only Germany, but also Britain and the United States, gave the Soviet Union only a few months to live.

The British government was less put out by the actual Swedish concessions than by the danger that they could be a foot-in-the-door leading to fresh ones of increasing extent and frequency. Definite British warnings of such a development were given to Günther, but the British government did not resort to any formal protest or any specific counter-measures.

The American government let it be known that it considered Sweden's foreign policy based on a realistic assessment of the current situation from a strictly Swedish point of view, and noted in particular the declaration that Sweden intended to resist by force of arms any military threat which endangered the country's sovereignty, integrity, or independence.

Moscow too showed understanding, possibly because it may have feared even stronger German demands, leading to Sweden siding with Germany and Finland. The Soviet government's first reaction to the transit concession was considered mild in Stockholm. Then it made a protest in a note of 24 July: the concession was an 'unfriendly' act (the sharper word 'hostile' was used when the note was handed to Assarsson) and constituted a breach of the neutrality Sweden had declared. But Madame Kollontay hastened to let it be understood that it was only after the Russians had heard of British representations that it was thought opportune to make their complaint. The protest should be considered merely formal and did not in any way imply a deterioration

119

in Russo-Swedish relations.

London, Washington, and Moscow thus looked at the substance rather than the shell of Sweden's policy. That the Swedish concessions to Germany were more or less incompatible with the formal rules of neutrality was a question of minor importance to them. What was crucial was Sweden's continued existence as a self-governing and free country inside the German sphere of influence, with a clearly held intention to maintain her independence and to keep out of the war. Sweden's compliance with Germany's demands, given the facts of power at midsummer 1941, they saw as a reasonable premium to pay for the continuation of Swedish independence, as a wholly understandable policy adapted to events.

When Schnurre had pressed the points in his list of 22 June to a conclusion satisfactory to the Germans, he tried to start another round of negotiations, this time of a more political nature. In a conversation at the beginning of July, he sounded out Günther cautiously. When Günther at once shrugged off his suggestions that an opportunity should be provided for Swedish volunteers to be enrolled in the German army, he drew back immediately. He produced instead an invitation for Swedish officers to attend the German army's Eastern campaign in order to gain experience. When Günther refused to be drawn into any soundings about Sweden's adherence to the Three Power Pact or to some German-Nordic pact, and emphasized that Sweden wanted to avoid the impression that she was taking the Axis Powers' side in the great conflict, Schnurre restricted himself to giving an animated warning against a purely negative Swedish attitude.

Günther was manifestly worried lest Schnurre's approaches, which were made during the enormous German advances and territorial gains of the first weeks of the Eastern campaign, presaged an increase in German pressure in order to force Sweden to conclude a written agreement binding herself to Germany and Italy against the Allies. The Swedish Legation in Berlin, on the basis of talks with its contacts, also expected a German diplomatic offensive aimed at getting Sweden into some treaty relationship with Germany.

Sweden was surrounded by German troops and economically entirely dependent on trade with Germany, Germany's allies, and areas occupied by Germany. Any treaty negotiations with Germany would in the prevailing circumstances have been extraordinarily difficult. However, at this time Hitler and Ribbentrop had neither the time nor the interest for any talks with Sweden about a treaty. Berlin judged the downfall of the Soviet Union to be close at hand and was busy with plans for the future on a worldwide scale. Still, it was noted with disappointment that Sweden had failed to take up a political stance in favour of the crusade in the East; that Sweden's adherence to the Three Power Pact could not be counted on; and that Swedish volunteers, unlike the Spanish 'Blue Division', were not to be seen on the Eastern front. On instructions from Berlin, Schnurre withdrew the invitation for military study-tours in the East. Sweden, it was noted in the *Auswärtiges Amt* at the end of July, did not wish to join Germany and her allies and, in accordance with Hitler's directions, should therefore be ignored.

Sweden, nevertheless, was not left in peace. A number of minor new transit demands were made in Stockholm; and were, as a rule, granted. However, when on 31 July Schnurre presented Günther with Hitler's request for passage through Sweden to Finland of a further German division — followed on this occasion also by a corresponding Finnish request — the Swedish response was an immediate refusal. The Swedish government, Günther affirmed, had publicly emphasized that the transit of the German division at midsummer had been definitely declared by both parties to be a one-time measure. It could not now depart from this standpoint. Transports to Finland on the German army's account, Günther continued, had for some weeks past gone by sea through Swedish territorial waters, escorted by Swedish warships, without suffering any losses; the request for railway transit facilities could not therefore be considered compelling.

Berlin's reaction to this instant refusal was tame: there were complaints, but the point was not insisted on. The Swedish government could take note of this as a sign that Sweden's negotiating position on matters where the German government was not specially committed was not completely hopeless. From now on what can be described as a more resolute Swedish approach to Swedish-German questions can be noted. It was attentively observed in Stockholm that the Soviet Union's armed forces had shown themselves surprisingly strong and resilient. But there was also a keen awareness that German reverses in the East could increase the risk of preventive German military action against Sweden, to complete Germany's control of all the territory within the boundaries of *Festung Europa*. Germany's increasing disillusion with Sweden's intention to stay out of what, according to Germany's interpretation, was a war for the liberation of Europe was closely watched. One could not, Günther told the Parliamentary Foreign Policy Committee at the end of August, say that Sweden's position *vis-à-vis* Germany had actually deteriorated, but it could be described as even more delicate than previously.

121

## German disappointment with Sweden

After August the Germans did not for a while come forward with new major demands on Sweden. All the same, their disappointment and disapproval over what they regarded as an utter lack of understanding by the Swedish public of Germany's crusade against Bolshevism and of her mission in Europe did not abate. On many occasions in September the Swedish Legation in Berlin reported a bitter German attitude towards Sweden, both among Germany's leaders and the general public. Particular exception was taken to remarks at a Trade Union Congress and in the press on conditions in Norway, where, on 10 September, the German occupation forces had unleashed a reign of terror against the trade union movement and had executed two trade union leaders. The handling of Norwegian ships in Swedish harbours which had been requisitioned by the Norwegian government in London and speeches by some Swedish ministers were further sources of annoyance.

Germany's displeasure was registered officially on 26 September when Ribbentrop lectured the Chargé d'Affaires, Eric von Post, during Richert's holiday in Sweden. Hitler, Göring, and other leading Germans, he said, had been insulted and lampooned in the Swedish press during the Trade Union Congress as well as on other occasions. The speeches at the Congress had been such as 'could only have been given in a country with a hostile attitude to Germany', and this at a time when Germany was carrying on a gigantic struggle to save not only Germany but the whole of Europe, including Sweden, from annihilation. Ribbentrop went on to administer a sharp warning about the Norwegian ships: 'If one single ship actually slipped out and reached Britain, the government of the German Reich would interpret this as an expression of a completely hostile attitude on the part of Sweden'.

The Norwegian ships, with a total tonnage of about 80,000, were loaded with goods of the greatest value to the Allied war industries, particularly ball-bearings. It was manifestly of prime importance for the British to bring them home to Britain and, correspondingly, for the Germans to prevent their departure. Nevertheless, in retrospect, the space and the weight allotted to the question of these ships in Swedish foreign policy for nearly three years of the war, 1941–43, evoke surprise. The explanation is that the prestige of Britain as well as of Germany was deeply involved, and that the general attitude of the Swedish government to the belligerents was judged in London and Berlin by the manner it handled the issue of the ships. Things came to a head in September 1941: the British government chartered the vessels from the Norwegians and appointed British captains to them. The Germans thereupon made those of their owners still to be found in Norway request that the ships be sequestered while a law-suit regarding the rightful ownership of the vessels was settled.

In considering its position in October 1941, the Swedish government therefore had to take into account an obviously growing annoyance at Sweden in Berlin, from Hitler downwards. At the same time the German attack on Moscow was making headway; and the possibility that before the winter the Germans would be victorious in the East could not be ruled out. True, of late several reports had reached Stockholm indicating disappointment among Germans at their failure to achieve all the successes they had counted on, and their surprise at the ability and determination of the Soviet army to hold out and to replace its enormous losses. But there was no escaping the fact that in the great offensive mounted against Moscow in early October the Germans registered very impressive gains and the Soviet forces very heavy losses. After Hitler had trumpeted out on 9 October through the Reich Press Chief, Otto Dietrich, that the campaign in the East had now been won, continued German successes in the next few weeks made Sweden's foreign policy-makers regard this assessment, weighted with propaganda though it was, as very far from groundless; the more so as cabled reports from the Swedish Legation in Moscow at this time spoke of growing doubts and defeatism on the Soviet side.

It is against this background that a number of measures taken by the Swedish government to prevent the disputed Norwegian ships from leaving Sweden must be seen, measures which facilitated German efforts, by means of a judicial process of sequestration. By November the Germans had reason to believe that they had achieved their object. The Swedish government's attitude had become quite ambiguous; statements to the Allies that in principle there was nothing to prevent the vessels from leaving were combined with various practical measures to keep them where they were. In a way this behaviour was understandable. As was clear from Ribbentrop's remarks, Germany's prestige was deeply involved, and repeated German warnings not to let the ships leave could not be airily disregarded. If the vessels broke out, the Gothenburg traffic would certainly be doomed. Further, German warships might enter Swedish territorial waters to capture the ships, and might then get into a fight with Swedish naval units. If this happened, there would be the danger of a conflict with Germany and such a conflict could not be risked in Sweden's precarious situation, where, as Boheman said to Mallet in the middle of October, her relations with Germany must actually take precedence over her relations with the Western Powers.

'In my latest discussion with Mallet', Boheman noted,

I strongly emphasized that the attitude we assumed towards Germany in this matter was based entirely on the fact that, on a question in which we considered the Germans were wrong, we could not afford giving in to German threats. The Germans would thereby gain the impression that they could obtain whatever they wanted from us by intimidation. On the other hand, our position was not dependent on our relationship to Britain. Certainly we were very anxious to maintain a good relationship with Britain and the United States, but concern for Sweden's own interests would be the decisive factor. Our policy must be based on the assumption that, in our present situation, we would try to steer a course through difficulties without being dragged into the war. The only advantage, in purely material terms, we had gained from our good relations with the Western Powers was for the time being the Gothenburg traffic. This for the British brought the great advantage that through it they could exercise a certain control over our trade with Germany. If the Gothenburg traffic were now to be completely cut in consequence of some Norwegian ships slipping out of Gothenburg, then concern over the maintenance of the traffic could not play any part in the appraisal of this question. We could also be pretty sure that, if, because of the Norwegian ships or for other reasons, we came into conflict with Germany, we might certainly count on British and American sympathy. But, apart from such sympathy, support would most likely in the main consist of a friendly advice to blow up our mines in the North.

In Sweden's exposed position it was imperative to make every effort to avoid friction with Germany. This theme also ran through Günther's arguments to his colleagues in favour of acting against disruptive political groups. Here, however, he finally found that a ban on the Communist Party could be misinterpreted as drawing closer to Germany, and he therefore did not press the matter to a head. The same efforts obviously influenced the text of a government declaration on foreign policy which he presented at the end of October. This declaration contained several concessions to present exigencies. It stated, for instance, that changes in Europe affected Sweden too, and that in the future she must pay due regard to the demands imposed by reality and could not ignore criticism from the belligerent powers. But at the same time the declaration contained a firm announcement of Sweden's desire and decision to stay out of the war, and her determination to order armed resistance if either belligerent party sought to involve her in action against the other. It also reaffirmed Sweden's faith in the future freedom of all the Northern countries.

In Berlin, the measures taken to immobilize the Norwegian ships were noted, as was the skilful construction of the Swedish government's statement. But Germany's annoyance had in no way been lessened. Complaints were often made about the unsatisfactory attitude of the Swedish newspapers, sometimes in very sharp terms. The Swedish government was not considered sufficiently quick, or sufficiently accommodating, in responding to various German proposals. This latter criticism the Swedes countered by handing over in Berlin a compilation of the services Sweden had rendered for the benefit of Germany and Finland to date. They were determined to resist German attempts to get soldiers on leave carried on Swedish railways between Germany and Finland, and endeavoured to meet new German demands by referring to what Sweden had already done.

When Schnurre laid the list before Ribbentrop about the end of November, he described it as an account of 'considerable services'. This appreciation is no understatement. During the months from July 1940 to October 1941, the account revealed that about 670,000 German soldiers – approximately 1,400 every day – had been transported through Sweden either to or from Norway, or between Trondheim and Narvik. During the period 22 June to 1 November 5,000 railway cars with military supplies, in all about 75,000 tons, had been sent from either Germany or Norway to Haparanda, and 70 German vessels, totalling about 420,000 tons, carrying troops and war material, had been escorted through Swedish territorial waters. In the coming winter 60 German courier aircraft a week would fly over Swedish territory, and a big transit depot for provision, fodder, and fuel had been built at Luleå. Sweden's trade with Germany had increased greatly during the war and was now carried predominantly in Swedish bottoms. After the destruction of Narvik harbour in the spring of 1940, the major part of the iron-ore shipments had gone through Luleå and there, despite technical difficulties, had reached a figure – 45,000 tons a day – which had previously been held to be impossible. Sweden had also helped Finland with deliveries of grain, and with credits and military equipment.

Swedish foreign policy towards Germany thus proceeded, balancing on a tightrope and with sidelong glances at the progress of the war. More or less appreciative statements and declarations alternated with attempts to limit concessions to German demands – partly yes, partly no, sometimes a flat no.

In November and December a great German offensive froze to a halt before Moscow. A few days later, through the Japanese attack on Pearl Harbor and Germany's declaration of war, the United States was drawn into the conflict. Sweden's situation did not immediately improve, but her prospects for the future became brighter. In mid-December the Swedish government rejected a German request for leave traffic from Finland – four trains a week, each carrying 500 men. Swedes by no means ruled out the possibility of German reprisals after this negative answer to Schnurre, who had been sent again to Stockholm as special negotiator, with a letter from Hitler to King Gustaf. Immediate repercussions were not, however, feared; the Gothenburg traffic went on and the tough negotiations on the exchange of goods in 1942 were concluded without any extra Swedish concessions being exacted. But it was noted that the situation could easily develop into a crisis. The Ministry for Foreign Affairs informed Richert on 20 December that the air of Stockholm buzzed with rumours of an impending German move against Sweden.

On 22 December the government discussed Sweden's military preparedness in the event of a German attack over Christmas. It was found to be deficient and improvable only through a general mobilization. Since this could be both alarming and provocative and since he did not expect a sudden German onslaught in the immediate future, Thörnell did not wish to go that far. The government concurred and resolved to take no disturbing measures over the holidays, but subsequently to increase preparedness little by little.

## German reverses. Swedish fears and assurances

Around the turn of the year 1941–42, the Soviet armies went over to the offensive in many sectors. They caused serious difficulties for the Germans, who were inadequately equipped for the severe winter weather and had no fortified lines to fall back on. The front was thrown into confusion and, for the first time in the war, the German armies found themselves on the defensive and were forced to give up vast areas. A German military move against Sweden, either in connection with an Allied move against Norway or as a preventive measure against this, had been envisaged in assessments of future developments which the Swedes had made in August 1941. Such a German move had not been considered as imminent, but as a reasonable possibility in the event of serious German reverses in the East at a later date. These reverses had now happened: the German armies in the East were clearly in a critical situation. The Swedes, in Richert's opinion, had at Christmas 1941 to realize that 'we are now entering a period which can be more dangerous for us than any other, in short, a time of desperation in Germany'.

Sporadic reports and rumours of an impending German preventive *coup* against Sweden, or at least of plans for one, in order to eliminate one uncertain factor in the event of an Allied landing operation in North Scandinavia later in the spring were reported by the Swedish Legation in Berlin in the first weeks of 1942, without, however, any special weight being given to them. Towards the middle of February rumours of an attack on Sweden became more frequent and reached the Legation even from generally reliable sources. Richert was no longer willing to take the responsibility for disputing that these rumours were, or could become, correct: Sweden, he now advised, should concentrate on the danger of the next few months and should take appropriate measures, first of all in military preparations.

From quarters other than Berlin similar warnings too reached Stockholm. The government considered that it could not disregard the rumours, even if it hardly thought an attack likely, and on 18 February ordered an increased state of readiness. No special political move or any particular gesture to improve relations with Germany was considered. The government found it useful, however, to repeat the assurances already given so many times earlier to Berlin, that Sweden's aim was to protect her neutrality in all circumstances. With this object, just as he had done when the situation was similarly deemed grave in spring 1940, King Gustaf sent a personal message to Hitler. To bolster credence in Berlin that Sweden had both the determination and the resources to oppose any intervention by the Western Powers by armed force the Swedish government also instructed Westman in Helsinki to give corresponding assurances to Witting: it was expected that the latter would pass this declaration on to Berlin, where such a pledge from Stockholm to Helsinki must be considered completely reliable. The press was urged to pay attention to the fact that for Sweden it would be 'absolutely essential to maintain a good relationship with Germany'. The heightened state of readiness was presented to the Germans as a seasonal phenomenon in preparation for the expected increase in activity on all fronts in the spring and, since the forces in the North especially were to be strengthened, as evidence that Sweden was on the alert in case an Allied move was made against north Norway. Such a move, however, Günther stated to Schnurre (he had got information from the Norwegian government in London), was not to be expected in 1942. At any rate no large-scale operation had to be feared.

Alarming rumours continued to come in for a while. Well on in March, however, Richert reported that a more favourable attitude to Sweden could be observed in leading German circles and that Sweden's true friends were obviously less worried about developments than some weeks earlier. Somewhat later Hitler himself declared that no danger threatened Sweden. On 14 March, Wied asked Günther to convey to the King Hitler's thanks for his message and, in addition, to declare that Germany on her side would not take any steps which would infringe on Sweden's neutrality.

In their discussions with Swedes German official spokesmen now began to reflect the satisfaction which Hitler had ostensibly shown with King Gustaf's message and thereby also with his government's policy. Their tone became noticeably more friendly and more cordial than in recent months. Particularly after the royal message and the Führer's reply, Weizsäcker assured the Swedish Trade Minister, Herman Eriksson, during the latter's visit to Berlin in the last week of March, Germany's relations with Sweden were very good.

At the end of January, Hitler expected an Anglo-American attack on north Norway. He was convinced that Sweden would take part in it and in return had been promised Narvik and the ore deposits at Petsamo. If the armed forces of the Anglo-Saxons occupied Sweden, all freedom of movement in the Baltic would in his opinion gradually be lost. The German navy must therefore do its utmost to strangle the British attack at birth. Accordingly a very powerful naval force, headed by the new battleship *Tirpitz*, was assembled in distant Norwegian waters during the winter and spring.

In view of these fears of Allied landings and of Sweden lining up on the Allied side, it is plausible that the question of preventive action against Sweden was discussed by Hitler with his closest military collaborators and that more or less detailed estimates were produced of how large a German force would be required for such a move. If a figure which appears in a Swedish report from Berlin – 30 divisions – is derived from those calculations, they must have been to Sweden's advantage. Thirty divisions equipped for winter fighting, even after operations on the Eastern front had more or less ended in February, Hitler simply had not got at his disposal. An attack with too small a margin of superiority could hardly be considered. The Western Powers would get time to hasten to Sweden's help. The Anglo-Americans could thus establish control over Sweden, and this possibility Hitler wished to avoid. If Hitler really harboured any intention of attacking Sweden, in all probability he must have realized pretty quickly that for the present adequate resources were not to be found.

All the same, even after the King's assurances, Sweden remained an uncertain factor in Hitler's eyes. 'Schlimmste Besorgnis Landung Nordnorwegen mit Rücksicht auf Schweden' (Greatest concern landing northern Norway considering Sweden), noted Halder, who did not usually show much interest in Sweden, on 28 March after Hitler's discourse on the situation and on his further plans. Hitler probably trusted the assurances of King Gustaf and the Foreign Ministry officials and military men in Sweden that they would oppose an Allied move against Swedish territory. But he was not certain that, under pressure of an Allied landing, public opinion would permit those now in power to remain in office. His fears that Sweden would side with the enemy persisted in spite of the assurances of the King and others, and in spite of reports confirming their sincerity from the German Legation in Stockholm. Yet it was in his interest outwardly to take them seriously and to respond with a similar pledge. He would thus strengthen as much as possible the present Swedish government's resolve and ability to carry through the policies it had laid down.

What effect the increase in Sweden's military preparedness had on German plans is an open question. The assurances given by Sweden were anyhow a good tactical move in a time of stress and contributed to an obvious improvement of Swedish-German relations. This improvement was achieved without any Swedish concessions, as the assurances did not involve any new commitments.

## The Balance of power begins to shift

On 17 March the Supreme Court gave a judgement in the case of the sequestered Norwegian ships, which acknowledged the right of the British government to dispose of them. The vessels were now free to leave port, but, owing to obstructions caused by ice, could not immediately proceed from Gothenburg harbour. Hitler had recently let it be known that he was counting on good relations with Sweden, and he could hardly change course suddenly, unless he was in a tight corner. Berlin's reaction to the release of the ships was also fairly tame. A *démarche* was held to be unavoidable; but, compared with previous wide-ranging declarations, was couched in moderate terms. In addition, Richert was able to pick up information that nothing was expected to result from it. When, therefore, on the night of 31 March the ten Norwegian ships sailed from Gothenburg, there was, in contrast to the situation at the end of October 1941, hardly any risk of grave German reprisals.

As Günther explained to Wied on 19 March, Sweden's policy on the sequestered ships had been to Germany's advantage. The vessels, with their particularly valuable cargoes for the British armament industry, had lain shut up in Gothenburg for about half a year. By the time they were able to go on their way, the nights had begun to shorten and in consequence the time was less propitious for a successful break-out. At the same time, however, Sweden's policy had been of real benefit to Sweden as well. Ribbentrop's warning, that the sailing of a single vessel would be interpreted as a thoroughly hostile act towards Germany, entailed less serious consequences now, six months after it was given. The exceptionally hard winter on the Eastern front had considerably limited Germany's freedom of action. Günther's policy in the matter of the sequestered ships was not so strait-laced, so closely in accordance with international law, as of necessity was maintained to both the Germans and the British. It sometimes moved forward by devious enough routes. But it was indisputably successful to the extent that it gained time – and thereby a better position for Sweden against Germany.

Whatever was to Germany's benefit in the question of the Norwegian ships was resisted by Britain. During the course of the legal proceedings in autumn–winter 1941–42 the British spared neither sharp notes nor unofficial warnings to express their displeasure, even their distrust of Sweden's neutrality. Boheman's assurances to Mallet that the Swedish government would fight Germany rather than submit to further political demands were, in the opinion of the Foreign Office, disproved precisely by the very important political concessions the retention of the Norwegian ships in Gothenburg implied. The harder the line taken with Sweden the better.

And a hard line was followed. After long and tiresome negotiations in London Marcus Wallenberg was at last able, in December 1941, to get a number of supplementary agreements to the 1939 War Trade Agreement, under which Sweden gained certain increases in, and additions to, her import quotas, but also had to consent to Finland being treated as an enemy country in the context of the Agreement. On the Norwegian ships London refused to negotiate at all; they had to come out. Repeated Swedish attempts to win British understanding of 'the larger political issues in the question' – that Britain would also lose by the counter-measures (including the ending of the Gothenburg traffic) which possibly Germany could take against Sweden if the ships left harbour – were as fruitless as a proposal that the vessels should remain in Gothenburg in return for the provision of some equivalent service by Sweden.

The attempt of the ten Norwegian ships leaving Gothenburg on 31 March to reach England had an unsuccessful outcome. Only two vessels made their destination, but they carried 6–7,000 tons of valuable cargo, mainly ball-bearings and ball-bearing steel. Three ships were sunk by German naval forces, three by their own crews to avoid their capture by the Germans, and two, *Dicto* and *Lionel*, returned to Gothenburg. No infringements of neutrality had occurred in Swedish territorial waters.

The break-out, however, had a lively sequel. From the interrogation of the captured Norwegian crews the Germans learned that, contrary to undertakings given, the ships were armed and that British diplomatic staff had assisted in arming them. The Germans immediately made sharp complaints in Stockholm. The Swedes in their reply rejected any intimation that Sweden had chosen to show bias towards Britain or had adopted an anti-German attitude. Günther, moreover, confirmed in writing an earlier oral statement that the two Norwegian vessels which had returned to Gothenburg would not sail out of the harbour again. It was also pointed out that the withdrawal of the official at the British Legation primarily responsible for smuggling the weapons on board, Sir George Binney, had been requested and that the Swedish Minister in London had been instructed to protest to the British government.

In recent months Germany had not resorted to any particularly harsh or threatening language about the Norwegian ships. Since her primary aim was to prevent the arrival of the vessels and their cargo in England, the partial failure of the attempt to break out may have largely offset German anger at the arming of the ships. If the Swedish government quickly made plain its resolve to clear up what had happened in a businesslike manner and made a determined complaint to the British government against the violation of Swedish laws and regulations as well as the infringement of diplomatic practice, which had been sanctioned from London, it would be able to say that it had observed the legal obligations of neutrality. But Günther went beyond this with his written undertaking to prevent the two Norwegian vessels form leaving Gothenburg.

The Germans very soon lost interest, although references to the incident went on well into the summer. Little by little the discussion turned towards the conditions for the Gothenburg traffic. Meanwhile, however, the traffic continued and no direct warning that it would be stopped was received from German quarters.

The British obviously had less to say than the Germans about what had happened when the Norwegian ships left Gothenburg. They complied with the Swedish government's demand that the official primarily responsible for the arming of the ships should leave Sweden. The Swedish protest led to regrets over the embarrassment which had been caused and to oral assurances that no attempt to take out the two boats that had returned was being planned for the coming months. The British, however, would not give up all plans to bring them to England at a later and more favourable opportunity. And the Swedish government's request that two more diplomats involved in smuggling the arms should be recalled was rejected. On the contrary, their retention was made a condition (among several) of an increase in Sweden's oil quota. The affair was not ended; two ships were still lying in Gothenburg and, in view of Günther's written undertaking that they would not sail, were later to cause much trouble.

For the time being, however, the matter was in limbo. Not without cause were those responsible for Sweden's foreign policy able to feel that on the whole they had so far got away with it quite nicely. In the autumn of 1941 the sailing of the ten ships would have caused great embarrassment, and even serious risks *vis-à-vis* the Germans. Now it was a passing incident without any particular consequences, above all without any ban on the Gothenburg traffic, which in recent months had assumed proportions of real significance to Sweden's essential supplies. The shift in Germany's attitude to Sweden could be seen as yet another indication of the desire for undisturbed relations, which had been manifested in Hitler's letter to King Gustaf. Germany's policy was not to exploit the situation by raising new demands, but rather to be satisfied with the advantages and concessions already gained in the last few years.

The British, however, immediately began to push harder — and in time the Americans pushed even harder — their claim that these advantages and concessions, above all those concerning the passage through Sweden of soldiers on leave and of German goods, must be reduced, if any increases at all were to be made in Swedish import quotas. Negotiations on these matters had started in mid-May 1942 in London. Sweden's foreign policy did not, in the Swedish view, meet with proper understanding in London, and particularly not in the Foreign Office, as Stockholm noted with disappointment. A factor in this was obviously resentment at Sweden's attitude in the affair of the Norwegian ships. First various interventions on legal and administrative grounds, then in

different courts delays in acknowledging, or even refusal to acknowledge, what in the British view was their government's clear right to the
chartered Norwegian ships, had prevented their sailing during the dark
season. Another and more deep-seated ground for Swedish disappointment, however, was the British conviction that a stern and threatening
attitude was the best and surest way to prevent the Swedish government
from granting Germany further concessions damaging to Britain. When
Britain's military situation improved at the end of 1941 and in early
1942, with the German setbacks in the East and the entry of the United
States into the war, this conviction grew in both strength and scope.
The Swedish government, through an acrimonious and exacting British
policy, should be made not only to refrain from making new concessions
to Germany, but also to withdraw those already given, as well as to
make concessions to the Allies at Germany's expense. This aim is
expressed very precisely in a Foreign Office minute of mid-March 1942:

I imagine that our desiderata as regards Sweden are:

1. We want the Swedes to be as united as possible, for that is their
only hope of effectively resisting German demands or German invasion;
we should therefore do nothing that is likely to put them in two minds.

2. We want to get as much as possible out of the Swedes in this war,
and to get them to give Germany as little as possible; as we are fighting
for our lives, ruthlessness is not to be excluded, subject however to 1.
above.

It has been said, rightly I submit, that in this war there is no such
thing as neutrals; there are only belligerents and non-belligerents, and
the latter trim their sails according to the strength of the wind blowing
from the various belligerents. Desideratum 2. above demands that we
should press the Swedes relentlessly for what we want out of them so
that when they take the line of least resistance it will be in our favour
and not in the Germans' favour. It is in the nature of belligerents to be
never satisfied, and each pro-Ally act of the Swedes should, I suggest,
be used by us to encourage more pro-Ally acts.

The Western Powers' policy towards Sweden was to follow this
principle to the letter.

## The tide of the war turns

With the arrival of spring, the British view was thus that, by stern
measures if need be, pressure should be put on Sweden to pay much
more regard to Allied interests in her relations with Germany than in
1940 and 1941. Ways of doing so were duly discovered. In April the
Swedes had asked that the oil quota in force since the spring of 1941

should be increased by 30,000 tons a quarter, an amount indispensable for her defence. Their arguments made no headway in London, where the increase was not deemed to effect a significant improvement in Sweden's ability to defend herself against Germany. However, willingness to agree to it was expressed if Sweden in return would cut down the German transit traffic. An opening bid in the negotiations was made in mid-June. The passage through Sweden of German military equipment and troops on leave should be restricted (to 2,500 tons a month each to Norway and Finland and to 75,000 men a year to and from Norway). Oil and oil-products in general should not be transported through Sweden and regular statistics of the transit traffic should be provided to the Allies. If the Swedes gave satisfactory undertakings on these points, they could, if need arose, count on more oil than the amount they had asked for.

Towards the end of June the Swedes delivered their reply, partly evasive, partly compliant. Meanwhile they were trying, without engaging in proper negotiations with the Germans, to achieve on purely technical grounds the reductions in the transit traffic held out to the British in this reply. The Germans, however, refused first to consider any curtailments without formal talks and then, in negotiations in Stockholm at the beginning of August, to bind themselves to accept a limit to military traffic; they did, however, hold out the prospect of a decrease. Nevertheless, no German measures to this end were noted subsequently. But when in September the Swedes, after due warning, reduced the transit traffic of goods to Norway and Finland (though by less than had been suggested in July), the Germans submitted to this limitation. It was maintained, however, that the reduction in transit traffic was a consequence of German efforts to increase traffic by sea in order to reduce the load on the Swedish railways; a unilateral Swedish ruling could not be accepted.

The Swedes had wished to avoid a political confrontation. Germany still had military superiority over her opponents. The 1942 summer campaign in the East had brought important German successes: in early autumn German troops stood on the Volga and at the gateway to the Caucasian oilfields. The Allies were still on the defensive, their prospects for opening up a new theatre of operations against Germany in Europe by an invasion in the West seemed uncertain. London and Washington were further delaying the all-clear signal for the trade negotiations, to which the reduction of German transit traffic would be Sweden's entry ticket.

As time passed, however, it became all the more clear in Stockholm that the difficulty in getting down to substantial negotiations lay less in London than in Washington. Here the uncertain authority of the State Department and the lack of united leadership in an expanding wartime administration complicated and confused the handling of the business. In influential circles too there was a very critical attitude towards Sweden's policy of neutrality.

Without the participation of the United States an agreement between Britain and Sweden alone would be illusory — certainly London could issue 'navicerts', but only Washington could guarantee that Sweden actually got the raw materials she wanted. Gradually, however, the British (after they had set forth in a long document how valuable Sweden was to the Allied cause, as, among other things, a supplier of certain tools and ball-bearings, as the owner of a considerable shipping tonnage in Allied service, and as a field for intelligence operations) persuaded the Americans to agree in mid-September to a joint proposal for negotiations on oil deliveries and other matters.

For these negotiations, which promised to be awkward, the Swedish government sent Boheman to London. Deliberations in Stockholm before his departure were based on an Anglo-American memorandum which had been handed to the Swedish Legation in London on 18 September. Here the conditions of the opening bid in June (see p.134) were stiffened in several respects. Thus a ceiling was set on the total amount of goods to be passed in transit to Norway and Finland, not just on the transit of war material. All Swedish escorting of German vessels carrying troops and military equipment must cease. Detailed statistics of Swedish exports must be given to the Allies monthly. At the same time as this memorandum was handed over in London, the screws were turned in Washington by detaining the cargoes of all the Swedish safe-conduct ships.

Boheman was given the opportunity to present Sweden's case not only to senior officials in the Foreign Office and Ministry of Economic Warfare and to senior military officers, but also to Cripps, Bevin, Butler, Eden, and Churchill; the latter invited him to the Prime Minister's weekend place at Chequers. The British wished to see Sweden remain undisturbed and to give her the oil and other goods directly necessary for her defence and her sustenance. Sweden's difficult situation was acknowledged and there was no desire to exact from her services which could bring her into conflict with Germany. But, at the same time, the danger of such a conflict was judged substantially less than formerly. Hitler had not the same means to hurl himself at a new country as before, and Sweden, according to London's assessment, could very well

*Erik Boheman, Secretary-General at the Swedish Foreign Ministry*

return to a stricter neutrality. Churchill and Eden merely touched on Boheman's negotiations in passing, but both made it quite clear that, to get what she wanted, Sweden must pay by some significant reduction of concessions to Germany.

To a large extent Boheman met the Allied demands, but on the most important points he inserted one or more reservations. He wrote home that when he held out the prospect of cutting down the leave traffic, he had said straight out that he presupposed Allied measures which would cause the Germans to restrict leave for their troops in Norway. Obviously he was not certain that his undertakings about reductions in goods traffic could be fulfilled. 'God knows if we can keep them, but one year is a long time, and if we cannot, we may resume negotiations'.

The Swedes in return were now waiting for some indication that the Allies were ready for an early start to negotiations for a general agreement on Sweden's imports from the Western hemisphere. But the American representatives in London lacked the authority to give any binding undertakings on the understanding about oil deliveries which the Swedes meant to have reached by now. To get the necessary American consent Boheman went on to Washington on 26 October. Churchill had promised to recommend him to President Roosevelt so that he would gain immediate access to him.

In London Boheman had explained his country's policy to Churchill and assured him that Sweden would rise up in arms against a German attack. Churchill had said plainly that no pressure would be exerted by the Allies to get Sweden into the war; that he wanted Sweden neutral, even if more strictly neutral than to date; that it would be a disaster if Sweden were to be occupied or conquered; that, if a serious risk of a German attack arose — Boheman had expressed the opinion that Stockholm would know of this 14 days in advance — the British government should be informed; that, in the event of a German attack, the Swedish troops should advance towards Trondheim, from where the Allies would try to join up with them; and that, after the war, Sweden with her traditions and her political maturity ought to play a leading role inside a Scandinavian federation, which would also include Finland. Such expressions of goodwill obviously did not rule out an Allied invasion of Norway, an event which could have dire consequences for Sweden. But the sympathy Churchill, and other leading British politicians as well, showed for Sweden was nevertheless an important asset for her policy.

Boheman's journey to Washington clearly signified that the real power of decision in the questions affecting trade relations between Sweden and the Western Powers now lay there. It was beyond doubt that this change was detrimental to Sweden. There was no war trade agreement to fall back on between the United States and Sweden, no established relationships between the negotiators, no fund of goodwill like that Sweden could draw on from Britain after the shipping agreements of 1940 and 1941. London had been aware of Sweden's problems for some years, and, even if critical, understood them to a certain extent. In Washington there was little insight into Sweden's position and her difficulties. Boheman also found a complicated negotiating situation there. The State Department certainly showed understanding. But other centres of power, above all the military, refused to accept the British line that Sweden should be supplied with oil and other necessities. Quite the opposite, they considered that a rupture of trade relations would better serve the Allied cause. If Sweden's economy was impoverished, they argued, Sweden's ability to supply Germany would be diminished and the war thereby shortened. Furthermore, there was little likelihood of Germany attacking Sweden and, even if this did happen, liberation would come soon; a little more or a little less oil and other necessities would scarcely affect the issue.

By and by, however, Boheman's pleas for an increased allocation of oil to Sweden were listened to. But at the same time new conditions were introduced over and above the concessions which Boheman had already made in London. One was an assurance that the two remaining Norwegian ships would be free to sail, another the right of the Allies to charter more Swedish ships outside the German blockade. The Americans were willing to discuss a war trade agreement and quotas for goods only when the oil question had been solved, and gave preliminary notice of far-reaching demands.

Boheman considered that he should seek an agreement in principle with the United States; even if the material advantages were less than hoped for, its political value was not to be underestimated. He was of the opinion that a number of concessions could be made, as the war was developing in such a way that Sweden could take greater risks with Germany than hitherto. The government was more cautious and wanted to put off detailed and final negotiations on a war trade agreement and quotas: postponement could allow Sweden to present more satisfactory proposals soon enough.

Boheman reported home that the situation in Washington was confused and problematical. President Roosevelt and the State Department were well disposed, but their good intentions were effectively frustrated at a lower level. It was difficult to convince them all that Sweden really was an independent country. Boheman's visit had, however, won appreciation and in many quarters been taken as an astonishing demonstration of Sweden's independence.

After an intervention by the President, the situation changed for the better for Sweden. On 1 December, Boheman was able to telegraph that oil shipments would now be resumed: two Swedish tankers would be allowed to leave without conditions. The question of the two Norwegian ships had been reserved for later discussions. A delegation from the Western Powers would be sent to Stockholm for further negotiations. The safe-conduct traffic to South America was to continue until further notice.

Certainly it had been hoped in Stockholm that Boheman's negotiations in London and Washington would get better results than could
now be reported. The agreement on oil-quotas and the guarantee of
early further negotiations on a trade agreement, in return for Swedish
concessions on the transit traffic and other matters which Stockholm
considered approved by the British, had still not been approved by the
Americans; and the concessions which the Americans had granted at
the last minute were only temporary. Boheman pointed out that his
negotiations had achieved a *modus vivendi*, which opened up various
favourable possibilities, while the safe-conduct traffic meanwhile
continued as before. But this *modus vivendi* was not to last long. Before
Boheman returned home on 27 December, the Western Powers had
already informed the Swedish government that, unless the two
remaining Norwegian ships were allowed to sail in the next few weeks,
they would block all imports to Sweden from the West.

During the exchanges of views on the transit question in the summer
of 1942 Swedish-German relations in general had been fairly unruffled,
and without serious friction. German discontent with Sweden remained,
however, more or less the same as before. In Party quarters very little
store was set by Sweden; more active participation in the fight against
Bolshevism and stronger support for Finland, were, as heretofore,
demanded. The Foreign Ministry represented an attitude which was
basically friendly to Sweden, but different officials time after time
complained about developments in Swedish public opinion – every
alleged Soviet success on the Eastern front was celebrated with
sensational headlines, while German victories were put in out-of-the-way
corners; about the progress of British propaganda, skilfully exploiting
the situation in Norway; and about the utter failure of both Swedish
press and Swedish public to appreciate Germany's achievements in
the East.

In the late autumn of 1942 Berlin's displeasure, not to say anger, at
the Swedish press increased. Several major newspapers had begun
openly to discuss a German defeat. Ribbentrop delivered a warning to
the Swedish Legation in Berlin of the consequences a continued anti-
German attitude in the Swedish press could have on political relations.
The Swedes for their part were anxious to avoid any raising of the
temperature in Berlin through an anti-Swedish campaign in the German
press and German fears of a change in Sweden's policy. Günther
appealed to Swedish journalists for a more subdued tone. He also

pointed out to the *Riksdag* the hazards which Berlin's anger at the attitude of the Swedish newspapers involved. To the Germans was emphasized the government's firm control of the country. Stockholm was anxious to soothe Berlin's fears that Swedish public opinion would, in the event of a successful Allied landing, force the government into war against Germany.

In November 1942 the tide of war turned decisively with Rommel's defeat at El Alamein, with the American and British landings in French North Africa, and with the major Soviet offensives north and south of Stalingrad. But, even if Germany was on the road to defeat, on that very road she dragged Sweden with her into an obvious danger-zone; the development of the war clearly did involve some risk of preventive German action to incorporate Sweden in 'Fortress Europe' in order to counter anticipated Allied moves, in particular against Norway and Denmark. The state of readiness of the armed forces was repeatedly discussed within the government and, immediately before Christmas, a decision was taken to increase it in February and March 1943. Before then no action in the North by one side or the other was expected. In the New Year, appeals were made by those in authority for continued national unity and preparedness. At the same time it was explained that no particular disquieting events or information lay behind the coming concentration of troops.

Those responsible for foreign policy early in 1943 were not so much concerned that Sweden might be drawn into the war than that they should adopt a harder line towards Germany, a course which events seemed to dictate. The Germans were handled more brusquely than previously. Approval for additional transit facilities over and above the agreements in force was not granted as often as earlier. A hard line was maintained in trade policy. Repeated German demands for new credits (something which the Americans had opposed with the utmost determination during Boheman's visit to Washington) were unsuccessful. Tentative German moves aimed at using the Gothenburg traffic to exert pressure on the Swedes to comply were rejected.

Nevertheless, this stiffening attitude did not satisfy the Allies: the Swedes should not just limit themselves to refusing new concessions, they should now hurry to withdraw those already given. And while the Germans now limited their demands on Sweden to 'no special sympathy for German views or war aims but simply the maintenance of neutrality', Allied pressure increased all the more.

The departure from Gothenburg of *Dicto* and *Lionel* had continually come up during Boheman's London and Washington negotiations. In London he succeeded in persuading the British not to raise the question at that time in official discussions. He envisaged such discussions in Stockholm later. In Washington he had more difficulty. But here also the question was eventually deferred to later negotiations in Stockholm.

In the middle of December, two British delegates from the Ministry of Economic Warfare came to Stockholm. Right from the outset they adopted a hard line: they had not come for a nice talk, but to get the two ships out. When this request produced no result, after a few days' wait they brought up heavier artillery. On 21 December, Mallet, together with both delegates, called on Günther and handed over an *aide-mémoire*, in which it was announced, tersely and to the point, that if within the next two weeks undertakings were not given that in accordance with international law the vessels would be permitted to sail, then the British and American governments would prevent all imports to Sweden from the West.

Günther argued against this view and refused to see the ships' departure as a question of law; 'as a consequence of the well-known smuggling affair in the spring the Swedish government considers the matter a political question and, for the time being, will not permit the vessels to leave'. No promises that the ships would stay had been made to the Germans, nor was there any agreement to that effect, 'but at the time I did inform the German Minister that they would not leave'; so if there was to be a change in this situation, the Germans had to be told. Günther further maintained that, should the vessels sail, the Germans would automatically block the Gothenburg traffic.

He immediately came under increased pressure from various quarters. The Americans associated themselves with Mallet's *démarche*. Boheman, who had just returned home from Washington, recommended acceptance of the Western Powers' demands, and his report to the government and the Parliamentary Foreign Policy Committee produced new pressures on Günther to permit the ships to leave. It could not be doubted that public opinion throughout the country, with its ever more open support for the Allies, would subject the government to harsh criticism, if it became clear that it had let the Western Powers cut off the Gothenburg traffic rather than offend Germany. Criticism at any rate could well take some such form. Finally, after talking to Boheman, Richert proposed to Günther that he should allow him to try in Berlin to induce the Germans to agree to letting the vessels sail without taking any measures against them.

Richert's first reports from Berlin indicated that no more offensive actions were to be expected from the Germans in the event of the ships' departure. Günther then decided to leave them free to go even without German consent, direct or indirect. The Germans, on the basis of Richert's first soundings, expected some Swedish gesture in return for their acquiescence, but Günther now did not consider such a gesture needful. Indeed, in the weeks around the turn of the year, he had moved rather swiftly towards a harsher attitude against Germany.

Boheman informed Mallet on 11 January that the two ships could sail on 15 January, provided that satisfactory assurances could be obtained on a number of points, among others that if the Gothenburg traffic was interrupted, Sweden should control the ships engaged therein and that Boheman's London Memorandum of 15 October should be considered a sufficient basis for the continuation of negotiations for a trade agreement, in which Sweden's import demands would receive favourable treatment. The Allies were possibly surprised at this lead from weakness, but returned a prompt reply, which did not give definite undertakings on all points, but was nevertheless of an accommodating character. At this Günther confirmed that both ships could leave. In the meantime, however, the Germans had made clear that if the Swedish government let the ships go without reaching an understanding with them, the very basis of the Swedish-German agreements concerning the Gothenburg traffic would be destroyed. When the Swedes did not yield, even after this warning, the German Naval Command stopped the Gothenburg traffic during the night of 15 January. However, the Germans hinted that they were willing to let it continue in return for some Swedish gesture, such as increased leave traffic or fresh credits. But on the Swedish side there was no disposition to make concessions. And in any case, it was considered best to delay new discussions with the Germans until the two ships had got away.

But the two ships never got away. After one abortive attempt to break out on the night of 17 January, they returned to Gothenburg and subsequently stayed there. The Swedes repeatedly pointed out in London the inconvenience this caused Sweden — strong German naval patrols outside Gothenburg and suspended safe-conduct traffic. The British stated to begin with that they still intended to make an attempt to break out at a suitable opportunity 'this season' (before the light nights of spring and summer). However, no attempt was made, and, in mid-March, the British announced that, because the season was well advanced, they wished to lay up the ships for the coming light period.

After an intensive diplomatic offensive the Western Powers had got the two vessels freed, and because of Sweden's agreement to their departure the Gothenburg traffic had been broken off by the Germans. Two months later the ships were still lying there. The importance of the vessels' cargoes for the British war industry had set the whole business in motion. But the actual volume of supplies had not merited so much fuss. On a general political plane, however, it was in many respects an important affair. Sweden, in a clearly prestige-loaded question, had openly put Allied before German demands. The Western Powers had demonstrated their negotiating advantages by (to put it bluntly) forcing Sweden to push the Germans to break off the Gothenburg traffic, and thereafter not bothering to take the two ships out. Britain and the United States had shown themselves well aware that even for far-reaching demands they got support, or at least understanding, from the Swedish public. It was obvious to them that the popular desire in Sweden for an Allied victory and also the present course of the war must cause the Swedish government to adopt a less accommodating and more negative attitude towards Germany.

The Western Powers meanwhile still delayed the adjustment in matters of commercial policy they had promised in return. Clearly they found no reason for special favours; the Swedish government had simply, at long last, acknowledged their manifest right to have the two Norwegian ships cleared for sailing. When Sweden, as a condition for letting the vessels sail, demanded from the Western Powers certain assurances about trade negotiations, a fairly heartening reply had immediately been given. After 15 January, however, the Western governments showed not the slightest haste in agreeing to any genuine negotiations. They limited themselves for the time being to sending to Stockholm an 'exploratory and fact-finding mission', which in the course of several weeks' deliberations, from the end of January to the beginning of March, obtained detailed statistics of the previous year's trade and memoranda on Swedish trade agreements.

On his first visit to the Foreign Ministry at the end of February 1943, the newly appointed German Minister in Stockholm, Hans Thomsen, told Boheman 'that before his departure he had, at conferences with the Reichs Chancellor, the Reichs Foreign Minister, and the Reichsmarschall, obtained assurances that they all appreciated Sweden's neutrality'.

This appreciation was taken as natural enough in Stockholm. In the early months of 1943 the Germans had been forced back on practically all sectors of the Eastern front. At Stalingrad a whole German army of 20 divisions had surrendered. The Allied bombing attacks on Germany had increased, and the German-Italian troops' bridgehead on the North African coast was being continuously reduced. From the end of January onwards the Nazi regime's earlier attempts to minimize setbacks were abruptly succeeded by dismal portrayals of the seriousness of the situation and of the fate which would afflict a defeated Germany. At the end of January, Richert had sent back very well-informed reports, based on private information, of serious differences between Hitler and the highest officer circles; senior commanders in the East had expressed the opinion that 'the war is lost, and that in the year 1943'. Richert himself was less categorical. He considered Germany's defeat certain only after a probable new German offensive in the East or South-east had failed, or any gains it made had again been lost. Nor did he believe in an internal collapse so long as the front, and morale at the front, could be maintained. But he entered reservations on unexpected events, such as Anglo-American landings in Europe, complications in countries allied to Germany, especially in the Balkans, and new differences between Hitler and his senior soldiers on the conduct of the war.

Very little contemporary information is available concerning the attitude of the Swedish government to the German opposition to Hitler and its attempts to establish contacts with the Allies. Through private Swedish connections, representatives of the opposition on several occasions got in touch with Englishmen in Stockholm. Another channel was via the Wallenberg brothers: Jacob Wallenberg had known one of the leaders of the German opposition, Carl Goerdeler, for a long time and Jacob's brother, Marcus Wallenberg, often met the British Minister in Stockholm, Sir Victor Mallet. Günther was fairly well-informed about these contacts, and undoubtedly thought it essential that he should know what was afoot. On a few occasions, he received representatives of the German opposition himself.

However, it is also clear that Günther avoided involving the Swedish government or the Ministry for Foreign Affairs in these peacemaking efforts. Hitler would, of course, have regarded official Swedish participation in such moves as a grave provocation, and considered himself obliged to retaliate in strong terms. Nor was it likely that Sweden in the role of mediator would be particularly appreciated by the British government. In the summer of 1940, the British had emphatically refused King Gustaf's offer to mediate and made it very clear that Sweden had gone to unnecessary trouble. Nor, of course, did information concerning the British and American attitude to the German opposition encourage Sweden to take steps: the Allies' insistence on

*Christian Günther, Swedish Foreign Minister, and Sir Victor
Mallet, British Minister in Stockholm*

unconditional surrender ruled out any negotiations. Finally, Günther
probably considered that the opposition had little hope of over-
throwing Hitler; the Berlin Minister, Richert, in whose judgement
Günther had great confidence, was sceptical of the opposition being
able to remove Hitler before the final collapse of the regime.

Germany's many reverses were reflected in Sweden's firm insistence
that the Germans must pay more attention to the regulations and
agreements in force and the clear notice that they could no longer
count on the same hearing and regard as before. The transit of goods to
Norway and Finland was further reduced in the spring of 1943. And
when, in mid-April, a German merchant ship in Swedish waters opened
fire on the submarine *Draken*, the protest notes, which were immediately
made public, used far sharper and firmer language towards Germany
than ever before. In conversations with German diplomats the deep lack
of sympathy with Germany among an ever-growing number of people
was emphasized, and the liveliest anxieties expressed over conditions in
Norway. From mid-March (when the British announced their decision
to lay up *Dicto* and *Lionel*) Germany's agreement to the resumption of

the Gothenburg traffic was repeatedly demanded with increasing emphasis.

On their side the Germans wanted in return some Swedish guarantee that the two ships would not sail. Sweden, by granting it, would in this way cancel an undertaking to Britain exactly as an undertaking to Germany had been cancelled in January. Moreover, German air and naval forces could be withdrawn with complete confidence from keeping watch over the two vessels. Various concessions were asked for as well. But Stockholm would not give a guarantee. It could, if the British suddenly changed their decision (an eventuality which could not be completely ruled out), lead to tiresome complications in both foreign and domestic politics. Nor was there any willingness to grant concessions.

When, in spite of repeated reminders, the Germans delayed their reply, the Swedish tone became sharper. On 27 April a German answer was requested within a week, since a decision on the disposition of vessels and cargoes in the suspended safe-conduct traffic could not be put off any longer; a failure to answer would imply a negative reply. Behind this forcing of the pace by Sweden lay the desire to elicit a favourable German answer before information reached Berlin of the approaching trade negotiations in London between Sweden and the Western Powers, to which the Swedish government had at last been invited. It was feared that information of this nature could induce the Germans to hold back their agreement to a resumption of the Gothenburg traffic in order to have available some brake on the concessions expected from Sweden in London.

The Germans finally gave their assent at the beginning of May in return for an oral Swedish assurance (which had got British agreement) that the two Norwegian vessels would not sail before 1 October. Immediately they received this assurance on 6 May, the Germans furnished the necessary notices and directives for the resumption of the Gothenburg traffic, only four days before the Anglo-American-Swedish negotiations on a new war trade agreement were to open in London on 10 May.

The Gothenburg traffic resumed in May where it had left off in January without Sweden making any concession in return. Repeated German feelers about a *quid pro quo* had been without result. On the contrary, Germany forced herself to agree to the resumption of the traffic, to which Ribbentrop had been adamantly opposed. After the *Draken* incident some gesture of reconciliation by Germany must have seemed called for in order to calm an ever more hostile Swedish public, which now began increasingly to turn its attention to the termination of the transit traffic.

## A time for diversion of policy. Negotiations with the Western Powers and Germany

The tripartite negotiations between Britain, the United States, and Sweden opened in the Foreign Office on 10 May. Lord Selborne, the British minister responsible for the blockade, in his introductory statement held out the prospect of agreements on quotas for essential Swedish imports and Allied efforts (not definite undertakings) to ensure that the goods on quota would be available and could be shipped to Sweden. In return, he continued, the Allies expected substantial reductions in Sweden's exports to Germany and to countries allied to, or occupied by, the Germans (in Allied terminology lumped together under the name 'Axis Europe'). He further gave a warning against credits for Germany and made it clear that, in the Allied view, help to Finland must be equated with help to the enemy. The transit traffic must be included in the agenda; it was not strictly a matter for trade negotiations, but no clear line could be drawn between one form of help to the enemy and another. The United States Ambassador in London, John Winant, was briefer; his main theme also was that the time had now come for Sweden to demonstrate by her conduct her sympathies for the cause of free peoples by reducing her help to the Axis Powers.

The negotiations in London went on for six weeks right up to 19 June. The Western Powers had now very thoroughly studied Sweden's negotiating position towards both the South and the West. The Swedish delegates were at a marked disadvantage and had slight success in their attempts to reduce the Allies' initial demands. In most cases they had to give way, sometimes after obtaining approval from Stockholm, sometimes on their own initiative. Swedish ministers felt some concern not only at the demands of the Western Powers, but also at the delegation's concessions to them. The demands went beyond what had been envisaged, and the concessions tended to determine Sweden's policy towards Germany without the government having the time for thorough investigation and the opportunity to give a ruling on how far Sweden could actually go. Accordingly, the delegation did not obtain authority to sign the texts agreed upon.

The London negotiations ended on 19 June with the delivery by Sir Orme Sargent, Deputy Permanent Under-Secretary in the Foreign

Office, to Gunnar Hägglöf, Head of the Swedish Delegation, of a letter with those texts attached. In all there were four unilateral declarations (two Swedish, one British, and one American) and six exchanges of notes. Sargent's letter anticipated the entry into force of a final agreement on 1 July; the Swedish Legation in London instead of the delegation would participate in the necessary formalities.

One Swedish declaration dealt with questions of transit traffic, passage, and escort, matters more of military and political import than of commercial policy. Sweden here undertook to cancel before 1 October all transit traffic both of German military or para-military forces and of war materials specified in a considerably extended list, which, however, because of energetic opposition from the Swedish side, did not in the end include oil. From October onwards the amount of goods carried in transit on the German account should be limited to 120,000 tons a year. This undertaking about ending the transit of men on leave and war materials was, however, not yet final; Sweden was at liberty to denounce it before 1 August. In the event of such a denunciation the parties would jointly review the date on which it was to be ended; if agreement could not be reached, the Allies could shut off imports to Sweden. Sweden further undertook not to allow German soldiers or military equipment to pass through the Falsterbo Canal and not to escort vessels with such cargoes anywhere.

The other Swedish declaration concerned restrictions on exports. In it Sweden undertook, among other things, to cut down her exports to the whole of Axis Europe in 1943 by 130 million crowns compared with 1942; not to grant any credits at all to Germany, and to Finland only a further 8 million crowns; to restrict her total exports to Axis Europe in 1944 to 700 million crowns and her credits to Finland to 10 million in all. In 1944 also exports of iron-ore to Germany would at most be 7½ million tons. (Under this ceiling there was another reservation: for every 2 tons of ore shipped to Germany, one ton of coal or coke must have been imported from Germany.) And exports of other goods of military significance would be stopped or limited (including, among others, ball-bearings).

The British and American declarations recorded undertakings by the governments 'to do their utmost' to make available amounts of goods laid down in a list; the oil quota had doubled from 1942, from 60,000 to 120,000 tons a year; but for the rest import quotas were on the whole unchanged.

More than a year had now gone by since spring 1942 when Sweden had asked for negotiations with the Allies to fix quotas for oil and other necessities from the West. During this time the Allied position in the war had improved step by step, and in consequence the terms they set for Sweden had continually stiffened. They now required an adjustment by Sweden to aid an early Allied victory. The restrictions they demanded on Sweden's exports disregarded the basic assumption of the 1939 War Trade Agreement with Britain that Sweden would be able to trade normally and to that extent pushed her to the brink of a trade war with Germany. In addition they brought appreciable difficulties for Sweden's supplies and economy. Here indeed, the exchange of goods with the Continent, vital deliveries of coal and coke especially, played a bigger role than that with countries outside Europe. An obligation to end the transit of soldiers and war materials could still mean a danger of German retaliation. Undertakings to co-operate in the Allied blockade policy must increase that danger further. Allied concessions were limited and indefinite; they did not guarantee, but merely held out the prospect of, quantities of certain goods. But Sweden was paying not merely for an allowance of goods but also for good relations in general with the West.

While the Western Powers were constantly putting pressure on Sweden to take their interests more into account, the Germans limited themselves to trying very unobtrusively to retain the benefits which they had got in the earlier, and for them more favourable, years of the war, and, by and large, to maintaining good relations with Sweden. They tried to keep the transit agreements working as long as possible. Leave travel was less important than the transit of goods; the goods traffic through Sweden was essential to supply German units in north Norway and north Finland. The traffic, especially of course the leave travel, was, however, for Swedish public opinion the most hated concession to Germany. For how long would the Swedes do regular service for the oppressors of Norway? Given the realities of power in 1940–42, it had generally been accepted as an unavoidable contribution to the price of Sweden's continued existence as an independent state within the German sphere. But about the turn of the year 1942–43, when Germany's setbacks became more serious, when the tide of war was definitely seen to turn, and when the German occupation regime in Norway had become harsher, influential opinion considered that the closing of this traffic could no longer be deferred. Articles in newspapers and resolutions at meetings demanding early termination of the leave and transit traffic multiplied during the early months of 1943.

The Swedish government did not doubt that in the trade negotiations the Allies would insist more strongly than ever on a reduction in, or an end to, all kinds of transit. The directive for the Swedish delegates going to London at the beginning of May envisaged, in fact, that the transit traffic could be wound up before 1 October.

The government obviously aimed at its early ending, and the sooner the better. The traffic was a departure from the neutral course which the government attempted to follow. It was an increasingly irksome burden, when ministers considered Allied and ever growing Swedish opinion. In principle, therefore, the government had before the London negotiations began decided to end it in a few months. It had already been gradually whittled down and, on 1 April, amounted to 60–70 per cent of the original volume. But all the same, the government, and first and foremost the Prime Minister, wanted to hasten slowly. The Foreign Minister, however, soon found occasion both in private conversation with Thomsen and in public speeches to make clear that Sweden could soon reduce it or even entirely break it off.

It was impossible to doubt that now Germany genuinely did desire the best possible relations with Sweden. At the beginning of June, Ribbentrop expressed the hope that the German and Swedish navies would work together to prevent German mines drifting into Swedish territorial waters. Germany courted King Gustaf and, to some extent, his country also, when, on the King's eighty-fifth birthday on 16 June, Hitler sent a very friendly letter of good wishes and the papers carried detailed and laudatory reports and articles. Inevitably, however, the announcement of an end to the transit traffic would aggravate Swedish-German relations. Should the Swedish government further strain them by entering into an agreement with the Allies according to the texts worked out in London, involving heavy limitations on Swedish exports to Axis Europe? A final Allied victory over a steadily weakening Germany could not readily be doubted, but the date of such a victory was still uncertain. The failure of an attempted invasion could temporarily tip the balance and prolong the war, and in such a situation, for a small country still militarily encircled by Germany to stake on an early German defeat could have serious consequences.

Björn Prytz, when commenting on the results of the negotiations just concluded, stated that in his opinion no significant improvements could be gained in the texts as they were, that both the Foreign Office and the Ministry of Economic Warfare had shown willingness to come to an understanding, and that, if Sweden signed the agreement, 'criticism of our neutrality to date would quickly be forgotten'. If

Sweden did not sign the agreement, however, it was 'difficult to see how a significant deterioration in our general political position towards the Western Powers could be avoided'. From the Swedish Legation in Washington it was stated that the American delegates in London had reported to the State Department about their favourable general impressions and about an atmosphere of honest co-operation; this, in the State Department's opinion, was the most valuable result of the negotiations for Sweden and would have long-term repercussions.

The general attitude and the policies of the Allies towards Sweden were also the main theme of the important account of the London talks the chief Swedish negotiator, Hägglöf, gave the government on 28 June. He made not the slightest secret of the fact that an agreement according to the texts now before them had both economic and commercial disadvantages; the sacrifices Sweden was making were greater than the gains obtained from the continuation of the Gothenburg traffic, and Sweden's trade relations with Germany could run into serious complications at the coming autumn's negotiations on next year's exchange of goods. However, he did not foresee any insuperable difficulties in regard to Germany. For 1943 there was a good prospect that the provisions of the trade agreement concluded in December 1942 would be met, and for 1944 imports from Sweden were of such great interest to Germany that an uncontrollable rupture of commercial relations need no longer be feared. Without an agreement with the Allies it was hardly possible to count on imports from the West. If anti-Swedish propaganda, taking up, for example, Sweden's exports of ore and ball-bearings to Germany, could not be restrained, particularly in Washington, then the more extreme elements there, namely the Secretary of the Treasury, Henry Morgenthau, and the military, would gain the upper hand in the United States' Swedish policy. On the other hand, with an agreement duly signed, Sweden would improve both her present and her future relations with the Western Powers.

Hägglöf did not carry the Prime Minister and the Foreign Minister with him. Günther sharply criticized the texts as going altogether too far to be accepted except in a desperate situation or as the price of something extremely valuable; the situation before them was not desperate and a good relationship with the Allies after the war — which one hoped for on general political grounds — was something which it was difficult to assess. A rejection of the agreement would bring certain difficulties, but no significant deterioration. It should

be stated in London that Sweden intended to carry out a policy which would to a large extent follow the lines of the agreement. Credits could then be refused to Germany and the transit traffic allowed to end. After this it would be easier to conduct new negotiations without such impediments.

Hansson emphasized that it was not wise to challenge Germany by ending the transit traffic and concluding the new war trade agreement with the Allies simultaneously – 'he was not so sure that Germany could not do something to us militarily'. He wanted to do

first whatever we can concerning the transit traffic. He proposed to move step by step. The agreement gave nothing. The improved future relationship with the Western Powers which the agreement should bring was uncertain. The outcome of the war was not clear. We should delay the conclusion of the agreement on these grounds.

The government then decided on 2 July that about 1 August it would give notice to Germany of the impending cessation of the transit traffic, having previously made particularly large increases in the armed forces' readiness. Towards the Allies it would stand on a declaration of principle that Sweden's trade policy would be conducted within the formulas of the London declarations.

As Hansson pointed out, this reply to the Allies was not far from an agreement; the government in the ensuing autumn must accept in essence the texts now before it. Still, the delay in taking this step was not entirely without significance. The important thing was, Günther emphasized, 'that a change of course in our policy should occur through our own choice and not from outside pressure'. Certainly Günther himself had earlier said that Germany would doubtless connect the cancellation of transit facilities with the negotiations in London and pressure there. But an independent cancellation of transit facilities was more than a formal matter: the cancellation would gain more credibility and respect from public opinion, both in Sweden and abroad, if it was announced as an independent move rather than as the result of obligations incurred under a treaty with the Western Powers. Circumstances of war dictated to Sweden a course more oriented towards the Western Powers, but it was wise to allow this change of balance to occur somewhat more slowly and in a somewhat more seemly manner than by the sudden lurch which a direct engagement to the Western Powers to repeal an earlier engagement to Germany involved.

Obviously Swedish diplomats had to make the most of the government's decision in presenting it to the Western Powers. They stressed to what a large extent London's and Washington's demands had in fact been satisfied. When Boheman on 13 July communicated to the British and American Ministers in Stockholm the Swedish government's written and oral declarations of principle, he emphasized that in general the London texts had already been followed in 1943 and would also be in 1944. And this involved a radical change of direction in the commercial policy Sweden had followed from April 1940. All the same, London and Washington did not find the Swedish declaration satisfactory and insisted in the main upon the agreed London texts. They deferred, however, for a while further pressure upon Sweden.

Towards London and Washington the change in Swedish policy should be played up, towards Berlin it must be played down.

During spring and summer 1943 Günther's and his closest colleagues' remarks to the Germans showed that the Swedish attitude to the transit agreement had stiffened step by step: it could be abrogated unilaterally, it could also be considered annulled for reasons other than the renewal of hostilities in Norway. At the same time, they continually stressed their desire for a smooth settlement and promised that prior warning should be given in order to provide time and opportunity for a solution by agreement. The more time passed, the better the prospects for such a solution. Good relations with Sweden became even more important for Germany at the end of July. In the central sector of the Eastern front a Soviet offensive launched in the middle of the month had still not been contained. In the South, after the Western Powers' landing there on 10 July, Sicily was well on the way to being lost, and on 25 July, Mussolini was forced to leave his post as Head of the Italian government — Germany's only Great Power ally in Europe was beginning to falter. The Allied air attacks and their material and psychological aftermath weighed ever more heavily on the German war industry and home front, and also, generally speaking, made deliveries from a sheltered country like Sweden even more valuable for Germany's economic life. But the Swedish government took no risks and ordered an extensive call-up, which, in spite of harvest-time, was planned to provide at the beginning of August a force of about 300,000 men at readiness.

There had not been such a large call-up since the spring of 1940. The military leaders, however, appreciated that great dangers lay ahead, not only German military activity in response to Sweden's withdrawal of transit facilities but also an Allied invasion of Denmark and Norway, with consequent German counter-moves. In addition,

153

there might well have been some desire, with an eye on any awkward situations that might crop up, to demonstrate to the outside world what considerable forces Sweden could mobilize in a short time.

It is hardly probable that either in the German Legation in Stockholm or in the *Auswärtiges Amt* there was any great surprise when, on 29 July, Günther handed to Thomsen, and Richert handed to Steengracht, Weizsäcker's successor as German State Secretary, a written declaration by which the Swedish government stated that all transit traffic of military personnel and of war materials through Sweden must cease. As justification for this step it was stated that the situation in Norway had not developed in the way the government had expected when, in summer 1940, it had approved transit facilities through Sweden for men on leave and for military equipment. It had then expected a military occupation regime which would bring fighting in Norway completely to an end and a certain measure of pacification to the people of Norway. Developments had instead reached a point where these transit facilities had become a continually heavier burden on the Swedes in their relations with the Norwegians. They had also become a burden on traditionally friendly Swedish-German relations. Three further points followed. First, the Swedish government had not found it possible to differentiate between the transport of war materials to Norway and that to Finland. On the whole, therefore, it would not co-operate in easing the passage of such material for belligerents. Second, the government wished to avoid unnecessary dislocation and difficulty while the present transit traffic was being halted. Third, it would be a great satisfaction if the transit facilities could be terminated in the form of measures taken in concert. This to avoid the spreading of the incorrect information that Sweden's policy, particularly towards Germany, had in some way altered. The note concluded with an express assurance that there had been no change in Swedish policy and that an unconditional and armed neutrality would be maintained to the utmost.

Günther thus presented the cancellation of transit facilities as a measure dictated by purely Swedish interests. In January the Germans had closed the Gothenburg traffic when Günther had very clearly put the Western Powers' claims in the matter of *Dicto* and *Lionel* before those of Germany. Günther's aim now must have been as far as possible to ward off the possibility of Germany reacting to the cancellation of transit facilities by again taking measures against the Gothenburg traffic. Quite in line with his arguments to his government colleagues that the cancellation had to appear as a completely independent Swedish measure towards Germany, he did not link it in any way with the Western Powers or the course of the war, but with the situation in Norway and Sweden's neutrality. In the exchange of views between Stockholm and Berlin so far during 1943 the Swedish side had spoken ever more openly of the adverse effects the occupation regime in Norway must have on Swedish-German relations, and had continually declared their government's determination to conduct a policy of resolute neutrality. Concern for Norway was now brought into the foreground at the same time as Sweden's adherence to a neutral policy was given prominence.

The transit of German goods in the summer of 1943 was far from being as extensive as a year earlier. The prospects of successful commercial or economic reprisals against Sweden were evidently seen as slight. And Hitler now had bigger questions to occupy him – under the new Badoglio government Italy was moving away from Germany and Germany in return was moving to occupy Italy. He decided to give way very soon, on 30 or 31 July, and Schnurre was given the task of negotiating, with the aim of keeping as much transit traffic going as possible. On 5 August, Schnurre and Richert signed an agreement stipulating that all transit of soldiers on leave and war materials should end during the month.

Sweden's abrogation of the transit agreements of 1940 and 1941 was completely overshadowed by the fall of Mussolini and Germany's acute fear of Italy's withdrawing from the war. In Hitler's headquarters it was quickly dealt with as a peripheral incident at a critical and unpredictable stage of the war; besides, on 3 August, a big new Soviet offensive had been launched in the southern sector of the Eastern front. In one week, without any difficulty, the Swedish government pushed through its demands with one exception, the ban on the transit of oil. Furthermore, the Germans allowed a separate unilateral Swedish decision to appear as an agreement, and this even in official commentaries on the joint communiqué. Germany's endeavours to have – and to be able to demonstrate to the world at large – good relations with Sweden were obvious.

The abrogation of the 1940 and 1941 transit agreements showed that Sweden could afford to talk to Germany more boldly than Stockholm had hitherto imagined. In subsequent months far-reaching Swedish moves were also to follow in the interests of Denmark and Norway.

A more direct consequence of the abrogation was that it opened the way for the regularization of the London June texts in the form of a treaty. Towards the end of August, after repeated prods from the Western Powers, the Swedish government declared that Sweden would sign, with certain minor modifications and reservations. In addition, a special clause was asked for, which had as its principal aim the possibility of increasing Swedish deliveries to Finland in the event of a separate Finnish-Soviet peace.

After several weeks of suspense the answer was received that the Western Powers had on the whole approved the Swedish communications; in this context the special clause was noted without comment. The proposals for modifications were referred to the Joint Standing Commission; on some points, however, it was directly stated that the Swedish demands could be met only to a limited, in some cases only to an extremely limited, extent. Through an exchange of notes on 23 September between Prytz, Selborne, and Winant, an agreement was brought into force, in essence identical with the texts which the delegations had submitted to their respective governments after the London negotiations had ended on 19 June. (The Swedish undertakings on the question of abrogating the transit agreement were now, as a matter of course, omitted.) The Anglo-Swedish War Trade Agreement of 1939 was thus succeeded by the Tripartite Agreement of 1943.

On 13 August, Boheman had informed Mallet and his American colleague, Herschel Johnson, that the end to the transit of war materials would affect 'also goods in accordance with the list discussed in London', and that the 'transit of non-war materials would not exceed the present amount'. It was considered that this undertaking was covered by the agreement negotiated between Richert and Schnurre on 5 August, and that it was unnecessary, or rather inappropriate, to discuss the matter further in Berlin. As for the suspension of oil transit traffic, which the Western Powers had been promised by 1 October, efforts were at first made to reach some compromise solution in Berlin.

The Germans, however, refused to negotiate on the basis of a time-limit already fixed for 1 October. They detained three Swedish safe-conduct ships carrying oil in Kristiansand for several days around 20 September. They let them go, however, when their attempts to start negotiations about continuing the oil transit traffic were answered by a warning that permission still obtaining for courier flights as well as for fieldpost and courier rail journeys might be withdrawn. The Swedes thereupon and without any repercussions cancelled the oil transit traffic with effect from the beginning of October.

The termination of transit for men on leave and for war materials brought indisputable gains, both politically and in regard to public opinion. They were considerable in Norway, but less in Britain and the United States, where they had already been anticipated, and in the Soviet Union, where people were suspicious and believed that the traffic continued all the same. But above all they were important at home. The government, and especially Günther, could take credit that it had succeeded in winding up an irksome service without having jeopardized the country or even, except for the Kristiansand incident, caused embarrassment. Certainly for some weeks after 5 August traces of irritation and criticism could be discerned in the press over the concessions to the Germans still existing on postal and courier traffic and transit facilities for civilian personnel and goods. Tendentious or exaggerated reports, however, could be countered with some success, by Günther, for instance, at a press conference on 25 September. This kind of traffic was in fact unimportant and, moreover, in terms of international law, fairly unobjectionable. By and large, Sweden, after more than three years, could now restore her transit railway traffic to its normal level. Not even strict overall neutrality, however, could satisfy the Allies for long.

## Increasing pressure from the Western Powers. Continued German withdrawals

During the final months of 1943 and in early 1944 continuous Soviet offensives pushed the German troops further and further back towards the West. The 1939 frontier between the Soviet Union and Poland was crossed at the beginning of the new year. On the Gulf of Finland the German front line was pulled back in January to the River Narva, the 1939 Soviet-Estonian frontier. The Germans were more successful in Italy. The Badoglio regime declared war on Germany in October 1943 and was recognized as a belligerent by the Allies, but the German front held firm in the south, and an Allied landing near Rome in January was successfully contained. However, even if the irruption into Fortress Europe from the South was making slow progress, another attempt to break in was awaited, most probably against the southern coast of the English Channel, possibly against Norway or Denmark. Allied air attacks on Germany became even more intense and more devastating. It was plain that time was working fast against Germany. Nevertheless, the German fighting spirit was still unbroken: Hungary, which had begun negotiations for a separate peace with the Allies, was occupied on 19 March 1944, and a clearly German-oriented government was installed in Budapest.

157

Swedish foreign policy took advantage of the increasing room for manoeuvre against Germany which events provided. After the various reductions in transit traffic in August-September 1943 came direct and openly acknowledged interventions in Danish-German and Norwegian-German affairs in October and December.

Even after 9 April 1940 Denmark was formally an independent country, maintaining regular diplomatic relations with Sweden. The policies of the Stauning, Buhl, and Scavenius governments to negotiate with the Germans, and their efforts to retain through skilful manoeuvring some control over their own country and prevent the establishment of as harsh an occupation regime as in Norway, were followed with sympathy by the Swedish government. But no *démarche* had so far been made by Sweden in Berlin on matters affecting Denmark or Danish-German questions.

Late in the summer of 1943 the basis for this restrictive attitude was shaken: Sweden's position towards Germany improved, while at the end of August the Danish policy of negotiation, caught between the German occupiers and the Danish Resistance, collapsed. The Danish government resigned, a state of emergency was introduced. The Danish armed forces were disarmed, their officers were interned. Five hundred Danish Jews were deported to Germany early in October; and now Sweden intervened: both before and after this action Swedish representations were made in Berlin. Richert warned the *Auswärtiges Amt* of the indignation and the serious anti-German repercussions which a persecution of Jews in Denmark would provoke in Sweden. On instructions from Stockholm he also offered to receive all Danish Jews in Sweden.

Richert's warnings of adverse repercussions in Sweden could hardly have much weight. After the cancellation of their transit facilities the Germans hardly expected new reductions in trade or traffic unless more specific statements were made. But Günther wanted to explore every possibility of helping the Danish Jews. Furthermore, through the publication of the representations he was able to demonstrate to public opinion both at home and abroad that he had come to the support of Denmark against Germany.

Although Sweden had been unable to prevent the deportation of the 500 Jews, many Danish Jews finally found a refuge in Sweden from German persecution — in all about 7,000. Of these a few hundred could travel legally through being accepted as Swedish citizens or issued with provisional Swedish passports, but by far the greater number fled across Öresund.

Sweden's desire to support Denmark to the best of her ability was reinforced by the accommodating reply given later in the autumn of 1943 to a request from leading Danish Social Democrats to Hansson for Swedish assistance in forming a Danish police force to be on hand when the German occupation ended. Hansson was, however, restrictive and careful. He avoided discussion on a possible Swedish intervention, which his Danish party colleagues had hinted at. And although he gave the Danish Social Democrats a generally favourable reply about training and equipping a Danish police force, the Danish demands were met only to a limited extent: training of a Danish police unit of 500 men and establishment of a depot with equipment for a further 2,500. Danish representations to increase these concessions followed immediately and continued for the rest of the war.

The limits within which Sweden was able to alleviate the German occupation of Norway were extraordinarily narrow during the first years of the war. Of course there was a great flood of sympathy and concern among Swedes in the face of developments in the occupied neighbouring countries, especially Norway. Events in Norway played a large and significant part in Swedish political debate. Here was often to be found a cleavage between the government and public opinion which could not in all respects be kept informed of the harsh realities which had to guide the government's policies and decisions, and which entertained illusions of Sweden's ability to intervene effectively in events. It is characteristic that, when a private enquiry in Berlin in the late autumn of 1942 whether an official offer to take into Sweden the Norwegian Jews, whose deportation to Germany had been ordered, could have any prospects of success was answered in the negative, the matter was dropped. Later, however, concern for Norway was more clearly demonstrated. Sweden's close relations with Norway were advanced as a compelling reason for the abrogation of the German transit facilities. During 1943 it was also pointed out, in firmer and stiffer terms than previously, that the German occupation regime's ravages in Norway could not fail to have an adverse effect on Swedish-German relations. At the end of the year Sweden intervened directly when, as the culmination of a long-standing conflict, over 1,200 teachers and students at Oslo University were taken to prison on 30 November for subsequent transport to Germany. The next day an appeal was made – and published – by Günther to Thomsen that the German government should cancel those measures.

The Swedish government, however, could not prevent the deportation of the Norwegian students, any more than it had earlier been able

*A Swedish ski patrol near the Norwegian Frontier in May 1942*

to prevent the deportation of the Danish Jews. Günther's appeal had an immediate success with the public, but when it was not followed by any concrete action against the Germans in spite of the fact that the deportations were continuing, disillusion arose in many quarters, in Sweden as well as in Norway. In the opinion of the Swedish government, and more particularly of the Prime and Foreign Ministers, effective reprisals should be taken only in response to German actions directed against Sweden or Swedish interests. Nevertheless, like the Danish Jews the Norwegian students were not lost sight of, and fresh Swedish attempts to help them were soon to follow.

Immediately before the intervention on behalf of the Norwegian students, the Swedish government had agreed to Norwegian proposals for the training in Sweden of a Norwegian police force of at most 1,500 men and a reserve of up to 8,000. Further evidence of the increased willingness to oblige Norway was provided by a communiqué of 15 December 1943 that the new Norwegian Minister in Stockholm, Chargé d'Affaires hitherto, J. S. Bull, would present his letters of credence to King Gustaf two days later. A far from insignificant cause of ill-feeling between Sweden and Norway was thereby removed – the Norwegians considered it derogatory for their country that Sweden, out of concern for Germany, had not for three years accepted a plenipotentiary Norwegian Minister. The post of Swedish Minister to the Norwegian government had meanwhile been revived during the summer.

The establishment of police forces, or rather police troops, for eventual use in Danish and Norwegian areas when the occupation had ended, was formally an exclusively Swedish-Danish or Swedish-Norwegian matter. But these measures were obviously, like the acceptance of a plenipotentiary Norwegian Minister in Stockholm, aimed at Germany. Both at home and abroad they brought not insignificant political advantages.

Germany for the time being refrained from making representations against the police training. The increasingly stiffer trade policy which Sweden now began to apply was a much more serious matter for the Germans. The reduction in Swedish exports to Axis Europe in the second half of 1943, made pursuant to the Tripartite Agreement, was carried through rather smoothly, not least because in 1943 Swedish-German trade reached unexpectedly large proportions; iron-ore and ball-bearings too, of such particular importance to the German war industry. But reductions in exports envisaged for 1944 were far more drastic than those for 1943. Furthermore, the Swedes wanted to include guarantees for the Gothenburg traffic in a new trade agreement. The Germans had closed this traffic in October 1943, claiming that naval measures were necessary to prevent an attempted break-out of the two Norwegian ships remaining at Gothenburg. The Swedish intention was now to press the Germans to allow and guarantee the resumption and uninterrupted continuation of the safe-conduct traffic.

The mood of leading circles in Berlin, confronted with a toughening Swedish policy, was bitter, Richert reported. Sweden, it was felt, was now definitely banking on the victory of Germany's enemies and making adjustments accordingly. The Swedes took notice of Hitler's and Ribbentrop's disapproval, but did not now, as they often had done before, consider it necessary to appease them.

In the New Year of 1944 an agreement on the exchange of goods for 1944 between Sweden and Germany was signed. Hägglöf succeeded in reducing Sweden's exports to Germany in accordance with what had been agreed in London six months earlier. Indeed in some cases the reductions went beyond the London figures. The final quotas for key commodities, such as iron-ore and ball-bearings, signified important concessions by the Germans. Also the Germans accepted the Swedish argument that, for Sweden, trade with Germany and the Gothenburg

161

traffic were interdependent and that, accordingly, a trade agreement presupposed guarantees for that traffic. They therefore undertook to allow the traffic to be resumed without any further reciprocal measures by Sweden and to let it continue for the whole of 1944, provided that compelling military reasons did not require its closure.

For the Western Powers, however, the important reductions thus achieved in Swedish exports to Germany were not sufficient. They were meeting stiffer opposition in Italy than foreseen. Despite frequent, and in pilots and aircraft very costly, air attacks on war industries and other targets, the German production of war materials continued at an unexpectedly high level. It looked as if the war would be both costlier and longer than had been thought likely in the spring and early summer of 1943, when the Tripartite Agreement was negotiated in London. Complaints came in from the Western Powers that the agreement had not been observed, and with them were linked demands that, after the accession of Italy to the Allies, Swedish exports to Axis Europe should be proportionately reduced and that exports of iron-ore and ball-bearings to Germany in 1944 should be kept down below the amounts stipulated in the Tripartite Agreement. Primarily in Washington, but also in London, influential military men called for further pressure on Sweden, whose exports to Germany even in their present reduced

*Gunnar Hägglöf, Head of the Commercial Department at the Swedish Foreign Ministry*

amounts were considered incomparably the most important neutral contribution to the German war-effort. On 17 March a memorandum from the Western Powers was handed over in Stockholm, in which various complaints of Swedish transgressions against the Tripartite Agreement were spelt out, particularly in respect of iron-ore and ball-bearing exports. It was requested that exports of iron-ore for the first six months of 1944 should be limited to about 2,600,000 tons and exports of ball-bearings for the whole of 1944 cut down further.

A Swedish reply of 6 April dealt with the Western Powers' complaints and demands point by point. On the Swedish side the stipulations of the Tripartite Agreement of September 1943 were obstinately upheld against the attempts of the Western Powers to force Sweden to submit to further export limitations for 1944 than demanded in it. For Sweden to accept additional obligations would mean withdrawing to a new and less firmly established line of defence while encouraging fresh pressure. On the other hand, deference had to be paid, at the end of the war just as at the beginning, to those Great Powers who were on the winning side. As Boheman explained in conversation with the two Ministers of the Western Powers, Mallet and Johnson, the Swedes intended to try to meet the Allies' demands in the matter as far as possible. They were trying to reduce imports of German goods and thereby reduce Germany's supply of money to pay for Swedish exports. Luleå harbour would be opened as late as possible and, as a result of mobilization, the number of miners in the orefields would be reduced by about 30 per cent.

The Swedish view that there was more to be gained by informal contacts than by official diplomatic representations, where prestige and principles were engaged, received some support in London, but less in Washington. In the demands on trade policy presented to Sweden by the Western Powers ball-bearings had now displaced iron-ore in importance. The change was clearly connected with the coming invasion. In Allied quarters it was considered that Swedish ball-bearings were essential to German aircraft production, and that it was therefore necessary in the next few months to reduce Swedish exports of ball-bearings to Germany to a minimum: 'The fewer German aircraft, the less blood shed by the invading troops'. On 13 April, Johnson delivered to Günther a new far-reaching note calling for a drastic reduction in Swedish ball-bearing exports to Germany. In a note delivered at the same time by Mallet the British government fully endorsed the American demands.

Johnson's note had been preceded by an obviously inspired

campaign in the American press against Sweden's ball-bearing exports to the Continent, and these were also attacked as important aid to Germany in a speech by the Secretary of State, Cordell Hull, broadcast on 9 April. The note demanded an immediate ban, valid in any case for the next three months, on exports to Germany and associated or occupied countries of ball-bearings, machinery, and instruments, as well as of steel for their production. The tone was threatening. The American government assumed that the Swedish government did not wish to harm Sweden's own long-term interests by directly supporting Germany's military power through the export of ball-bearings. However, if its demands were not met, the American government would seriously consider using all means at its disposal to achieve the desired result.

The Swedish government in its reply of 22 April refused to believe that the government of the United States was considering measures against Sweden to stop exports which took place within the framework of a treaty with the Allied governments. It regretted that it could not comply with the demands put forward. At the same time, however, Günther let Boheman pass on by word of mouth the information that the Swedish producer Svenska Kullagerfabriken (SKF) was investigating whether the Allies' wishes could not to some extent be met within the scope of existing contracts.

Formally the Swedish government thus adhered to the provisions of the 1943 Tripartite Agreement and the 1944 agreement on the exchange of goods with Germany based thereupon. As Günther and Boheman explained to Johnson and Mallet, the government did not want to make the requested cuts in ball-bearing exports for two reasons: they were afraid of German reprisals, and they were afraid that concession on this point would immediately be followed by new Allied demands, perhaps for air bases. However, in the situation prevailing a blank refusal to the Western Powers was hardly feasible. By suggesting that SKF should investigate the possibility of making cuts, a definite reply could be postponed — and gaining of time had in several difficult situations during the earlier years of the war proved to be particularly helpful. The Western Powers had themselves already considered opening direct discussions with SKF and some weeks later in May they began, through special emissaries, Griffiths and Waring, regular negotiations with the company.

In the summer and autumn of 1943 various transit concessions granted to the Germans were rescinded, but a few still remained — as mere ordinary commercial transit facilities. The Western Powers wanted all concessions and facilities cancelled and time and again made representations on this point. In the final months of 1943 and the early months of 1944 the Swedes refused, exactly as they rejected Allied demands for reductions in iron-ore exports. A British proposal in October 1943 that the German mail-coach traffic through Sweden should be abolished was turned down and a fresh proposal in the New Year was left unanswered. A demand in November that the transit of coal, coke, and cement through Sundsvall and Härnösand to Trondheim and through Luleå to Narvik should be reduced was similarly rejected: this traffic, it was pointed out, had never been discussed earlier, and it was only in respect of the transit traffic through the ferry-harbours of Hälsingborg, Malmö, and Trelleborg that certain limitations had been imposed. Meanwhile it was made clear that the Swedish government was determined to maintain traffic in the Gulf of Bothnia at its existing level.

German mail-coaches – and coaches for military couriers – through Sweden were also a nuisance in terms of domestic politics; they were mentioned much more often in the Swedish press than in Allied circles. When on 14 April 1944 in Hälsingborg a search of goods which had come from Denmark in transit to Norway revealed 28 packages containing maps of Sweden, Günther was presented with a suitable justification for telling the Germans that the special mail and courier coaches would not be allowed after May. Immediately afterwards on two other occasions maps were discovered during the customs examination of German goods in transit to Norway and Finland, partly large-scale maps of the Scandinavian peninsula, partly small-scale maps of northernmost Norway and neighbouring frontier districts of Sweden. These discoveries aroused considerable alarm in Stockholm: were the maps just routine deliveries – or a move in a war of nerves – or evidence of preparations for action by Germany to oppose an expected invasion by the Western Powers?

Meanwhile on 13 April the German government had, in a clear and thoroughly argued *démarche*, expressed its hope that the Swedish government would end police training for Danes and Norwegians in Sweden as being contrary to international law. It was, the Germans argued, comparable with military training, and a neutral power must not permit military formations to be trained or recruiting centres established on its territory for the benefit of a belligerent. This argument was rejected in a Swedish note of 19 April as being based on incorrect information about the nature and aims of the training, which was concerned only with pure police duties. The weapon training only corresponded to the instruction required for every modern police force;

165

the trained police formations would not be transferred from Sweden to Norway (or Denmark) except with the Swedish government's approval; and this would not be 'before Norwegian (or Danish) territory had been evacuated'.

The Swedish standpoint was hardly indisputable in international law. The German government, however, limited itself to a very moderate reply on 6 May, which maintained that in this question Sweden had violated her duty as a neutral. One explanation of this cautious approach may be that, through the discovery of the maps, Berlin was put at a disadvantage in discussions with Stockholm; another could be that the question scarcely had any importance just then. A general deterioration in Germany's negotiating position was anyway taken for granted in Stockholm. It was noted that, although Hitler and Ribbentrop were reported to be as bitter and suspicious of Sweden as ever, they nevertheless avoided deeds and words which could act as irritants in German-Swedish relations, and that, despite air attacks on their factories and communications, the Germans executed their deliveries under the 1944 trade agreement with admirable efficiency. No warnings of interference with the Gothenburg traffic were forthcoming. To be sure, the Germans took exception to various obstacles which the Swedes put in the way of the exchange of goods agreed in 1944, but in hurt rather than threatening language. The Western Powers' severe pressure for a ban on ball-bearing exports brought no official reaction at all from the Germans. Good German-Swedish relations and uninterrupted Swedish deliveries to Germany had now become the Germans' chief aim in their relations with Sweden.

Günther was, however, not willing to rule out the possibility that Hitler might suddenly decide to take military action against Sweden. Hitler could suspect, as did the Swedes themselves, that the Western Powers' *démarches* on ball-bearings, made quite publicly, were intended to drive Sweden more and more into the Allied camp before the invasion of the Continent. Hitler was unpredictable and, as Germany's occupation of Italy and Hungary had recently shown, did not shrink from drastic measures. Günther had for a long time been worried lest Swedish public opinion should mislead Hitler and others into believing that the Swedish government, if threatened by drastic Western measures, would readily move towards meeting their demands, including even a demand to join their side. Fears of a German preventive action against Sweden in the face of an expected Allied landing in Norway had been a permanent anxiety in Stockholm. Warnings from the Berlin Legation at the end of March in connection with Sweden's demonstrative advice to Finland to come to terms with the Soviet Union and the many finds of maps in April kept these fears alive. Respect for the German army's striking power still remained. The Swedish government was by no means alarmed but, primarily at Günther's instigation, decided on 5 May on a minor increase in readiness. The situation was uncertain. The Western Powers' long-awaited invasion must now be very near.

Around the end of May the Berlin Legation again warned Stockholm to be ready and alert. An invasion of Norway by the Western Powers might still lead to a more or less simultaneous German action against Sweden. And even if events during and after an invasion took place away from Sweden, they could have repercussions there. The Swedish government had a clear interest in disposing as soon as possible of the Western Powers' latest *démarche* on ball-bearings, which certainly opened up a vast area of contention both with them and with Germany. On 8 June therefore the government approved an agreement between SKF and the Western Powers which severely reduced ball-bearing deliveries to Germany in the next few months. The deficit in deliveries contracted for 1944 should, however, be filled during the last months of the year. In so doing, the Swedish government formally maintained its standpoint that it was abiding by its agreements on the exchange of goods in 1944 with the Germans as well as the Allies: SKF's agreement with the Western Powers was the firm's affair, not the government's. But in fact there was no doubt that a retreat from the earlier Swedish line had taken place. During discussions on 8 June ministers openly expressed the opinion that approval of SKF's move sanctioned a breach of definite agreements with Germany. The Prime Minister declared that 'he certainly wanted to stand by agreement . . . but it was not always so easy . . . we must take the situation into account'. On 19 April Günther had told the *Riksdag* of the Western Powers' demands on ball-bearings and the government's refusal. As one argument for this reply he had said: 'It has also to be pointed out that developments in the war from the Swedish point of view have not produced such fundamental changes as to cause us to disregard obligations which we have undertaken'. On 8 June, two days after the start of the Normandy invasion, when the bridgehead had been established, the government considered that such fundamental changes had occurred.

The Swedes had in vain insisted that the September 1943 Tripartite Agreement with Britain and the United States was binding not only on Sweden but on the other two signatories as well. This attitude could count on understanding (at any rate in principle) in London. But not in Washington, where the agreement was considered purely temporary.

'You in Sweden must understand', a prominent and well-informed American explained to Hägglöf in London,

'that right from the USA's entry into the war American public opinion has been set on waging war one hundred per cent. In the view of the average American the task of the USA is now, as in 1918, to decide the war through real American toughness. To act tough towards neutrals is a really easy task. That Sweden has so far come off so lightly is very surprising. Right up to the middle of 1942 Sweden certainly could always and with justice maintain that she was in an emergency situation. But afterwards it has certainly been difficult to find reasons for her behaviour acceptable to the man in the street. Without the continuous discussions in 1942 and 1943 and even without the agreement last summer, things would probably have come to a crunch in Swedish-American relations. There is', he continued, 'certainly nothing to be surprised at in a dispute arising in the spring of 1944 in a dull season before the invasion. On the contrary, the Swedes should consider themselves lucky that this dispute has been restricted to a single, comparatively technical field like ball-bearing exports'. Leading people in Washington – I imagine that he meant the State Department in particular – were ready to accept some form of compromise; the main thing was that public opinion should be satisfied with the result.

I naturally maintained that the agreement had been construed as a settlement for the whole of 1944. If, in April 1944, the American government was already insisting on revising one point of the agreement, what would prevent it from taking up other points as the year went on? To this my interlocutor replied: 'The agreement has already achieved its main purpose. Without an agreement Swedish-American relations would have gone crash. Now the invasion is coming. If the invasion succeeds, our small quarrels about ball-bearings will pretty soon be forgotten. If, against all expectations, it does not succeed, and the war be prolonged for some time, our war trade problems should become really embarrassing'.

'Toughness' towards neutrals an American aim, a dispute during a 'dull season' a completely natural event, the State Department ready to approve 'some sort of compromise', if only a success could be recorded for public opinion. To survive as an independent state encircled by German military power Sweden had had to execute several awkward manoeuvres, some of which had strained her neutrality to the utmost. Early in 1943 the German threat began to recede, by the spring of 1944 Sweden had regained much of her freedom of action against Germany. Only to be taken in tow by the Allies?

# 6 Sweden and Finland's war

## From the start of hostilities to the start of peace discussions

On 22 June 1941 Germany invaded the Soviet Union. The Finnish Prime Minister, Johan Rangell, announced on the evening of 25 June that the Soviet Union had commenced hostilities and that Finland was defending herself with all military means at her disposal. In the opinion of the Finns, the Swedes in the face of permanent Soviet plans for expansion and conquest ought to see this new war as for Sweden's defence too. Therefore Sweden should grant Finland extensive and generous help with those 'necessary deliveries' and 'credits required' which were requested in a comprehensive list submitted by Wasastjerna on 22 June. The Swedes felt, however, that the Finns went too far both in their claims and in their methods of negotiating. In summer 1941, unlike winter 1940, the Swedish public was not at all united in the view that it was in Sweden's own interest to support Finland in her war. Quite the contrary, an influential body of opinion, particularly firmly rooted in left-wing circles, considered that help to Finland now was help to Germany in her offensive against the Soviet Union. Chauvinistic statements and articles in the Finnish press in support of 'Greater Finland', not infrequently accompanied by a hostile, or at least cool, attitude towards Sweden, also caused concern.

An offensive opened in mid-July brought the Finnish troops in early September to the old frontier on the Carelian Isthmus. On the other side of Lake Ladoga they reached the River Svir well to the east of the frontier; and on 1 October they pushed their way into Petrozavodsk, the capital of the Carelian Soviet Republic. The Finns now occupied considerable areas of Soviet territory and their official argument, that they were conducting their own war quite separate from the trial of strength between the Great Powers, was treated by the outside world with scepticism. Furthermore, after pressure from Germany, Finland had broken off diplomatic relations with Britain in the summer. In

November the British government threatened to declare war, if Finland did not halt operations at her 1939 frontiers. In this situation Günther expressed both to the British and to the Americans his doubts that Britain's assistance to the Soviet Union really had to take the form of a British declaration of war on Finland. Although he lacked reliable information on Finland's strategic and political objectives, he thus gave Finland rather strong diplomatic support. As a matter of fact Sweden herself had an important interest in trying to prevent a British declaration of war on Finland, as it would drive Finland closer to Germany, reduce the possibilities of a separate peace, and increase the risks for Allied military actions against northern Scandinavia.

Günther's move proved ineffective. The British government announced on 6 December that a state of war would exist with Finland from the following day. Simultaneously Finnish-American relations deteriorated. Finland's attitude to Sweden, in the opinion of the Swedish Legation in Helsinki, remained exacting: as the present war was just a continuation of the Winter War, Sweden, both in her own interests and on general moral grounds, should help Finland as far as possible in her fight against the Soviet Union and Bolshevism.

On Christmas Eve 1941 Madame Kollontay called on Boheman to ask him, without instructions from home and only 'in a purely personal capacity and as an old friend', whether he believed that a willingness to settle with Finland, which she thought she had reason to discern in Moscow, could find any response on the Finnish side.

It may be that Madame Kollontay was more concerned to introduce thoughts of a separate peace into the calculations of the planners of Sweden's foreign policy than to ask for specific Swedish action in Helsinki. To undertake to mediate, as in the Winter War, was anyhow, as she herself said, far too risky for Sweden. Germany had in Finland not only a valuable military ally, but also a political trump card to play in support of the thesis that the states of Europe must join in a crusade to eliminate once and for all the permanent threat to their existence which the Soviet Union presented. Consequently the Germans must be expected to react violently against any Swedish attempt to extricate Finland from the war. The Swedish government, therefore, had repeatedly assured the Germans that no Swedish mediation between Finland and the Soviet Union was contemplated. Nonetheless, Günther allowed Madame Kollontay's remarks to Boheman to reach Ryti informally. Furthermore, on 2 January, Wasastjerna obtained for the President's ear information about Anthony Eden's negotiations with Stalin in Moscow, which had just ended. According to this information, which Assarsson had got from his British colleague, Sir Stafford Cripps, Stalin had declared straight out that he had no intention of challenging Finland's independence, provided 'that Finland got rid of the present ruling clique and people like Paasikivi took control'.

Helsinki had also received information through other channels on the negotiations between Stalin and Eden. The Finns, however, did not interpret them as an invitation to make contacts for peace, but as a warning to Finland — and to Sweden — that Britain had now accepted the Soviet Union's claim to have the final word on Finland. In spite of her great war-weariness, her considerable losses in dead and wounded, her anxieties over her food-supplies, and the beginning of a certain disquiet at military developments on the Eastern front, Finland, Karl Ivan Westman summed up early in the New Year of 1942, had no thought of abandoning the foreign policy followed up till now. An authoritative confirmation was provided by the President's speech at the opening of the Finnish parliament on 3 February 1942. Ryti addressed himself directly to Stalin's and Eden's discussions and declared that Finland, at the side of Germany and her allies, must bring her defensive struggle 'to a victorious conclusion, since Bolshevism remains the greatest danger threatening us and the whole of Europe'. Approaches for a separate peace were rejected.

When the Finnish troops reached the northern point of Lake Onega at the beginning of December 1941, Mannerheim halted operations. No further advance towards the Sorokka rail-junction to cut supplies from Murmansk was ever made. Repeated German proposals on pressure for such a move were resisted by Mannerheim with great deftness. On the Svir front Soviet attacks were repulsed in the spring of 1942. Thereafter the Finnish-Soviet fronts on the whole were quiet.

Hitler's visit to Mannerheim on his seventy-fifth birthday on 4 June 1942 and his optimistic forecasts for the war, German successes in North Africa, where, on 21 June, Tobruk was captured, and German promises of help, particularly with deliveries of food, obviously strengthened the Finnish expectations that their policy would yield good dividends. In the press the dominant note was one of confidence in the government's policy and in the future. The atmosphere towards Sweden was not exactly friendly. When Westman left his post as Swedish Minister in Helsinki early in October 1942, he recorded some worry there about Finnish-American relations and about a gradual cooling-down of Swedish feelings for Finland, but he foresaw no alteration of course in the Finnish government's foreign policy.

In the next few weeks, however, unambiguous signs appeared that

171

concern for the future was beginning to influence Finland's policies towards greater friendliness with Sweden. During his first discussion with the new Swedish Minister in Helsinki, Hans Beck-Friis, Witting announced that the President and the government's Foreign Affairs Committee were unanimous in wanting to maintain ties with Sweden, and in working to prevent any rift arising. The press, especially the main Helsinki papers, began to change their strong leaning towards Germany. This development became yet more obvious in November under the impact of the British victory at El Alamein and the Western Powers' landings in North Africa. Towards the end of November 1942, some days after the great Soviet offensive north and south of Stalingrad had begun, the Swedish Legation in Helsinki concluded that 'the increasing care for relations with Sweden, caused by concern over general developments, is put more clearly on record every day by Finland's leading newspapers'. The Swedes, however, were cautious and Hansson and Günther, it appears, warned against precipitate Finnish action to break loose from Germany.

Towards the end of 1942 the United States stiffened her attitude towards Finland and recalled her Minister in Helsinki. The successful Soviet offensives in the East and the Western Powers' progress in North Africa at the same time increased the doubts that already existed of Germany's final victory. Faced with constantly unfavourable developments, Ryti wanted to explore the prospects of Swedish reinsurance. On 9 January 1943, the President summoned Beck-Friis for a private discussion. He referred to the Minister's account several months earlier (29 October 1942) of Churchill's remarks to Boheman during his stay in London about a Nordic bloc, which would also include a free Finland (see p.137). Ryti asked Beck-Friis whether he had heard any more about it after Boheman's return to Stockholm from Washington. When Beck-Friis replied in the negative, Ryti went on with a long exposition primarily of the economic prerequisites for such a bloc. He said it would interest him to hear the results of any pertinent investigations which might have been made in Sweden. Beck-Friis promised to pass his question on to Günther.

Ryti clearly wanted to start a discussion on Nordic and above all Finnish-Swedish co-operation. As if to underline these aspirations further, about a week later an interview with Witting appeared in a Swedish newspaper. The Foreign Minister disassociated himself from 'Greater Finnish' plans of conquest and defended himself against accusations of belittling Nordic co-operation and the ideals of a democratic society, of which, on the contrary, he was a convinced protagonist. Finally, at the same time the Finns asked for Swedish support for their Minister in Washington in his efforts to maintain good relations between Finland and the United States.

Günther agreed to provide the support requested in Washington, even if not exactly in the desired terms. Ryti's question about a Nordic bloc he answered in a friendly enough, but completely non-committal, manner. Ryti was told that Sweden's neutral position could not conceivably undergo any change while the present war was in progress, but that Sweden was ready as a matter of course to provide neighbouring countries with all the humanitarian aid and diplomatic support which circumstances allowed. Günther then very cautiously hinted at Swedish help in soundings for a separate peace. But when Beck-Friis brought Günther's message to him on 26 January, the President carefully avoided taking up this hint.

For a long time Moscow refrained from any sharp admonitions on Swedish concessions and other services to Germany and Finland in their war against the Soviet Union. The important thing was that Sweden was keeping out of the war. Moscow, Assarsson reported in autumn 1941, was anxious not to adopt towards Sweden a provocative attitude, which could subject Swedish-Soviet relations to undue strain, and to avoid everything which could provide a fair wind for anti-Bolshevik feelings in Sweden. Nor were there any special Swedish-Soviet difficulties worth mentioning right up to the summer of 1942.

Then, however, Moscow found it appropriate to remind Sweden that, as the war had now developed, benefits hitherto given to Germany and Finland should be reconsidered. In somewhat sharp notes it refused to acknowledge blatant attacks by Soviet submarines on shipping in Swedish territorial waters and maintained instead that they were German provocations. Moreover, the Soviet government protested against alleged breaches of neutrality by which Sweden, it was asserted, afforded direct support to Germany and Finland in their military operations. These protests were repeated in late autumn, despite refutation by the Swedish government. Around the end of 1942, the Soviet Union's general attitude towards Sweden was further stiffened. No dramatic outburst took place, but the Soviet view was made clear: in the changed war situation Sweden ought to pay less regard to the interests of Germany and Finland and more to those of the Soviet Union.

Through an intermediary, the Soviet authorities had informed Assarsson that there was some interest in a Swedish initiative for a separate Finnish-Soviet peace. Günther, however, had good reasons for caution. In spite of defeats on the Eastern front and in North Africa, Germany still dominated the Baltic war theatre and thus the situation in Finland. Ryti had shown no interest in discussing the prospect of a separate peace when an opportunity to do so had been offered him. Further, Günther distrusted Witting and on several occasions gave information to Wasastjerna subject to the specific restriction that it should go only to Ryti and Mannerheim. He did not want to risk it being passed on through Witting to Berlin. Altogether Günther and his colleagues doubted whether anything could be done about peace before there was a change in the Finnish government, perhaps also a change of President. In December 1940, Ryti had been elected only for the remaining term of Kallio's office and new elections were to be held on 15 February 1943.

Should such changes occur in Finland, declared Günther on 9 February, chances of a separate peace were not so bad. Both the Soviet Union and Germany had a major interest in shortening their fronts. There were many signs that the Germans could be expected to take a separate Finnish peace fairly calmly. One must assume that Germany had lost the war. An early Finnish peace was in Sweden's interest, said Günther to his colleagues.

Without making any direct proposals, Günther then raised the question of whether Sweden should not advise Finland to seek peace through American mediation. He did not consider any major Swedish contribution to help Finland possible for the present: 'presumably Finland would be obliged to settle with the Soviet Union in the same way as happened in 1940, but so far as supplies are concerned, we could help to eke out'.

Herschel Johnson called on Boheman two days later to present a message to the Swedish government from Cordell Hull about an exchange of views on the Finnish question. Boheman, whose remarks were endorsed by Günther later that same day, gave him clearly to understand that Sweden wished to remain in the background, in any case for the time being. In return, however, he tried energetically and eloquently, citing the Atlantic Charter, to get the Americans to work for a separate peace for Finland on favourable terms, including full freedom to co-operate with the other Nordic countries after the war.

Johnson told Boheman that an American initiative to mediate between Helsinki and Moscow presupposed that the Finnish government 'would be ripe for an approach on this problem'. It was thus in Sweden's interest to guide Helsinki's thinking in this direction. When Wasastjerna announced on 12 February 'that Helsinki was considering

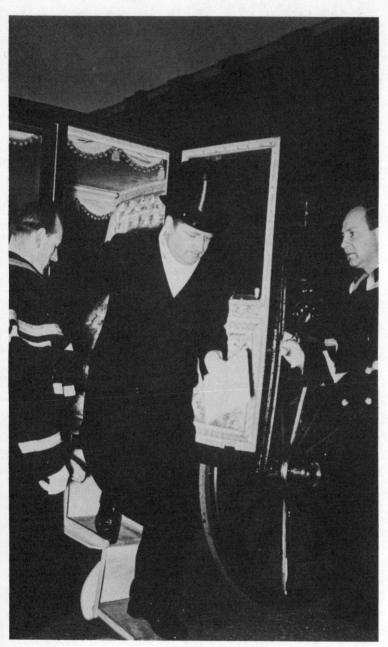

*Herschel Johnson, American Minister in Stockholm*

asking the Swedish government to pass to the British government proposals for peace negotiations with Great Britain', Günther replied that this initiative would certainly be rejected in London; everything indicated that peace negotiations should be started simultaneously with Britain and the Soviet Union. He also turned down a feeler from Wasastjerna about a study of a Swedish-Finnish union on the lines sketched out in 1940. Beck-Friis was instructed to forward to Ryti, who on 15 February had been re-elected President for a further two years, a personal message from Assarsson. Sweden's envoy in Moscow earnestly recommended that Finland should exploit the opportunities of the present political and military situation to 'seek and achieve a peaceful settlement with the Soviet Union, satisfying the demands of honour and the nation's security'. The time was ripe for a bold initiative. Günther added that he had not 'wished to deny to Assarsson in his capacity of custodian of Finland's interests in the Soviet Union the right to put his personal opinions to Finland's President'. Obviously his sanctioning of such an unusual step implied that he approved of Assarsson's viewpoint.

Ryti replied to Assarsson's message on 20 February. He contented himself with general remarks, but did hold out the prospect of discussions later, as soon as a reconstruction of the government was completed. Some weeks later, on 5 March, a new coalition government took office with Edwin Linkomies as Prime Minister and Henrik Ramsay as Foreign Minister. But the anticipated discussions never took place. Beck-Friis was inclined to detect a change of mood in Helsinki. Thoughts of a separate peace were receding, and in authoritative circles a more optimistic view of Germany's position prevailed — towards the end of the winter the Germans had succeeded in stabilizing their Eastern front.

In Stockholm some Finnish initiative had been expected. But nothing happened. Sweden's advice was plainly neither sought nor desired in Helsinki. Günther therefore held back, but all the same let a message be passed to Ramsay from Assarsson: what had become of a Finnish peace initiative? Ramsay expressed his thanks, but underlined the difficulties: at the beginning of April he saw the possibility of peace as 'very dark'; it was, in his opinion, 'very difficult, indeed almost impossible'.

A few days later, on 10 April, Ramsay told Beck-Friis that the Finns had rejected an American offer to get peace negotiations under way. The United States had in fact offered, Ramsay commented, to bring about contact with the Russians. This the Finns could naturally achieve themselves whenever they wanted. They had hoped for something more from the Americans, but this had not been granted, so the answer had to be no. Günther knew that Ramsay had made a journey to Berlin before this reply to Washington, whereby Germany had been given the chance of tightening the screws. About this journey Ramsay was very reticent. A fairly accurate guess of what had happened could nevertheless be made in Stockholm; and later in May it was noted that in an official speech Linkomies delivered a lengthy and uncompromising declaration of war to the bitter end against the Soviet Union. Any change of course by Finland was obviously out of the question.

So Günther limited himself to keeping Ramsay apprised of particularly interesting information, and trying to work in Washington for a better American understanding of Finland's position. For the time being, there was little more to be done. To get Finland to take further and decisive steps towards a separate peace it would obviously have been necessary for Sweden to guarantee Finland's frontiers under it, or even in fact to send troops across to Finland before it was signed. Both these measures had been repeatedly suggested in Helsinki, but were considered out of the question in Stockholm. Moreover, it was to be feared that too pressing Swedish advice in Helsinki would adversely affect mutual relations and make any Swedish intervention later more difficult.

In the course of the London American-British-Swedish trade negotiations in May and June 1943, pressure was put on the Swedes to impose strict limits on trade with Finland. The Swedes managed, however, to a certain extent to preserve a special position for Finland compared with Germany. Even if the London texts in a sense were to Finland's disadvantage, it was Günther's opinion that in a broader view they served Finnish interests. In terms unusually pathetic for him he explained to Mallet at midsummer 1943 that Sweden was bound to the utmost possible extent to help Finland, 'Sweden's daughter', out of the dangerous situation into which her leaders' foolish policies had brought her. Therefore relations with the Soviet Union, which just now harboured unfounded suspicions of Sweden, had to be improved, and therefore, in their turn, the proposals just worked out in London for a Swedish-British-American agreement had a significant political value: if Sweden could enter an agreement which was so disadvantageous to Germany, this should make an impression even on Moscow and help to convince the Russians of Sweden's sincere desire for the best possible relations. Her standing in Moscow improved, Sweden would be able to speak more effectively for Finland.

At the same time, Swedish assistance in Finland's withdrawal from

177

the war would obviously advance Sweden's own interest in Moscow. The Soviet attitude towards Sweden had become harsher in recent months. The Soviet press gave its readers the impression that Sweden was running Hitler's errands. The Swedish Legation in Moscow encountered a more unfriendly atmosphere than at any time earlier. The Kremlin not only criticized the continued Swedish concessions to Germany, but also openly expressed suspicions of a secret Swedish-German understanding. It was further maintained that, by protestations of sympathy and deliveries, Sweden was prolonging Finland's agony instead of resolutely helping the Finns to perceive the real need of the moment. If Sweden adopted this latter course, the Soviet Union's attitude would obviously become more friendly. A separate peace for Finland thus was both desirable in itself and a means of improving Sweden's general position.

During the summer of 1943 no significant changes occurred in Finland's position. On the Finnish-Soviet fronts still no real operations took place. The Finnish government stubbornly refused to comply with repeated German demands for assurances that it would not enter into a separate peace. But it did not consider that there was any hurry to negotiate either. In August it replied to a Soviet feeler with an opening bid in quite general terms, giving the 1939 frontiers as the starting-point; extensive areas of East Carelia were by now in Finnish occupation. The Soviet government found this bid much too high to want to discuss it. Under the impact of Germany's continued reverses, Mussolini's downfall, and the Swedish-German agreement on the ending of the transit traffic, opinion in Finland grew in favour of direct negotiations with the Soviet Union and disengagement from a Germany doomed to defeat. All the same, Finland's leaders thought they should wait. Developments in Italy also provided a drastic incentive for caution in the matter of a separate peace. On 8 September the Western Powers' Supreme Commander in the Mediterranean theatre, General Eisenhower, publicly announced Italy's surrender. During the next few days the German troops, which had been pouring into the country, moved to an open occupation and disarmed the Italian troops. Also in September the Eastern front had begun to fluctuate through widespread German withdrawals and big Soviet attacks, which, at the end of the month, had in some places crossed the River Dnieper, where the Germans had planned to establish their new main line of defence. But Hitler's will to fight was manifestly unbroken.

The Finnish government was anxious to keep the door to the West open. Accordingly in September it put forward a request that the

Swedish government, through its envoy in Washington, Wollmar Boström, should emphasize Sweden's lively interest in Finland's survival as a free and independent state. Günther complied, but, with Finnish consent, instructed Boström also to impart Finland's readiness to enter into an agreement with the Soviet Union, provided that such an agreement did not entail 'a continued threat to Finland's integrity'. Boström found interest in his information at the State Department. Cordell Hull told Boström he was convinced that the Finns no longer wanted more than their old frontiers. He stated that he understood their difficulties in getting out of the war, and promised to bear in mind the Swedish point of view at the coming Moscow Conference between the Foreign Ministers of the Big Three – although he was uncertain whether the Soviet Union would be willing to discuss the question there. Hull also said that he would firmly abide by the principles of the Atlantic Charter. 'He was in general very well informed and sympathetically disposed', Boström concluded.

Immediately after Finland's April rejection of the American government's offer of its good offices in Finnish-Soviet contacts for a separate peace, Washington had come near enough to breaking off diplomatic relations with Helsinki. Later, in August, through his Chargé d'Affaires in Helsinki, Hull had informed Ramsay, who had asked whether Finland could count on the United States telling her when the time was appropriate for peace contacts with the Soviet Union, that Washington had nothing to add to what it had already said about Finland's relations with Germany. Against this background the considerable understanding which Hull showed Boström was promising. It could almost seem as if Günther was on the road to success in achieving his aim of making Washington Finland's advocate in Moscow. Since Hull had shown understanding for Boström's arguments he would probably say something in Finland's favour at the impending meeting in Moscow. Günther concluded thus when relating Boström's report to the new Finnish Minister in Stockholm, Georg Gripenberg. For the present, in his opinion peace efforts should wait. Ramsay concurred in this view.

Moscow's displeasure with Sweden had not diminished during the summer of 1943. The termination of the German transit traffic in August produced no turn for the better: the Kremlin let the press cast doubts on the efficacy of its cancellation. Assarsson argued strongly against this view, but was not listened to: his assurances were countered by references to reports in the Swedish newspapers. Towards the end of September, Assarsson spoke of a campaign against Sweden in the Soviet press. When Assarsson called on Molotov on 18 September, the

Foreign Commissar was very bitter. He maintained that Sweden had granted, and continued to grant, the use of her railways and her territorial waters for the transport of war materials, which Germany and Finland used to fight the Soviet Union and its allies. Assarsson rebutted the charges. The discussion gradually centred on Finland, which Molotov in harsh terms accused of sharing the blame for the terrible sufferings of the inhabitants of Leningrad and the destruction of their city. Assarsson touched on the possibility of a change in Finnish policy, if the prospect of an acceptable peace could be found, and tried to get Molotov to talk about these matters, but without success. Further discussion about an eventual peace served no purpose, until the Finns themselves had some proposal to contribute. This was Molotov's closing remark. Assarsson's impression was that the Russians, in spite of being at present almost drunk with victory after their recent great military successes, nevertheless continued to be anxious to make a separate peace with Finland, having regard particularly to the Leningrad front. But the good chances to obtain favourable conditions the Finns had had in the previous winter were now forfeited. Stalin would now insist on the 1940 frontiers and in addition the Petsamo district, and there was no question of any compensation for Finland.

In a report to the government of 22 September on Sweden's relations with the Soviet Union, Günther dealt also with the chances of a Finnish-Soviet peace. He was not completely pessimistic. Moscow, his argument ran, wanted to establish a favourable position in the North against Britain and possibly the United States. It opposed every sort of union between Sweden and Finland and also a Nordic bloc, while it probably wanted a Scandinavian (a Danish-Norwegian-Swedish) coalition which could defend its neutrality against Britain. In one way or another, Günther continued, Finland would come into the Soviet sphere of influence. The Soviet Union's attitude, however, was not yet definitely settled. There was uncertainty in many matters, including the problem of frontier delineations. In addition, the Soviet Union had to think of its allies, who now played the same role in the Nordic question as Germany had done earlier. Efforts to achieve a separate Finnish-Soviet peace were certainly not pointless.

The Moscow Conference of 19–30 October 1943 between Molotov, Eden, and Hull was a greater success than expected, this primarily because Stalin now obtained sufficiently convincing assurance of a coming invasion of Europe during 1944. Certain of this, he did not push a proposal which Molotov had put forward right at the beginning of the conference, that the Big Three should jointly ask Sweden to make available airfields for use in the struggle against Germany. When the Western Powers, in the first instance the American military representatives who did not believe that men and machines in sufficient amounts were available, returned a negative, or at least a procrastinating, reply, the Soviet Union did not insist.

Apart from the published texts, among them a declaration demanding the enemies' unconditional surrender, very little real information about the conference came to the knowledge of those responsible for Swedish foreign policy. But Assarsson's reporting showed clearly that the Finnish government ought not to count on any help against the Soviet Union from the Western Powers, particularly the United States: expectations of such help had not been fulfilled, although Hull had shown himself well disposed towards Sweden. When Günther passed on to Ramsay his information on the Moscow Conference, he did not give him any direct advice to seek an agreement with Moscow. But a hint that some form of Finnish initiative was now called for could doubtless be read into his message.

Ramsay, however, was unwilling to take action. Stalin, he explained to Beck-Friis, had referred in a speech on 6 November to the liberation of the Carelian-Finnish Soviet Republic, but Finland was not willing to accept the 1940 frontier and the loss of Viipuri. Ramsay was also dubious about the importance of the concert achieved between the Soviet Union and the Western Powers. He was not persuaded either of Germany's downfall or the Soviet Union's wholly decisive role in Finland's future. Beck-Friis further noted that for a policy of wait and see the Finnish government was undeniably able to rely on a virtually united front in the press, which had been stiffened and welded together through the Moscow communiqué's request for 'unconditional surrender', and Stalin's remarks on the liberation of the Carelian-Finnish Soviet Republic.

Moscow, on the other hand, was more willing to take an initiative. It wanted to dispose of the conflict with Finland in order to have troops available on more central fronts for the approaching final settlement with Germany. It still wished to get Finland to the conference table. If the Swedish government at last interpreted the signs of the times aright and, as it had done in 1940, spoke out in Helsinki resolutely in favour of peace, it was in Soviet eyes a suitable intermediary for peace.

## Swedish attempts at mediation

On 13 November 1943, immediately after she had returned to her post

181

---

after a lengthy illness, Madame Kollontay invited Boheman to exchange personal views on Swedish-Finnish-Soviet relations. Boheman stressed that the Finns genuinely wished to reach a peaceful settlement but, before they began negotiating, wanted to have some knowledge of the main conditions on which such an agreement would be based. Boheman reiterated time and again Sweden's earnest desire to maintain a good political and economic relationship with the Soviet Union and her concern lest the Finnish question should develop in such a way that, despite the Swedish government's good intentions, this relationship would be destroyed. That, Madame Kollontay agreed, was precisely her chief worry too.

Madame Kollontay spoke appreciatively of Sweden. Assarsson's reports, on the other hand, warned that there was growing Soviet impatience and irritation with the neutrals, who in Moscow's opinion actively or passively supported the Axis Powers and thereby contributed to prolonging the war. Moscow was evidently expecting greater regard for its views and interests.

On Madame Kollontay's advice, her government was nevertheless willing to accept Sweden as its intermediary in an exchange of views with Finland about a separate peace. On 20 November she informed Boheman for transmission to Helsinki that a Finnish delegate would be welcome in Moscow for preliminary discussions. The Soviet Union, she declared, had no intention of encroaching in any way on Finland's autonomy and independence, so long as it was not forced to change its attitude by Finland's policies in the future. The Moscow communiqué's call for unconditional surrender was thus not repeated. Helsinki should send its reply through Boheman.

Moscow's direct call for Swedish mediation must have been very welcome in Stockholm. Sweden should now be able to promote a separate peace for Finland more effectively than before – and in so doing fortify her relations with the Soviet Union. The task could not be expected to be easier than it had been in 1940. Nonetheless, the prospects had just recently improved. Madame Kollontay, with her manifest goodwill towards Sweden and Finland and her good standing in Moscow, was back again at her post. And Sweden, as the abrogation of the transit facilities had shown in the summer, could now better afford to disregard German displeasure.

Hansson and Günther, however, at least for a start, did not want the Swedish government to get involved in peace talks. They decided to remain officially in ignorance of Boheman's activities as middleman between the Finnish and Soviet envoys in Stockholm. But both

Günther and Boheman exhorted the Finns in unequivocal terms to make good use of the chances of getting discussions going with Moscow. The Finnish government concurred in this opinion. After a short time, Boheman was able to hand over a reply to Moscow from Helsinki which took the 1939 frontier as its starting-point. But on 20 December Madame Kollontay informed Boheman that her government did not find the Finnish statement satisfactory. Moscow stood by the 1940 frontier and could not accept any other; all other questions could be discussed during the negotiations.

The tone of the conversation between Madame Kollontay and Boheman on this occasion was probably more subdued than previously. A few days earlier, on 17 December, she had told him that, according to precise information in the hands of the Soviet government, Assarsson and his Military Attaché had abused diplomatic privilege and passed to the German High Command very important secret information about the Soviet army; the Soviet government demanded their immediate recall. Boheman rejected the accusations as completely groundless, not to say ridiculous. Madame Kollontay had no comment to make beyond the statement that her government's decision was irrevocable, and Assarsson was instructed – unless he believed he could clear up the matter promptly and effectively on the spot – to come home immediately together with his Military Attaché.

Moscow did not further explain its actions against Assarsson. On 4 January, however, Madame Kollontay informed Günther on instructions from home that the Soviet government wished to maintain friendly relations with Sweden and that Assarsson's recall was an isolated event. It had no significance as far as Moscow's attitude towards Stockholm was concerned. A welcome declaration obviously – but the Swedish government could hardly believe that this drastic and sudden step was not intended as an indication of Moscow's displeasure at Sweden's policies.

No new Finnish messages to deliver to the Soviet government were forthcoming – nor any Soviet messages for the Finns. Madame Kollontay told Boheman that the silence of her government must be considered disconcerting. Meanwhile, Soviet offensives continued in the South and were beginning in the North as well; in mid-January the German forces were compelled to make substantial retreats west and south of Leningrad, and in consequence the Finnish front on the Isthmus of Carelia became more exposed than at any time since the summer of 1941.

In this situation Günther deemed it necessary to play a more active advisory role to get the Finns to renew contact with Moscow. Some Swedish promptings in this direction were made in Helsinki and certainly contributed to the Finnish government's decision in February to send Paasikivi to Stockholm in order to obtain more precise information on the Soviet Union's peace conditions through Madame Kollontay. Moscow, Paasikivi learnt, now set conditions for opening negotiations. The Finns should therefore give a prior undertaking to revert to complete neutrality, including the disarming and internment of the German troops in Finland (in which the Soviet Union was willing to collaborate), to withdraw to the 1940 frontier, and to send prisoners-of-war home. Further conditions could then be discussed in Moscow. Consulted by Paasikivi, Günther advised the Finns to accept.

Moscow had caused its conditions to be published and, in the American, British, and also the Swedish press they had been judged a suitable basis for negotiations. The British and American governments demanded, and the Swedish government recommended, that they should be accepted. Frequent bombing raids were made on Helsinki. South of the Gulf of Finland Soviet troops crossed the River Narva and broke through the position to which the Germans had withdrawn during the big Soviet offensive in mid-January. But the situation had also other aspects. There were about 150,000 German troops in Finland whom the Finns had no real prospects whatever of interning. The Finnish army still stood victorious, strong, and unbroken on Soviet territory, far from the 1940 frontier, which Moscow persistently claimed. On 4 March the Finnish government handed to the Swedish intermediaries the text of a reply: it was making serious efforts to reach an early peace, but could not accept the proposed Soviet conditions; it was nevertheless willing to negotiate on specific questions.

When Gripenberg produced this text on 4 March, Günther and Boheman told him that to pass it on 'would be like helping one's best friend to commit suicide'. They suggested instead a formula expressly proposing negotiations in Moscow, but not committing the Finnish government to the Soviet conditions given to Paasikivi.

Gripenberg promised to submit Günther's suggestions to Ramsay. Günther put further pressure on Helsinki by demonstratively emphasizing King Gustaf's worry that the Finnish government would return a negative reply to the Soviet proposals. The King, he told Gripenberg, had asked him whether any signs indicated that Mannerheim might come forward and rally the people of Finland in a united decision to negotiate for peace. The King desired 'that his personal views in the matter should be brought to the attention of the President and the Marshal'. Not since the last weeks of the Winter War had Sweden's foreign policy-makers sent such outspoken advice to Helsinki.

The Finnish government's new reply, which Boheman handed over to Madame Kollontay on 8 March, clearly took into account the views which Günther had put forward in the name of the King, the government, and himself and which also completely dominated the Swedish press. It was now prepared to negotiate, without, however, definitely committing itself to accepting the conditions put to Paasikivi in Stockholm.

Madame Kollontay was pleased with the Finns' reply. Her government was not. She had to report back by return, on 10 March, that the reply was quite unsatisfactory; that the conditions for the armistice, which Paasikivi had got, were 'minimal and elementary'; and that negotiations would be possible only after the Finnish government had accepted them. The Soviets expected a positive answer within a week — by 18 March at the latest. Otherwise they would consider their conditions rejected.

Günther and Boheman still considered that the Finns should try to start negotiations and told Helsinki so. But Ramsay was sceptical and, reported Beck-Friis, 'called into question, as usual, the value of the interpretations one got in Stockholm', that is, by Madame Kollontay. In Ramsay's opinion the Swedes relied far too much on her explanation of Moscow's intentions. 'Here through bitter experience one had reason to be sceptical'. In several discussions Beck-Friis repeated his superiors' assessment of the situation, but was unable to convince Ramsay. The Finnish parliament also, on 15 March, unanimously approved the government's motion that Finland should not negotiate on the Soviet Union's terms as then known. The new Finnish answer, which Boheman gave to Madame Kollontay on 17 March, laid great stress on Finland's desire to resume peaceful relations with the Soviet Union, but also pointed out the impossibility of accepting in advance conditions affecting the nation's very existence without knowing for certain how they were to be interpreted and what they involved.

Madame Kollontay found this reply better than expected and agreed with Boheman's opinion that 'the best that could happen would be that the Russians took up the point that the Finns wanted to know what an authoritative interpretation of the conditions involved'. As Moscow did want to reach a settlement with Finland, this also came about. On the night of 19 March, Madame Kollontay presented an invitation from her government for one or two Finnish delegates to have the Soviet Union's conditions for an armistice interpreted for them in Moscow.

Nor did Madame Kollontay now spare appreciative comments on Sweden's role. The advice given to Helsinki by the King and government, which had become generally known on 16 March and had then also been confirmed by the Foreign Ministry, and the attitude of the press were a turning-point in Soviet-Swedish relations, she enthused to Boheman on 17 March. Previously Moscow had believed that Sweden encouraged Finland and worked against a settlement with the Soviet Union. Now this deep-rooted opinion, which she knew to be unfounded, had to be changed. Some days later, on 21 March, on instructions from home she handed over to Günther a letter to the King, in which was expressed the Soviet government's sincere gratitude for his contribution to the great work of peace. She also spoke of her government's appreciation of the exertions of Hansson, Günther, and Boheman. Stockholm had received no such praise from Moscow since its mediation in the Winter War, if even then.

Günther was convinced that clear speaking was needed in 1944 as in 1940 to get the government, parliament, and people of Finland to see that there was no escaping a harsh settlement. In pressing his advice on Helsinki and in suggesting that the Soviet government would later soften its attitude, provided definite negotiations were started, he in fact went very far. This policy had also brought a good dividend in Moscow. If his expectations of Soviet generosity did not turn out to be justified, in Helsinki, conversely, the dividend would no doubt be negative and the wisdom of Sweden's foreign policy would be more than ever in doubt there.

But what consequences did Günther's manoeuvres have in Berlin? In recent months Germany's position had gradually deteriorated and Sweden's attitude towards Germany had gradually stiffened, not least in respect of the German occupation regimes in Denmark and Norway. In this situation the prospects for Sweden's policy of eventually getting Finland out of the war – and thereby depriving Germany of her now foremost military and political ally – must have seemed comparatively bright, the more so since the reports from the Helsinki and Berlin Legations towards the end of 1943 and early in 1944 hardly gave the impression that German pressure on Finland, isolated warnings apart, was strong and steady.

Although Sweden's activities to promote a separate peace between the Soviet Union and Finland were reported in the international press, Germany exercised the greatest forbearance. After press reports on 16–17 March of King Gustaf's and his government's advice to Finland to start negotiations with the Soviet Union, Hitler himself declared in an interview that, if King Gustaf had sent a message of this sort, that would be an exclusively Swedish affair. The German Legation in Stockholm got no instructions at all to take up the question. The Swedes on their side intended, should a discussion arise, to fall back on their 1940 argument that a secure peace for Finland was the earnest desire of every Swede.

Fears of a German move in the North were, however, still entertained in Stockholm and led at the end of March to a minor increase in the armed forces' state of readiness. Through their occupation of Hungary on 19 March the Germans had demonstrated that they still had both the will and the capacity to intervene ruthlessly against wavering allies. On 16 February, Hitler had ordered that, in the event of Finland changing her policy, the Åland Islands and Hogland should immediately be occupied; the former measure to secure supplies of ore from Luleå, the latter to maintain the blockade against Soviet submarines in the Gulf of Finland. But planning for such moves had scarcely progressed very far, and no directive had been given for military action.

Molotov gave the two Finnish delegates, Paasikivi and Carl Enckell, more precise information on the conditions for a peace agreement during their visit to Moscow in the last week of March. His statements included no Soviet concessions at all of the sort which Madame Kollontay and, after her, Günther and Boheman had held out to the Finnish government. If anything, the terms were perhaps stiffer. So far as the German troops were concerned, mere 'isolation' – mentioned by Madame Kollontay in her conversation with Boheman – would not be sufficient. The troops were to be interned or expelled before the end of May. The Finnish army was to be placed on a peace footing before the end of July.

Repeated Swedish messages to the Finns that a softening of Soviet demands could be possible had shown themselves without foundation. Swedish representations in Moscow through Madame Kollontay that, in the interests of Swedish-Soviet relations, the Finns should be granted better conditions than those notified had been without result.

Günther nevertheless considered that the negotiations should continue and so informed the Finns. But in their turn those responsible for Finland's foreign policy let it be known that, after the new Moscow statement, they must consider themselves better qualified to assess the Soviet Union's intentions than the Swedes. In Helsinki, Beck-Friis reported, there was pretty widespread criticism of Sweden's contributions to the talks. Ramsay, not without a certain bitterness, recalled his earlier strong scepticism towards Madame Kollontay's interpretation of Soviet aims against Finland. He further criticized Swedish newspapers, which kept on talking of modifications to the original Soviet conditions. When Beck-Friis enquired whether any Finnish counter-proposals were being considered, Ramsay's reply was negative. A statement by the Finnish government that it was unable to accept the Soviet government's peace proposals, which in important respects were altogether too onerous for Finland, but that it nevertheless wished to make peace, was transmitted to the Soviet Legation in Stockholm on 18 April.

Günther soon resumed his efforts. The Kremlin had hinted that it still considered the door open for peace negotiations. Since the Finnish government had refused to be drawn into fresh discussions on the Soviet conditions, Günther sent Beck-Friis to Ramsay on 8 May with a cautious feeler: could contact with Moscow be resumed through a proposal for an armistice, under which the Finnish troops would be withdrawn to the 1940 frontier (if nothing better could be arranged), while the problem of the internment of the German troops, the question of war damages to Russia, and Finnish demobilization were postponed until the final conclusion of peace?

Ramsay listened to Beck-Friis with polite scepticism and made no direct reply to Günther's proposal. A message, brought by Gripenberg at the end of May, that for the present nothing much could be done, could be interpreted as an answer. Some weeks later a big Soviet offensive on the Isthmus of Carelia brought about a new and dramatic situation.

During February and March 1944, Sweden, exactly as she had done four years earlier, in February and March 1940, actively sought to promote an agreement between Finland and the Soviet Union. In 1944, as in 1940, Sweden tried to persuade Finland to go along with the Soviet Union's conditions. But the essential requirements for success were not so propitious in 1944 as in 1940. Finland's army was not in retreat inside her own frontiers and was not fighting alone. Sweden was not now indispensable as a supplier of war materials and other necessities to Finland. The Soviet Union was already engaged in a Great Power war and ran no risk of worsening its position by continuing its war with Finland.

## Finland's withdrawal from the war

In the morning of 9 June 1944, after more than two years of calm on the Finnish-Soviet front, three days after the invasion of Normandy, Soviet troops launched a big offensive on the Isthmus of Carelia. They advanced both faster and further than the Finnish Military Command had expected; within less than a week the main line of defence had been broken, and the Finns were compelled, under great strain, to pull back troops from the East Carelian front to man a rear defence line.

In a conversation on 17 June with Gripenberg, Boheman recommended negotiating before Soviet troops crossed the 1940 frontier and also a reconstruction of the government: 'the Marshal should bring about a change and support the new government with all his authority or perhaps even head it himself'. Boheman added that if the Finns so wished, he was willing to try to make contact with Madame Kollontay. Two days later Gripenberg, who had just returned to Stockholm from a visit to Helsinki, announced that a new government would be formed, whose first task would be to seek peace with the Soviet Union, and that a message to Madame Kollontay could be expected in the very near future. Ramsay was to be designated Head of the new Government. Boheman made an appointment to meet Madame Kollontay later in the day, and the government decided to give a favourable reply to Gripenberg's question whether Finland could get 40,000 tons of grain from Sweden, if imports from Germany were cut off.

The message to Madame Kollontay was, however, delayed. Boheman could only arrange and then cancel meetings with her time and time again and beg Gripenberg to convey to Ramsay 'the Swedish government's deepest concern at every hour's delay'. The Soviet armies had now attacked the Finns' last line of defence on the Isthmus of Carelia. But when at last a Finnish message did come for Madame Kollontay on 22 June, it had a reservation which Gripenberg had not envisaged: the change of government had been made dependent on Soviet agreement to receive a Finnish peace-negotiating delegation. Moscow answered by laying down as a condition for meeting a Finnish delegation that the Finnish President and Foreign Minister should sign a declaration that Finland would be ready to surrender and ask the Soviet Union for peace. After this, nothing was heard of any further Finnish message to Madame Kollontay. On the other hand, Beck-Friis reported in telegrams which followed closely one upon another that the Finnish government appeared in the process of swinging away from a separate peace in the direction of closer links with Germany. Ribbentrop had arrived in Helsinki on 23 June. Beck-Friis feared all thoughts of reconstruction had been abandoned or, in any event, complicated through the arrival of help from Germany.

When the Swedish government discussed the situation in Finland on 26 June, it unhesitatingly took the view that the path Finland now seemed to be treading would lead to disaster and defeat in the company of Germany. The idea that a Swedish military emissary should be sent to Helsinki to explain the Swedish High Command's appreciation of the general war situation came up, but led to no decision.

The Swedish government received direct and detailed information on Ribbentrop's visit when Gripenberg called on Günther on 29 June with a message from Ramsay. The Finnish government, according to Gripenberg's account, was convinced that Moscow's demand for Finnish surrender was tantamount to Finland's ruin. As a condition for German help in holding the front on the Isthmus of Carelia, Ribbentrop had asked for some equivalent response from Finland, and this had taken the form of a letter from Ryti to Hitler on 26 June. In this the President had bound himself to make peace with the Soviet Union in present difficult circumstances only in full concert with the government of the German Reich, and not to permit any government appointed by him to sue for peace. Ramsay denied that Ryti and his government, through some unconstitutional procedure, or some sort of *coup*, had permitted Finland to enter into an agreement with Germany. (Reports and speculation to this effect were common in the Swedish press.) He also let it be understood that the President's letter was looked upon as binding Finland to Germany for only a limited period.

The Finns were able gradually to bottle up the Soviet offensive in their last line of defence on the Isthmus of Carelia: German help, the arrival of the East Carelian divisions, an improvement in fighting spirit were significant factors in an indisputable defensive victory. When the Soviet High Command moved troops from the Finnish to the German front in the second half of July – Berlin was a more important war target than Helsinki – the war against Finland entered a quieter phase. On 30 June the United States broke off diplomatic relations with Finland, but, after the considerable earlier deterioration of those relations, this step caused more sorrow than alarm in Helsinki. Finland's policy continued in its old rut, although pessimism and concern for the future increased.

Sweden's role in this latest phase of the Finnish problem had only been that of a go-between. The discussions Boheman had with the American, British, Finnish, and Soviet envoys without doubt clarified the Swedish government's attitude for them. But the government had still launched no appeals, nor did it order any corresponding *démarches* in the various envoys' capitals. Its influence with the Great Powers was limited, especially in the present state of the war, some weeks after the invasion in the West and the great Soviet offensive in the centre of the Eastern front. In the dramatic shifts through which Finland's policy ran in the latter half of June, Sweden, whence nothing beyond deliveries of food could now be expected, must equally have been a factor of purely secondary importance. Further, the regular and cocksure reports and comments on Finnish questions in the Swedish press were undoubtedly in Finnish government circles considered as a source not only of annoy-ance, but also of difficulties. Nor did Finland's foreign-policy planners consider that Sweden, where in their opinion there was an altogether too trusting and optimistic view of the Soviet Union, was a particularly suitable mentor in foreign affairs.

On 14 July, Beck-Friis called on Madame Kollontay in Stockholm at her request. In the course of their conversation she expressed 'her lively hope that it would not yet be too late to reach an agreement with Finland'. In her view Moscow was looking for a Finnish initiative by a new government, which should make a written declaration that it desired peace, but which need not directly announce its surrender. However, a move must be made soon, events were rushing ahead, and Finland must extricate herself from the war 'before they got to Helsinki'. Beck-Friis immediately reported Madame Kollontay's remarks to his ministry and then to a representative of 'the peace opposition', the former Finnish Foreign Minister, Erkko, whom he met later that day and with whom he had previously discussed the problem of peace in Helsinki. Beck-Friis was not instructed to pass on Madame Kollontay's advice to the Finnish government.

The Finnish 'peace opposition' was not a united and tightly knit opposition, but a motley group of politicians and industrialists working together. After Ribbentrop's visit to Helsinki and its outcome, they began to investigate the possibilities of working outside Finland, particularly in Stockholm. to get Finland quickly out of the war. The Swedish Foreign Ministry, which probably knew of their connections with Mannerheim, now saw them as more suitable recipients of Madame Kollontay's message than their government, which had so recently approved Ryti's promise not to enter into negotiations for a separate peace. As Mallet reported home at the beginning of July, official relations between the Swedish and Finnish governments were the chilliest possible.

From the Swedish side attempts were also made to influence Mannerheim in the desired direction. The Chief of the Swedish Defence

Staff, General Carl August Ehrensvärd, an old acquaintance since 1918, sent him a survey of the general military situation dated 22 July – two days after the attempt on Hitler's life. It ended with the conclusion that 'the hour of Germany's defeat is rapidly approaching'. Ehrensvärd's memorandum, the despatch of which one must assume to have been made with government approval, was followed a week or so later by an offer from Hansson to Judge Holger Nystén, the peace opposition's link to Mannerheim's close confidant, the Finnish Minister of Defence, Walden. If Mannerheim wanted it, said Hansson, he would allow a leading Swedish officer, most probably Ehrensvärd, to visit him 'to put before him personally the Swedish High Command's appreciation of Finland's position in relation to the general development of the war'. At the same time Hansson directed an appeal to Mannerheim to take over the political, as well as the military, leadership of Finland in order to bring about an unavoidably harsh, but all the same necessary, settlement with the Soviet Union. He did not believe, in spite of bitter experiences from the period after the Winter War, that the Soviet Union would afterwards have any interest in, or intention of, subjugating Finland.

In addition, Boheman passed on to Walden through Nystén information from a conversation on 25 July with Madame Kollontay which he summarized thus:

> After a change of government and a plea for peace, Finland, according to Madame Kollontay, can proceed on the assumption that negotiations could be started in which Finland can count on an agreement preserving her self-government and independence.

Boheman added that she based this statement on a telegram from the Ministry for Foreign Affairs in Moscow, in which great interest had been shown in various Finnish soundings in Stockholm.

Sweden's political and military leaders clearly wanted to give both information and advice to the men they hoped would come to power in Finland. In July 1944 enormous Soviet advances in the East and the progress of the Allied invasion forces in the West brought the final defeat of Germany nearer. Finland must now as quickly as possible be snatched away from Germany to avoid coming under Soviet occupation.

Mannerheim was urged to assume political, in addition to military, leadership. His unrivalled prestige could take Finland out of the war with national unity preserved. Such promptings came not only from the peace opposition and the Swedish government, but also, and certainly with greater weight, from the inner circle of the Finnish government, including Tanner, the Social Democrat leader who had prevented the Marshal's election as President in 1943. After Ryti had assured him that he was prepared to step down, Mannerheim decided on 28 July to make himself available. Ryti then announced in a letter to the government on 1 August that he had relinquished his post, and, by a law unanimously approved in parliament on 4 August, Mannerheim was appointed President of Finland.

Madame Kollontay's many statements that her government genuinely wanted an agreement with an independent Finland, her patent eagerness to pass this on to Helsinki, and also Swedish reports of all this to the Finns, had obviously encouraged the change of President. Whether other Swedish statements had any importance must be left open. Mannerheim did not allow himself to be greatly influenced by outside advice. Tanner and his colleagues had no particular regard for Sweden's political acumen.

Mannerheim's assumption of the Presidency on 4 August did not result in a direct appeal to Moscow. The Swedes gave emphatic warnings against postponing a peace initiative: Finland had to reach agreement with the Soviet Union before Germany was defeated or Stalin could conclude that Finland after all did not want an agreement. Mannerheim appointed a new Finnish government on 8 August. Contrary to expectations he did not send any message to Moscow asking for negotiations in the weeks immediately following. There was alarm, and impatience, among the peace opposition as well as in Stockholm and Moscow.

The Swedes passed on to the Finns several Soviet reminders that Finland really must hurry, if Moscow was not to lose all interest in a settlement. Moreover, the prospect was held out of large deliveries of food and other goods from Sweden in the event of Finland getting out of the war. Conversely, credits for pilotage fees, harbour dues, and so forth were refused so long as Finland waged war against the Soviet Union. On 22 August when Gripenberg, on Mannerheim's express instructions, asked Günther for his personal opinion on the probability of Finland getting Swedish and possibly American help to pay war damages to the Soviet Union, Günther foresaw a favourable attitude in Sweden and he hoped in the United States as well. Further, he considered that in the next few days Finland should make contact with the Soviet Union. Otherwise, Günther does not seem to have given any direct advice to Helsinki.

On the afternoon of 25 August, three weeks after Mannerheim's accession to the Presidency, Gripenberg asked for a Swedish intermediary to arrange a meeting with Madame Kollontay. Several Finnish and Soviet statements and elucidations were thereafter exchanged in Stockholm, before a Finnish negotiating delegation, with Prime Minister Antti Hackzell at its head, arrived in Moscow on 7 September. Since the parties had now made direct contact, Sweden's contribution as intermediary was over, even though she continued to help by providing technical assistance with telegraphic communications for the Finnish delegation and in other practical ways.

Reports from the Swedish Legation in Helsinki hardly indicated that the new Finnish government would have any greater interest in Swedish contacts and advice than its predecessor had lately shown. Sweden's assistance to Finland mainly consisted of practical measures to mitigate the consequences of her break with Germany: in addition to earlier undertakings to deliver food and other necessities, it was decided early in September to receive evacuated inhabitants from north Finland, out of the way of retreating German troops. Finland was on her way out of Germany's sphere of interest into the Soviet Union's. Sweden could do nothing beyond carefully watching events. This was all she had been able to do at the end of 1940 and the beginning of 1941, when Finland was moving away from the Soviet Union's sphere of interest and into Germany's. As had been the case earlier in tripartite confrontations between Finland, the Soviet Union, and Germany, now also there was a special problem to look after: the Åland Islands.

Rumours of a German occupation of the Åland Islands in connection with the Finnish-Soviet peace contacts in the spring were followed by silence. About the end of June Swedish newspapers, while discussing the course of the war in Finland and Ribbentrop's visit to Helsinki again began to speculate on a possible German occupation. Günther must have found these speculations a suitable occasion for reminding Helsinki of Sweden's interest in Åland; and in the period immediately after Ribbentrop's journey to Helsinki it was also considered convenient to give a warning against allowing the Germans too free a hand. On 6 July, Beck-Friis told Ramsay informally that the Swedish government assumed that Finland would not permit German troops to establish themselves on the Åland Islands on any pretext or in any form. Ramsay gave definite assurances that there had never been any question of sending German troops there and that, in negotiations with the Germans, Åland had never been mentioned. He declared without any reservations that what Beck-Friis had suggested would be heeded, and added that it would be sensible if the Swedish papers did not draw attention to Åland through statements and comments.

Fears of a German move against Åland during these weeks were not altogether without foundation. From 20 June, Hitler, faced with the risk of a Finnish collapse, had issued several directives for preliminary preparations for action against the Åland Islands. The units earmarked for such a move against Åland were, however, successively used to plug the gaps on the Eastern front. So it seems doubtful whether the action could ever have materialized. A further restraining factor, with thoughts of Swedish deliveries of iron-ore and ball-bearings in mind, was the desire to avoid making an unfriendly Sweden even more unfriendly.

The information on Finnish-German relations in the reports from the Swedish Legations in Helsinki and Berlin was not alarming, even if doubts about Germany's or, rather, Hitler's real intentions were evident. Expectations that he would pull his troops out of Finland, without letting them be dragged into hostilities against the Finns, were neverthe-ess stronger than fears that he would try to set up a satellite regime, as n Hungary. In view of the general state of the war these expectations nust seem soundly based. Soviet troops had entered Bucharest on 31 August, British and American troops Brussels and Lyons on 3 September.

The reaction in the German press and radio to the Finnish govern-nent's official announcement about the negotiations in Moscow was conspicuously tame; the commentaries on it were in general remarkably noderate. In this situation Günther limited himself to instructing Richert, when a suitable opportunity arose and without mentioning his rders from home, to point out to the German Foreign Ministry that othing had come to the knowledge of the Swedes which indicated any oviet intention of occupying Åland.

Attention was instead concentrated on the negotiations in Moscow. Molotov demanded that the Finns should make up their minds quickly n the Soviet conditions which were put before them and which he was ot willing to discuss. The conditions included the previous demands elating to the 1940 frontier, as well as the disarming of the Germans, emobilization (the Finnish army was to be on a peace footing after nly 2½ months), the surrender of Petsamo, and war damages: 300 million dollars to be paid in six years. But there were amendments: for he lease of Porkkala (20 kilometres from Helsinki), in exchange for anko, surrendered in the 1940 peace settlement; and for an Allied ontrol Commission to supervise the implementation of the terms f the settlement. From a military viewpoint, Mannerheim said to anner, the conditions were appalling: by complying with them

Finland would fall almost completely into the hands of the Soviet Union. The possibilities which the vaguely defined conditions opened up for Soviet penetration and internal subversion were generally feared, and Beck-Friis reported a deep pessimism, not least among the friends of peace, who, in spite of everything, had expected something better. However, there was no realistic alternative, and on 19 September, the Finnish delegation in Moscow signed an armistice agreement with the Soviet Union and Britain. (Finland had been at war with Britain also since December 1941.) When Boheman described the terms for the government the same day, it was concluded that 'in practice these conditions meant that Finland had become a Soviet vassal state'.

Against this background it was certainly noticed with satisfaction in Stockholm that with regard to Åland the armistice only provided that the islands, as after the Crimean War and the First World War, would continue to remain unfortified and demilitarized. This outcome was received with all the greater satisfaction because it was known that, during the Moscow negotiations, the Finnish government had wanted to find out whether the Kremlin might be willing to lease Åland instead of Porkkala, which lay so near to Helsinki. The new Finnish chief delegate, Foreign Minister Enckell (Hackzell was paralyzed by a stroke), had, however, not complied with the instructions from Helsinki on this point.

Gripenberg, in a conversation with Günther on 9 October, gave an assurance on behalf of his government that it 'would obviously have never taken any steps which involved making Åland available to a foreign power, either in whole or in part, without having first informed the Swedish government'. Günther replied that such an assurance was not satisfactory.

In the event of the Finnish government having any plans which involved a change in the status of the Åland Islands as laid down in the 1921 Convention, mere notification could not conceivably be sufficient. The Swedish government, both as a signatory Power and, together with Finland, indubitably the party most closely concerned, must be given beforehand a chance to state its position in the matter.

On the other hand, Günther avoided disputing, or even questioning the Finnish statement that Helsinki had never decided to offer Åland. When he gave an account of his talk with Gripenberg to his colleague the following day, he proposed that, as the question of the truthfulness of the Finnish declaration could not be raised, the Swedish government should not go beyond giving Gripenberg a written statement of its view according to which Finland alone could not dispose of Åland. The ministers agreed, and a corresponding letter was despatched to Gripenberg next day. A summary of what had happened, which was sent at the same time to the King, the Prime Minister, and others, shows clearly, however, that the Foreign Ministry did not accept at their face value the repeated Finnish assurances that no decision to offer Åland to the Russians had ever been taken. Günther's letter was never answered by the Finns, and there was no Swedish desire to pursue the matter.

Günther had thus firmly asserted Sweden's interest in a permanently neutralized and demilitarized Åland, while he simultaneously avoided addressing to the Finnish government any specific observations on the position it had taken or on its subsequent denial of this. Maybe he had not actually been surprised: Ryti, then Finnish Prime Minister, on his way to the Moscow peace negotiations, had told him in Stockholm on the night of 6–7 March 1940 that there were very influential circles in Finland which wished to offer Åland to the Russians in place of Hanko. Maybe he had a certain sympathy for the Finns' desperate situation; a Soviet garrison on Åland seemed less of a danger to Finland than a Soviet garrison at a distance of 20 kilometres from Helsinki. At all events he considered that he ought not to criticize a Finnish government already under strong pressure, but should confine himself to trying to prevent similar occurrences in the future. Åland in Soviet hands would mean an extraordinary deterioration in Sweden's general strategic position. The Soviet Union was already — or within a short time would become — a more dominant factor in the Baltic area than Tsarist Russia had ever been. Soviet troops on Åland in these circumstances would place Sweden in a situation which recalled 1809. In deciding to offer Åland to the Soviet Union the Finns had from the Swedish standpoint been playing with fire. That was unacceptable and should not be repeated.

Restraint, sympathy, and help, so far as help could be provided, were the guidelines of Sweden's policy towards Finland in her new situation. Sweden could do no more than try in different ways to facilitate Finland's adjustment to it. After the conclusion of the negotiations in Moscow, the Swedish government, as had been envisaged in August, gave Finland a credit for 150 million crowns to make possible the purchase of food, fertilizer, fuel, and iron and steel during the six months from October to March. In the New Year of 1945 this credit was increased to provide for Finnish purchases of certain goods, primarily metal products, essential for war-damage deliveries to the Soviet Union. As promised at the beginning of September, Sweden for a time gave refuge to civilians from north Finland, about 50,000 in all, who had fled from the ravages of the retreating German troops.

These Swedish gestures were noted in Helsinki and contributed to a more appreciative attitude to Sweden that steadily gained ground there. Articles on Finland and her government in Swedish papers, however, were still a source of complaint. On the whole, Finland's freedom of manoeuvre in the tight grip of the Control Commission was slight, and official Swedish-Finnish contacts were correspondingly sparse. There was little business to be done. In the light of events during the war years Stockholm was well aware that Moscow saw Sweden's Finnish policy as a significant factor in Swedish-Soviet relations. It was therefore essential to avoid any suspicion of meddling in Helsinki, where the Allied Control Commission, with Zhdanov, one of the top men nearest Stalin, at his head, was now established as the most powerful body.

# 7   Waiting for Germany's defeat

## End of the war in sight

The Allied landings in Normandy on 6 June 1944, Ehrensvärd noted
later that day, reduced the pressure on Sweden for the moment. In his
opinion, however, Allied landings in Norway and – although less
likely – in Denmark might be possible, and for this reason arrangements
should be made to increase the not particularly high state of readiness
of Sweden's forces. This was in fact done to a limited extent after
Johnson and Mallet, instructed by their governments, had inquired on 9
June 'whether an assurance could be given that any German attack on
Sweden would be met by force'.

During the following weeks the Germans lost ground on all fronts.
By the end of July, Soviet troops had reached the Baltic at the Gulf of
Riga: the German troops in Estonia and Latvia were now cut off from
land communications with Germany. At the beginning of August the
armies of the Western Allies which had landed in France succeeded in
breaking out from their bridgehead in Normandy. The 20 July
Stauffenberg *coup* against Hitler had failed, but had shown the existence
of a widespread German opposition.

During this unfavourable development for Germany it was not
difficult for Sweden to effect, as promised earlier to the Western
Powers, reductions in exports from Baltic harbours on the coast of
north Sweden and in the conveyance of coal, coke, and cement to
Trondheim and Narvik. The Western Powers, however, relentlessly kept
up the pressure for further reductions. In July an agreement was
reached on how the decisions of the 1943 Tripartite Agreement on
reductions in exports to Axis Europe would be applied as the Allied
forces liberated countries under German control. Informal suggestions
by the British and Americans in July that Swedish trade or, at any rate,
trade in Swedish bottoms with Germany should be ended, were rejected,
but Günther at the same time let it be clearly understood that the

course of the war could perhaps soon enough lead to a different attitude. Continued Anglo-American demands during subsequent weeks that all Swedish traffic to German harbours must be suspended were made against a background of ever-increasing air activity by the Western Powers over Germany. On the Swedish side war-risk insurance for journeys to German harbours was now gradually withdrawn. Without insurance, owners were reluctant to risk their ships and in September all Swedish shipping to Germany — except for some safe-conduct traffic in Red Cross service — was suspended; about half the tonnage used for the exchange of goods between Sweden and Germany was in this way withdrawn.

The Americans, however, were not satisfied. They wanted to put an early and definite end to all Swedish exports to the enemy: in a personal message in July, Roosevelt asked Churchill to take this matter up. London had the same final goal, but considered that it could be more surely achieved through successive applications of pressure than through the shock tactics which the authorities in Washington proposed — with the aim of influencing not only Sweden, but also the American public before the election later that autumn. For this latter purpose, formal notes in admonitory and high-flown terms which could be given suitable publicity were preferable. The British disapproved, but did not want to fall out with the Americans, whose support they so much needed, in such a relatively minor matter. A written joint message from Hull and Eden was delivered to Günther on 24 August. Their governments, they stated, had refrained from asking Sweden to adopt a policy towards Germany which could endanger her independence. The same understanding had been shown Sweden by helping her with the import of goods, even of goods in very short supply. Now, there was no longer any danger of a German attack. The time had come for a complete change in Sweden's policy towards Germany. Hull and Eden asked what steps the Swedish government contemplated taking in consequence.

Herschel Johnson spoke about this message at length but in somewhat imprecise terms, particularly warning that Sweden's performance now would be decisive for her position after the war and above all for the continuation of her imports of raw materials, food, and oil. Mallet, using more precise terms, emphasized that above all Sweden should now immediately end all commercial ties with Germany, a statement which Johnson hastened to confirm. Later that day Madame Kollontay arrived to announce that her government supported the Western Powers' *démarche*. However, the wording she used was markedly moderate and she said outright that 'her government wished to express its satisfaction with Sweden's policies both in the Finnish question and with reference to shipping to Germany and, in consequence, trade between Sweden and Germany'.

A demonstrative adherence to the Allied side would be inconsistent with Sweden's traditional policy, followed through two World Wars, of trying to keep out of the alliances and wars of the Great Powers and to create trust in, and respect for, these aims abroad. Least of all could the Swedish government think of abandoning its policy when faced with a perhaps imminent division of Europe into spheres of interest, with Sweden just on the borderline. A rupture not only of commercial but also of diplomatic relations with Germany, something which in any case could be considered an American aim behind the imprecise exhortations in Hull's and Eden's message, would deprive Sweden of the possibility of intervening with German authorities for mediatory or humanitarian purposes. On the other hand, the answer could not merely be a curt refusal. The war was nearing its end, and in such a situation to ignore demands which the Western Powers were pressing really hard could have serious consequences.

Günther's reply of 4 September again emphasized Sweden's intention to abide by her policy of neutrality. The Swedish government had taken the Western Powers' *démarche* as an expression of their desire to do everything to shorten the war. The Swedish people also ardently hoped that the war would soon come to an end. But, if a neutral Sweden was going to have any influence on the development of the war in general, such influence could only apply to her trade with Germany; this trade had already been so reduced that it could no longer be said in any way to prolong the war and, moreover, further reductions could be expected. A general change in Sweden's political attitude towards Germany could make no more contribution to the shortening of the war and – if only for this reason – did not need to be contemplated. These statements, the Swedish text concluded, should tend to show that the points raised in Hull's and Eden's message of 24 August 'are looked upon by the Swedish government in a spirit of understanding and due consideration and that in all essentials the wishes expressed by the Allied governments are and will be met by a continuation of Sweden's present policy'.

These views were further emphasized by Günther, when Johnson and Mallet called on him on 4 September to receive the answer. Trade with Germany had declined steeply, Günther explained, and coming events could lead to yet further reductions. German transit traffic through Sweden to north Finland had stopped in connection with the cease-fire between the Finns and the Russians the day before. An end to German transit traffic from Finland to Norway was being considered.

A week or so into September the Swedes had in fact strong reasons to believe that Germany was now well on the way to final collapse and that, accordingly, an end to the war was very near. Belgium had been completely liberated. The invading armies had reached Germany's western frontier. In the Balkans, Romania and Bulgaria had come completely under Soviet control. On the Eastern front the mighty Soviet offensive kept on rolling forward. Finland had initiated armistice negotiations. The Germans' tone towards Sweden was courteous, their criticism of the discontinuance of Swedish sailings to German harbours and the consequent decline in iron-ore deliveries was subdued, their efforts to change the situation were not forceful. This state of affairs obviously invited further Swedish restrictions during September, and these followed in rapid succession as far as payment for goods, export licences, and transport were concerned.

When the Finnish armistice, which had been signed in Moscow that same morning, was discussed by the government on 19 September, Günther proposed that it should be followed by the closing of Swedish territorial waters in the Baltic to German shipping. The government agreed and, a few days later, on the 23rd, he informed Thomsen that, with effect from the 27th foreign merchant ships, including ferry-traffic, would not be allowed in Swedish territorial waters from the River Torne down to and including the Falsterbo Canal. The reason for changing the regulations was baldly stated as 'regard to the completely different military position in and around the Baltic'. In addition, he seized the opportunity of giving prior warning of further Swedish moves affecting relations with Germany as a result of the anger which recent German measures in Denmark and Norway — mass deportation of Danish policemen and of imprisoned Norwegians to Germany — would inevitably arouse in Sweden.

For the benefit of the Western Powers and the Soviet Union the Swedes hastened to point out the extraordinary decline which would now ensue in Swedish-German trade and to emphasize that this was completely in line with what had been stated earlier in the Swedish note to Washington and London of 4 September. Bearing in mind reports of American dissatisfaction with this note and warnings of fresh Allied actions which had reached Stockholm, Günther had an obvious interest in providing concrete evidence of such further Swedish measures directed against Germany as he had envisaged in his statements to Johnson and Mallet that same day. But care was also taken to defend the remaining trade of the west coast harbours and Narvik: it was of little significance; the military situation was different from that of the Baltic harbours; a complete ban on trade would bring with it the rupture of diplomatic relations which could conceivably destroy Sweden's few remaining chances of helping Danish and Norwegian prisoners and endanger her Red Cross activities and her task as a protecting Power.

The American government, from moral and electoral motives, wished to put pressure on Sweden to break off relations with Germany. The British government considered it inappropriate to force the issue, as this would worsen Britain's relations with Sweden after the war, would give the Russians the chance of establishing themselves in Stockholm at the expense of the Western Powers, and – certainly not the least important consideration – would hinder negotiations on British purchases of Swedish lumber for post-war reconstruction. After talking to Churchill at the Quebec Conference in mid-September, Roosevelt decided not to impose any sanctions against Sweden. Sweden's closure of her Baltic harbours to German ships was therefore well received in Washington; at last Sweden was moving in the right direction. But the Americans in no way abandoned their resolve to shut off Swedish exports to Germany completely, even if, following the British pattern, they now relied on strong and continuous pressure rather than on violent thrusts.

By the autumn of 1944 some of the principles of international law habitually proclaimed and followed in Swedish foreign policy had been considerably diluted. The principle that Swedish territorial waters were open for foreign shipping had been abandoned – a principle which had previously been of great political value as an argument when the Germans were urged to transport troops by sea rather than by rail through Sweden. The principle that agreements must be faithfully observed was now disregarded, although only six months or so earlier it had been stubbornly maintained in order to avoid being drawn too deeply into the Allied trade war. Neutrality was still professed. But even more than before neutrality now was practised subject to the needs of the hour. The ease with which these needs took complete precedence in discussions, by ministers and in the Parliamentary Foreign Policy Committee, is striking considering the unwillingness caused by similar previous concessions in Germany's favour. However, explanations are not far to seek. The closure of territorial waters in the Baltic was in tune not only with the changes in the general political situation, but also with the general mood in Sweden. Public opinion was united and emphatic in desiring an early end to the war, the annihilation of Hitler's regime, the liberation of Denmark and Norway, and good post-war relations with the Allies. Decisions and measures by government and *Riksdag* which facilitated such a development were welcomed, even demanded. Decisions and measures which delayed it, such as continued deliveries of iron-ore and ball-bearings, could not count on the sympathy, or even the forbearance, of the public except in an emergency. In addition, there was, as Boheman maintained to the press on 30 September, 'the definite conviction that the war had now reached its final phase, and that its further duration could be counted in months'. As for the Germans, there was simply no need to pay any regard to them. As for the Western Powers, certain victors, Sweden had certainly gone far along the path of concessions.

Germany, on the other hand, had to pay considerable regard to Sweden. Germany could not afford to see a state which still remained neutral and which perhaps could be relied upon as a mediator changed into another enemy, who, apart from other things, could expose the German troops in Norway and Finland to a flank attack. Germany was obliged to do her utmost to keep vital imports from Sweden coming in and, despite the many restrictions the Swedes continued to place on transport, shipping, and trade, the Germans accordingly tried hard to maintain good, or at least tolerable, relations with Sweden. Thus in September, after earlier Swedish appeals in support of Denmark and Norway had been sharply rejected or left unanswered, they privately let it be known that there would be no more prisoners transported from Norway to Germany. When SKF, citing 'ökonomische *force majeure*', decided with effect from 12 October to end all further exports to Germany of ball-bearings, roller-bearings, and ball-bearing machinery, a letter to Günther from Thomsen of 18 October recapitulated Swedish measures against German-Swedish trade in recent months, but in temperate language and with limited demands. Sweden's bargaining advantage was demonstrated again some weeks later, when on 11 November, Germany declared large areas in the Baltic, including the Gulf of Bothnia, an operational zone, where attacks would be made by gun and torpedo without warning. After strong Swedish representations the Germans immediately indicated their readiness to satisfy legitimate Swedish interests. All in all, Swedish-German relations worsened step by step, but without any incidents occurring, and not beyond the maintenance of normal diplomatic relations. Opportunities to obtain concessions to Sweden's wishes, not least in the humanitarian field, from the desperately struggling Nazi regime were constantly looked for.

The Western Powers, particularly the Americans, no longer asked that Sweden should break off relations with Germany. Nevertheless, they wanted to limit Sweden's remaining exports to Germany still further. On 20 October, Johnson and Mallet proposed that, through measures by the Swedish concerns responsible, exports to Germany of iron-ore, pig-iron, certain speciality steels, machine tools, cold-rolled steel, and some additional goods should immediately end. In return their governments would allow Sweden, in the interest of maintaining relations, to permit German ships to use for the present ports on her west and south coasts (up to Malmö).

By its note of 4 September, by its ban on German shipping in Swedish Baltic ports, and by other measures to limit Swedish-German relations, the Swedish Foreign Ministry had clearly gained both time and ground. The war had come nearer its end, even if this appeared further away than was believed in the early autumn. The Western Powers did not now raise the question, as in August, of a complete Swedish break with Germany. In these circumstances, an accommodating reply to the Western Powers' fresh proposal had to be considered pretty much a matter of course, the more so as Sweden had now begun to get ready for, or even to start, negotiations on her trade with the West after the war. The government, however, refused to approve without reservations the Allied requests, which Boheman told them should probably be considered 'final, at least for the next few months'. The government held that the reductions demanded in exports must be carried through with great caution to avoid endangering the Gothenburg traffic and that the exports of ore, which reached only insignificant figures, should be allowed to continue until the turn of the year. Moreover the Allies in return should agree to the delivery of about 3,000 tons of rubber products ordered in the United States and planned for shipment in the safe-conduct vessel *Saturnus*.

Negotiations about the *Saturnus* in subsequent weeks became more difficult than Stockholm had expected. The cargo of rubber was finally released in return for a Swedish undertaking to stop all exports to Germany after *Saturnus* had arrived — not, as proposed by the Swedes, all 'dangerous' exports, but all exports without exception — and in the meantime to reduce all deliveries to Germany to an absolute minimum. Once again the Western Powers had followed up a Swedish retreat with new demands. Once again Sweden had given in.

Although Germany would thus be cut off from all Swedish deliveries, efforts were made to get the Germans to assent to continued Gothenburg traffic. The guarantees to the Allies of a complete ban on exports after the *Saturnus* had arrived, were concealed from the Germans behind remarks about negotiations at the beginning of 1945 on the exchange of goods that year. They were then gradually informed that more or less temporary and widespread new restrictions could become unavoidable. The *Saturnus* entered Swedish waters on New Year's Day 1945. The same day the Berlin Legation was instructed to inform the *Auswärtiges Amt* that, since no clear picture of the prospects for Swedish exports to Germany in the New Year had so far been obtained, a provisional ban on exports had been introduced; Swedish efforts in London and Washington, however, were continuing. A week later on 9 January a new message was sent to Berlin: the Swedish government did not wish for the present to push the matter with the Western Powers, but intended to resume its endeavours at the earliest possible moment. The Swedish government hoped that the Germans, for their part, while waiting for the situation to be clarified, would approve applications for safe-conduct traffic from one occasion to another; if the safe-conduct traffic were to be broken off, all further attempts to bring about trade between Sweden and Germany would be ruled out.

In fact, a certain amount of safe-conduct traffic went on in 1945. In the beginning the Germans allowed it to run for some weeks to complete the 1944 programme. On 25 January the German Naval Command summoned the Swedish Naval Attaché in Berlin to warn him that, since a new agreement about the continuation of the traffic had not been reached, there was no agreement in force. During the subsequent months safe-conduct was, however, granted on separate occasions for a total of ten ships. At such times the Germans vaguely suggested Swedish concessions on certain deliveries and talked about trade discussions in the near future, but without any emphasis and without producing any concrete proposals. The Germans did not really have a policy any longer. The German Foreign Ministry hardly functioned any more.

The near closure of the safe-conduct traffic cut deep into Sweden's slight direct trade connections with the Western Powers. Swedish negotiations in London and Washington came to an increasing extent to concern the post-war period and its problems: post-war trade, aid shipments, the disposal of tonnage, fugitive German capital. But even the very limited Swedish foreign trade of the last few months of the war led to a number of clashes of views. The Americans at first maintained that the *Saturnus* deal should also include exports to Norway and Denmark, the British that these exports were not authorized by the war trade agreement for 1945. (Around the end of 1944, the 1943 agreement had been provisionally extended to cover the time to the end of the war.) In the final months of the war difficulties arose over keeping the safe-conduct ships and their cargoes at the disposal of the Swedes. But these arguments concerned only minor problems. There was no longer any Swedish trade with the two hostile Great Power blocs: the balance of strength between them had completely tilted – and with it the very basis of Swedish trade policy.

A recurrent theme in Mallet's reporting to the Foreign Office during the war years was Günther's and Boheman's concern with the balance of power in Europe after Germany's defeat. They deplored the Western Powers' rigorously upheld demand for unconditional surrender, which welded the Germans together and hindered a revolt against Hitler. They looked for an early landing in force by the Western Powers in Europe to offset the Soviet advance from the East. Günther, so Mallet reported in December 1942, hoped that Germany and the Soviet Union would exhaust each other in the war. In a conversation at the beginning of February 1944, Mallet found the Swedish Foreign Minister nervous about the growing power of the Soviet Union. He doubted whether its expansion would stop at its 1940 frontiers. Just as in 1940 it had incorporated the Baltic republics in its territory, it could, after a victorious war, gradually take over neighbouring countries like Bulgaria, Romania, Poland, and Czechoslovakia: perhaps these lands would still have a reasonably tolerable existence as not fully sovereign states 'within the fold of the Soviet Union'. Günther did not rule out the possibility that the Soviet occupation zone in Germany might include the whole of the Baltic coast from Kiel onwards, and expressed his hope for a zonal division which left the Western Powers with at least some say in the question of developments on the Baltic coast.

Obviously Sweden's chances of influencing the balance of power in Europe were extraordinarily small. Stockholm could hardly do more than place its views before the government in London through frequent discussions with Mallet. Certainly intervention in the war would give Sweden the status of an Allied Power and a seat at the future peace conference. But such intervention was absolutely ruled out: the Swedish people, as Günther and Boheman time and again explained to Mallet, had no intention of going to war except to defend themselves against external attack.

Nor did the Western Powers put pressure on Sweden to bring about an intervention. As a neutral state Sweden was for them, and especially for Britain, extremely valuable as an area for intelligence operations and for links with resistance movements in German-occupied countries. By contrast, the importance of Sweden in the Western Powers' military plans was slight – as it had been for Germany in the early war years. But even if London and Washington did not ask for direct Swedish participation in the war, they still tried to obtain 'facilities' from Sweden. They were assisted in matters such as meteorological reports, information on crashed German rocket-projectiles, and release of British and American airmen. The goodwill that Sweden could thereby gain in Britain and the United States should not, however, be exaggerated. In both the British and the American view Sweden's main contribution to the Allied cause was increasing reductions in her exports to Germany – and in this respect the Swedish government, at least in American eyes, was often remiss.

As 1944 came to its end, London was on the whole satisfied with Sweden, which had now clearly come as far on the road to 'pro-Allied

*Exchange of English prisoners-of-war, managed by the Swedish Red Cross at Gothenburg in 1944*

non-belligerency' as Britain's interests demanded. Sir Alexander Cadogan, in conversation with his Swedish colleague Boheman towards the end of November, expressed 'in unambiguous terms his satisfaction with Sweden's policies in general'. Also, as was known in Stockholm, the British government had of late adopted throughout a more flexible and responsive policy towards Sweden than the Americans. The British government could furthermore be expected to look for a strong and independent Sweden in post-war Europe. But the longer the war lasted, the more Britain's attitude came under the influence of the United States, and her future power would certainly be less than before the war.

Equally the authority and strength of the United States would certainly be more dominant than ever before throughout the world, and not least in Europe. But it was scarcely possible to arrive at a reasonably firm assessment of America's future attitude to Sweden. For the present, in Washington the military wielded a decisive influence with Roosevelt. Their primary aim was to win the war as quickly as possible, and to this result they wanted Sweden to contribute. The State Department showed greater understanding of Sweden's arguments and interests. Its observations, lately so often repeated, on the impossibility of small countries remaining neutral in future must, however, arouse concern in Stockholm, where the continuation of the traditional policy of neutrality, hitherto so successful, was taken as self-evident.

During 1944 the Soviet Union had been less critical of Sweden's foreign policy than the United States or even Britain. Sweden's co-operation in Finland's withdrawal from the war and her tacit acceptance that Finland had now entered the Soviet sphere of influence seemed to satisfy Moscow's present demands. No notice was given of any assistance, in one form or another, expected from Sweden in the final struggle against Germany. Swedish affairs in general appeared to have been laid aside for the time being in Moscow. Stockholm's alarm at the growing power of the Soviet Union led to especial concern for good and secure Swedish-Soviet relations. But Swedish proposals for negotiations about agreements on post-war trade and aviation were left unanswered.

No discussions appear to have taken place among ministers on coming events in Europe and the North and on Sweden's place in them. Indeed the government's own continued existence after the end of the war was not very likely. A national government was an exceptional occurrence in Swedish political life, and recently, as outside pressure on Sweden decreased, strains on the coalition had grown.

For the future Swedish politicians aimed at political collaboration among the Nordic countries as a neutral group. For the present, however, this was neither a topical issue nor a certain development. What Sweden could do now to further it was to work to the best of her ability for an end to the war which would speedily and bloodlessly abolish the German occupation regimes in Norway and Denmark and immediately bring democratic governments to power in Oslo and Copenhagen. Allied troops ought not to succeed the Germans as rulers, nor should militant and armed extremist groups usurp a decisive influence. The liberation of Norway and Denmark became the great problem of Swedish foreign policy in the final months of the war.

## The question of Swedish intervention in Norway and Denmark in the last phase of the war

When, in the late autumn of 1943, it gave its approval to the establishment of Danish and Norwegian police forces on Swedish soil, the Swedish government decided that they would not be allowed to leave Sweden without its consent.

In summer 1944 the Swedish attitude was still that the Norwegian police-troops could move to Norway only after the German occupation had ended. But in September, Günther and Boheman gave the Norwegian government to understand that the transfer of the troops to Norway would not encounter any difficulties when the time came to use them in their own country. The situation was now different from that in the summer. The final collapse of Germany seemed near. Finland had been brought out of the war. The German troops' retreat out of Finland and into Norway and the Soviet forces' entry into Finnmark, Norway's most northerly county, were now an immediate prospect. In connection with a possible Allied intervention in Denmark, the Swedish government also was prepared to approve that the Danish police-troops should be transferred there.

Well into October 1944 Günther invited the Norwegian Foreign Minister, Trygve Lie, to come on an unofficial visit to Stockholm. After some hesitation the Norwegians accepted. The immediate occasion for the invitation was certainly the problem of the police-troops. But other important topics were also to be discussed. Furthermore, with a new era dawning in the North, it was highly desirable that Swedish-Norwegian relations should as far as possible be cleared from the encumbrance of events and decisions belonging to the war years.

In a speech broadcast at the beginning of 1944 Lie had concluded that, in the course of 1943, the main difficulties in the relations between the Norwegian and Swedish governments, the German transit traffic through Sweden and the inadequate Norwegian diplomatic representation in Stockholm, had been removed. He had also expressed his appreciation for the Swedish *démarche* in Berlin in December 1943 in support of the Norwegian students. During 1944 he was able to record afresh important Swedish moves in Norway's favour. The training and arming of the police had gone ahead. Provisions had been sent to Norway in greater quantities. Representations had been made in Berlin for the return to Norway of the Norwegians interned in Germany, or, if this was not acceptable, to Sweden as an alternative. In this connection Richert had warned that Swedish-German relations might be completely broken off. These representations had had some success. Unofficial information had been received from the Germans in September that there would be no more transfers of prisoners from Norway to Germany (see p.204). While Lie was visiting Stockholm, a further German concession could be recorded: on 2 November the German Legation reported that Hitler had decided to return to Norway Norwegian students interned in Germany who were sick; a number had already been sent back.

Lie's discussions with Hansson, Günther, and other members of the government revealed a great readiness on their part to go further to meet Norwegian demands. The Norwegians set the greatest store by Sweden's consent to send 2,000–3,000 police over to north Norway, which the German troops were now beginning to evacuate, and her promise to supply more equipment for them (full infantry equipment); however, transport could not be provided beyond the Swedish frontier. When further Norwegian territory was set free, more police-troops were to be moved there. Günther and Lie together also went through political developments from 1940 onwards and cleared up misunderstandings.

'We are extremely pleased with the outcome and have every reason to believe that the Norwegians are as well'. Thus the Swedish Foreign Ministry summed up its appreciation. Presumably the extent of the agreement achieved also exceeded both parties' expectations. But the mutual irritation – on the Norwegian side even the bitterness – of several years could not be dissolved by a few days' discussions, however cordial.

The Norwegians had for some time believed that Sweden had often run Germany's errands, in direct conflict with Norway's interests. In April 1940 Günther had let Koht believe that there was no danger of a

211

German attack, although he knew much better. King Gustaf was thought to have urged Hitler to depose King Haakon in June 1940. Swedish railways had been used during the spring fighting to transport German soldiers to Norway, and the transit traffic had subsequently been of exceptional benefit to the German occupation regime. Norwegian refugees to Sweden had been treated in a heavyhanded and unsympathetic manner. The circumstances surrounding the treatment of the Norwegian ships and their departure left room for criticism. Newspapers which had taken the part of occupied Norway against her oppressors had repeatedly been confiscated. The Swedish government had taken up altogether too cautious a position, and the Norwegian government's wishes often merited a larger measure of acceptance than they had received.

On the Swedish side, however, there was an impression that the Norwegians had come forward much too often with too many complaints and criticisms; if the Norwegian government now really accepted that Swedish independence was a net gain to an occupied Norway, then it should permit the Swedish government to judge its policy towards Germany, the better to achieve the continuation of this independence. An additional irritant was the information and the views about Sweden given to the British government by the Norwegians, quite often found not to be correct. There was strong criticism of the Norwegian Legation in Stockholm, which was held in no small measure responsible for what the Norwegians considered the inadequate and negative handling of their refugees in Sweden.

Even if Günther and Lie between them had cleared up a great deal of misunderstanding, not all others concerned, particularly on the Norwegian side, adopted such a positive attitude or were so willing to let bygones be bygones.

Swedish-Norwegian affairs were handled in the next few months on the lines which had been agreed during Lie's visit. Deliveries of food to Norway and the Allied approval necessary for them were discussed at several meetings. Police training was expanded to comprise bigger units and heavier weapons than previously. The police-troops were given yet more equipment – arms, vehicles, medical and quartermaster stores – when they left Sweden for areas of north Norway from which the Germans had withdrawn. The transfer of the troops proved, however, to be slower than the Norwegians had anticipated at the time of Lie's visit. Up to March 1945 less than a thousand men had left Sweden.

The Swedish government was unwilling for the time being to commit itself to further measures. When, on 30 November, the Prime Minister sounded out his colleagues on the question of a possible Swedish volunteer corps going to Norway later, the weight of opinion was that there was no prospect of such a corps. Recruiting and training on the same lines as were followed for Finland in 1940 could involve a risk of war with Germany. On the other hand, individual volunteers who wished to travel to Norway would be treated in the same way as volunteers for Finland in 1940. Nor did the government believe there was a particularly strong Norwegian interest in a Swedish volunteer corps. Günther expressed himself forthrightly: the Norwegians would certainly be unwilling to see a big Swedish volunteer corps: at most they wanted a few volunteers to witness their own victories.

What the Norwegians primarily had in mind, however, was not Swedish volunteers, but Swedish regular soldiers. The Norwegian government viewed with alarm the continued German retreat southwards through Norway, leaving behind devastation in evacuated areas. The suggestions for Allied landings in Norway had been turned down; the Western Powers had to concentrate their available resources in other places. Only Sweden was in a position to make an effective military intervention. After a rather drawn-out discussion and with some hesitation – to ask for Swedish help was politically not so easy for the Norwegian government – Lie presented on 1 February an official written notification of a possible later Norwegian request for Swedish measures to prevent German ravages in Norway, possibly a *démarche* in Berlin with a threat of armed intervention, and thereafter actual intervention, if the Germans did not comply.

The basic aim of the Swedish government's foreign policy was still to keep Sweden out of the war. By a *démarche*, including a threat to intervene, Sweden would be committed. In addition, it was to be feared that an intervention would add to the terror and cruelties in Norway. No pledges should be given, even if – and this was not ruled out – the situation could later call for Swedish intervention. Moreover, Günther and his colleagues felt that the Norwegians did not really want any intervention by Sweden, even though Lie had given notice of a possible request for it. On 15 February it was decided to send Boheman to London to explain to Lie his government's position, though not in too negative a way. When Boheman gave Lie this message on 22 February, Lie expressed his complete understanding of it and said he had not expected any other answer.

Lie had handed to Johan Beck-Friis, Swedish Minister to the Norwegian government in London, his note about possible coming proposals for a Swedish intervention. About the same time, Per Albin Hansson in Stockholm had received from the Norwegian Minister of Defence, Oscar Torp, who was visiting Sweden, a request which Lie had presaged earlier, that about twenty military depots of different sizes should be established along the Swedish frontier with Norway. Equipment for the Norwegian Home Forces would be kept in them; some of it would be moved to Norway now; but it would primarily be available in the event of a German collapse. Small units should also be stationed there, normally of twenty, in exceptional cases of a hundred, men who would maintain contacts with the Home Forces and would later cross the frontier to support them.

Acceptance of this Norwegian request would imply *de facto* approval of Norwegian operations from Swedish bases against German troops in Norway – an indisputably un-neutral procedure. Apart from the fact that such operations could lead to German counter-measures against Sweden, it was to be feared they would inspire a harder German line in Norway and thereby endanger a peaceful termination of the occupation. Since Sweden was exerting herself to facilitate such a peaceful termination, measures counteracting this aim should obviously be avoided. Hansson delayed his reply but, after Norwegian promptings, sent a message on 10 March, half accepting and half refusing the request; weapons could be brought from England in transit to the liberated areas of Norway but, when they arrived in Sweden, should be put under Swedish control; the government had not yet decided its final position on the depots, but, in preparation for further action, the Norwegian authorities should discuss their establishment, their supervision, and anything else with the Swedish Defence Staff.

Immediately thereafter Stockholm received information that the British government fully approved its general policies so far. At Yalta early in February, Churchill, Roosevelt, Stalin, and their senior assistants had said nothing detrimental to Sweden and no suspicions were noted on the part of the Soviet Union. That much Eden had told Boheman in London by mid-March. Eden had further stated 'that, so far as Britain is concerned, no Swedish intervention in the war is either expected or desired, whether in Norway or anywhere else'. Nor did any demands for Swedish intervention, in Norway or elsewhere, come from Washington or Moscow. A military move by Sweden against Germany was clearly as little expected there as in London.

In 1941 Sweden's neutrality was regarded by Germany with dislike, to some extent with bitterness. In Germany's New Europe there was no place for a country on the sidelines, and therefore Sweden should lend a hand in the struggle against the Soviet Union, especially since in fact only small services were required from her. At least, her government and people ought to show in their utterances their appreciation of Germany's battle for civilization and culture.

In 1943 Sweden's neutrality was rated far higher in Berlin than two years previously. Deliveries essential to the German war economy from a source of production shielded from the war; resistance, more or less successful, to Allied pressure to cut down the deliveries; facilities for transit, and other traffic through Sweden — these were services below German expectations in 1941. But for a Germany so much harder pressed, their value had increased considerably in both a material and a political sense.

In 1945 even these services were withdrawn. Sweden's neutrality now clearly inclined to the Allied side. Yet, for all that, the value of this neutrality to Germany was to some extent greater than the more German-oriented variety practised during the earlier years of the war. Swedish intervention on the Allied side would hasten the final military catastrophe, which Hitler did his utmost to avoid seeing or, at all events, tried to postpone in the expectation of deliverance through some reversal in the fortunes of war. Accordingly, Sweden should be kept on the path of neutrality, if necessary by suitable concessions and blandishments. Hitler himself in the autumn of 1944 had ordered compliance with Swedish interventions in Norway's interest and, at New Year 1945, had spoken of Sweden in not unfriendly terms, although he had criticized the Swedish press. According to Ribbentrop's assurances in February, Hitler had a friendly feeling for Sweden and looked up to the King of Sweden as to no one else.

For Hitler, Sweden was of value as being a neighbouring country at peace. For those circles inside Germany which wanted to make contact with the opposite side to reach some agreement before Germany was completely crushed, Sweden was of even greater value as a remaining window to the outside world. In the final months of the war, the foremost and most powerful man among those seeking a compromise peace was Himmler, who in this respect was now continuing on the same path as the resistance movement had trodden earlier. In the reporting of the Swedish Legation in Berlin Himmler was again and again described as a person favourably inclined to Sweden and Swedish interests. Behind his affability was discerned his hope of Swedish co-operation in some form for an agreement with the Western Powers. During February and March 1945, thanks to Himmler's collaboration, a big Swedish relief expedition, formally under the control of the Red Cross, but in reality under that of the Swedish state, could be sent to Germany to collect in a big assembly camp near Hamburg Norwegian and Danish internees, with the aim of transferring them later to Sweden. An invaluable go-between in contacts with Himmler was his Finnish masseur Felix Kersten, with whom Günther often talked in the winter and spring of 1945 to smooth the way for various Swedish demands.

As the military situation early in 1945 moved towards a final catastrophe for Germany, the time and scope dwindled for any German initiative for some kind of agreement with the Western Powers. On several occasions Himmler let it be known to the head of the Swedish Red Cross expedition, Count Folke Bernadotte, King Gustaf's nephew, that he was reluctant to act against Hitler's wishes. But, at the beginning of April, he asked Bernadotte through his trusted favourite, Walter Schellenberg, to be ready to go to Eisenhower to serve as intermediary in discussions about a German surrender on the Western Front 'if the situation concerning Hitler changed – a possibility that could materialize in the near future'. If Hitler was removed and Himmler became Führer – and in Stockholm both eventualities were considered likely – a German offer of surrender to the Western Powers could thus be expected.

The feelers for a separate peace which Ribbentrop was simultaneously holding out to the Western Powers were considered by the Swedish Foreign Ministry to have no prospect of success. So it refused to be implicated in them. But an offer to surrender was something different from a peace feeler. Himmler was willing and able to provide invaluable assistance in questions of great importance to Sweden, and Bernadotte, in view of his position (and his earlier involvement in the exchange of prisoners-of-war), was a suitable go-between. The chance of taking part in subsequent peace moves should not readily be turned down, the more so as Sweden could possibly facilitate a German capitulation in Norway and Denmark. If the German occupation of Sweden's neighbours could be ended through Himmler, the risk of pillage and disorder would be reduced, even if it was not entirely removed. At the same time, a military intervention by Sweden would be rendered superfluous. Conditions on the spot, according to information coming in from Oslo and Copenhagen, were not unpropitious.

Meanwhile Stockholm was receiving requests from the Danish and Norwegian governments for preparations to be made for armed Swedish intervention in their countries. The Swedish government, however, for the same reasons as earlier in the year, was not inclined to adopt an interventionist policy. In his answer to the Danes on 14 April, Hansson shied away from committing his country to hypothetical situations and pointed out that it was the endeavour of the Swedish government to keep Sweden out of the war. The Norwegians received a harsher answer, as they had in a note of 12 April rather pretentiously requested preparations for a later intervention by the Swedish army. The note emphatically stated that only an early and full Swedish mobilization could make it clear to the Germans in Norway that their situation after Germany's collapse would be untenable. Lie had also said that he intended to communicate the contents of the note to Britain, the United States, and the Soviet Union on the same day. Stockholm could well have feared that Lie's aim was Allied pressure on Sweden to accept the Norwegians' demands. The Swedish government therefore answered at once to avoid the possibility of Allied *démarches*. On 13 April, Boheman commented sharply on the Norwegian note to Norway's Minister in Stockholm, August Esmarch. The course of action it envisaged was seen as 'very unwise', since a Swedish mobilization with the threat of intervention would hinder rather than facilitate a quiet ending of the occupation of Norway. That the Norwegians had communicated their request to their chief allies before obtaining the reaction of the Swedish government was 'not exactly pleasant'. But since this had happened, it was Sweden's opinion that the Allied Ministers in Stockholm should also be presented with the Swedish view.

The Swedish government's written answer on 16 April was somewhat milder, culminating in an assurance that, as heretofore, it was following developments in Norway with close attention, but was obliged to take the view that Sweden playing a waiting game was also in Norway's interest; it would be unwise to take measures which could cause the Germans to fear a Swedish attack. It was added orally that, according to well-informed circles in Norway, the *Wehrmacht* could be expected to lay down its arms, while Reich Commissar Terboven, the SS, and others would continue to resist even after Germany had disintegrated. They would exploit every attack or threat to weld all Germans in Norway together, and the Norwegians should not encourage from London rash behaviour which could have this effect. The Swedish government thus let the Norwegian government know that it considered itself to be the better judge of the situation in Norway.

On 16 April the Soviet armies launched a big attack across the Oder. A week later they had surrounded Berlin. On 22 April, Hitler decided to stay in his beleaguered capital rather than move to mountainous Bavaria, while communications were still open, and direct the fight from there. This decision gave Himmler the impression that now at last he had the opportunity of trying to reach an agreement with the Western Powers. On the night of 23—24 April, he met Bernadotte in Lübeck. He asked him to pass to the Swedish government a request to forward to the Western Allies a message that he was willing to surrender on the Western front. Bernadotte expressed his readiness to do this, if Himmler would also include Norway and Denmark in the surrender — a condition which originated in briefings received by him in Stockholm. Himmler immediately replied that he agreed to these terms and that he was willing to allow American, British, or Swedish troops to occupy Denmark and Norway, whereupon the German troops would lay down their arms.

The Swedes immediately forwarded Himmler's message to the Ministers of the Western Powers in Stockholm. Three days later Bernadotte handed over their reply to Schellenberg in Odense: the Western Powers refused to agree to anything except a total surrender on all fronts to the three Great Powers simultaneously. In his expectation of splitting Germany's opponents Himmler had completely miscalculated.

All the same, the Swedish government was inevitably anxious to continue to exploit both the good connections with Himmler, which Bernadotte had established, and Himmler's obvious inclination to come to terms over Norway and Denmark. When Bernadotte returned with the Western Powers' reply, he had instructions to advise Schellenberg to propose to Himmler that he should follow his original plan of surrendering both on the Western front and in Denmark and Norway, and to persuade him to carry through at least the latter part. This advice, however, must be presented as purely private; the Swedish government must not be suspected of taking part in an attempt to split the Western Powers from the Soviet Union. Bernadotte should also express as his personal opinion that, if the Germans surrendered in Norway, their troops would be allowed to enter Sweden to be interned. In fact Bernadotte succeeded in persuading Schellenberg, who in turn succeeded in persuading Himmler, to consider the Swedish offer about the troops. On 28 April, however, news of Himmler's message to Eisenhower had become generally known throughout the world. Himmler had then become disappointed and alarmed over the difficulties which the news of his contacts with the West through Sweden could cause him. Nevertheless, he allowed Schellenberg to start discussions at the Swedish Legation in Copenhagen on the internment in Sweden of the German troops in Norway. The German troops in Denmark he wanted to deal with later. The Chief of the Political Department of the Swedish Foreign Ministry, Eric von Post, was delegated to represent the Swedish government. (Bernadotte had acted only as a private person.) In the afternoon of 30 April agreement in principle was reached between von Post and Schellenberg on a settlement. German military and other personnel in Norway could be interned in Sweden for subsequent transfer to Germany (not to be handed over to a particular Allied Power). In return for this, the German occupation of Norway would be ended in the best way possible. The negotiators then left to obtain the necessary instructions from their principals, the Swedish government and Himmler.

At the same time, however, the basic prerequisites of such a settlement disappeared. Information about Himmler's offer to surrender had reached Hitler in his bunker in Berlin. Before his own disappearance from the scene, he chose Grand-Admiral Dönitz as his successor and ignored Himmler. After Hitler's suicide, Dönitz on 1 May assumed the political and military leadership of Germany; his attitude to the question of German troops in Norway and Denmark was unknown in Stockholm.

The negotiations with Himmler and Schellenberg must have sustained the Swedish government in its view that the German occupation of Denmark and Norway could be brought to an end without armed Swedish intervention. In consequence the government also maintained its restrictive line towards any preparations to intervene. To be sure, it at once agreed, on 30 April, to a proposal from the Western Powers for Staff discussions about operations against the German troops in Norway, in case they decided to continue their resistance. But the Western Powers let it be known that they neither asked for, nor expected, any operations by Swedish troops on their own, either now or at any time. Hansson in fact warned the Germans about Swedish intervention, but characteristically enough it was a private warning without the Danes and Norwegians being told and without any significant strengthening of the armed forces: he obviously wanted to avoid any sort of challenge.

Reports of Dönitz's accession late in the evening of 1 May produced no change in Sweden's foreign policy. The next day a somewhat ambiguous reply was sent to a fresh Norwegian representation of 24 April on the necessity of Sweden preparing for a military intervention in Norway. On the evening of 4 May, Schellenberg announced through the Swedish Minister in Copenhagen that he had full powers in writing

219

from Dönitz to negotiate with the Swedish government and conclude an agreement for the termination of the German occupation of Norway. He would be coming to Stockholm the next day.

Schellenberg had full authority to negotiate with the Swedish government. But the Swedes, who had now been in touch with him for quite a time over the German surrender in Norway, had no actual legal powers to negotiate. They had to try to get them post-haste from the Western Powers, now that definite negotiations were to begin. Günther thus immediately informed the Ministers of the Western Powers in Stockholm of Schellenberg's impending arrival. Schellenberg, Günther announced, was bringing with him full powers from Dönitz 'to arrange for surrender to the Swedes of the German troops in Norway', a move which most probably would involve their internment in Sweden until the Allies could take them over. The Swedish government would be grateful for 'most immediate' information on the view of Washington and London. The Soviet authorities had not yet been informed, for the Western Allies were not thought to be bringing the Soviet Union into the proposed Staff talks. If, however, they felt Moscow should be informed at this stage, then the Swedish government particularly wished to take the first opportunity of doing so. Günther asked for complete secrecy; the Norwegian Minister in Stockholm, however, would be informed forthwith.

When Schellenberg came to Stockholm on 5 May, the government consequently limited itself to passing on his message to the Ministers of the Western Powers and to proposing that a delegation from Eisenhower should immediately be sent to Stockholm for negotiations on the German surrender in Norway. The government for its part was prepared to agree to any proposals from Eisenhower for the temporary internment in Sweden of the German troops in Norway. The Western Ministers were also informed of Schellenberg's wish to negotiate with Eisenhower for a general surrender as well.

Not only Schellenberg's news but also developments in Denmark must have increased to near certainty Stockholm's belief that the occupation of Norway would end peacefully. The previous day, 4 May, the German troops in the Netherlands, north Germany, and Denmark had surrendered to Field-Marshal Montgomery. News of this had become known in Copenhagen the same evening and, although the capitulation was not to come into force until the next day, a Danish government had been formed (preparations for which had long ago been completed) and had immediately started work. Overnight the Danish police-troops had been transported to Hälsingborg, whence they began to be shipped over to Denmark the following morning, 5 May.

Besides sending Schellenberg to Stockholm, Dönitz had also sent a negotiator direct to Eisenhower, who refused to discuss anything except a general German surrender on all fronts. In the afternoon of 5 May, a reply came from Churchill to Günther's message to Mallet about Schellenberg's arrival. In it Churchill briefly but firmly advised the Swedish government not to meddle in Eisenhower's doings by itself initiating negotiations with Schellenberg. Churchill had his way. A message from Herschel Johnson that his government had ordered Eisenhower to send representatives to Stockholm, and also expressing the view that Moscow should be informed of Schellenberg's mission, was never followed up beyond Boheman giving this information to the Soviet Charge d'Affaires in the evening of 5 May. That evening a meeting also was arranged at the Swedish-Norwegian frontier between representatives of the German Legation in Stockholm and the German Commander in Norway, with the aim of impressing on the latter that his surrender was unavoidable. But with this meeting all moves by Sweden in connection with Schellenberg's mission ended.

The capitulation of the German troops in Norway was arranged instead through negotiations in Eisenhower's Headquarters at Reims where, during the night of 6–7 May, Dönitz's representatives signed the surrender of Germany on all fronts, to come into effect on the night of 8–9 May. The Norwegian police-troops now entered Norway, and the Norwegian military depots along the frontier, whose number had been increased in recent weeks, were used to the full. The different measures taken by Sweden to facilitate a rapid and smooth end to the occupation of Norway came to a close here; the question of Swedish co-operation in interning the occupation troops was never raised.

In the closing weeks of the war Sweden's foreign policy was trying to navigate in previously uncharted waters. Promises had been given to the Western Allies of talks on operations against the German forces in Norway, while the prospect of interning these same forces in Sweden had been held out to the Germans. At the same time, there was concern to avoid worsening relations with the Soviet Union through one manoeuvre or the other. The final balancing-act was also performed successfully. At the end of it Sweden had not been drawn into the war, her relations with the victorious Powers were unchanged, and she had rendered not entirely unimportant services to Denmark and Norway: police-troops, despatch of equipment, repeated appeals to the Germans to end their occupation peaceably when the time came. More could not reasonably be expected by the Swedish government. It must

221

*The Swedish-Norwegian Frontier is opened by a German Customs officer in May 1945*

have felt some relief that it had avoided discharging an undertaking to intern several hundred thousand Germans in Sweden. The Swedes' offer to do this had served a purpose by providing, as long as it was open, some guarantee that the Germans in Norway and Denmark would not resort to desperate and destructive measures, which could force the Swedes to intervene. Because, even if in the interests both of Sweden's present situation and of subsequent relations with her neighbours the Swedish government wanted to avoid such intervention, it was certainly ready to order it in the event of pillage and chaos in Norway and Denmark.

# 8   Retrospect

In the spring of 1939 the Foreign Ministry's document quoted as an opening to the events described in this book, laid down the guiding principles for Sweden's policy of neutrality in the approaching conflict between the Great Powers. It was expected that in the new World War respect for international law would be slight or non-existent, and that therefore Sweden's neutrality would be subjected to stronger pressure than in 1914–18. The chances of Sweden remaining outside yet another Great War were summed up as follows.

The prospects for the maintenance of neutrality must be considered to lie in the fact that it will be to the interest of both coalitions involved in the conflict that Sweden should not be dragged into the war; in the fact that the Swedish military establishment is of a size sufficient to command respect; and, finally, in so strong an internal unity in Sweden that any foreign interference is ruled out.

In the spring of 1945 the Great War in Europe was over. During the previous six years the map of Europe had been altered many times. In 1939 twenty or so European states had chosen to stay out of the war. But nearly all had gradually been dragged into it. Among the few remaining outside it was Sweden.

The 1939 forecasts had understated the difficulties confronting a policy of neutrality in a war between the Great Powers. They had mistakenly assumed that the Soviet Union would join in the fight immediately as the Western Powers' ally against Germany. They had grossly underestimated the Great Powers' strategic interests in the North — Finland, Norway, and Denmark were brought into the war and prevented from following, in company with Sweden, a policy of Nordic neutrality.

Nevertheless, the forecasts turned out to be substantially correct. In

1939–45, as previously in 1914–18, Sweden was able to keep herself out of a major war extremely close to, and indeed encircling, her frontiers. But to what extent had the basic assumptions of the pre-war calculations – the Great Powers' interest in not having Sweden dragged into the war, the respect felt for Sweden's military strength, and Sweden's internal cohesion – contributed to this outcome, and what had been the relative significance of each?

The national government's course during the war years and its relationship to parties, *Riksdag*, the public, and the press still await detailed research. It is, however, obvious that all its members, in spite of serious differences and difficulties, were determined to preserve the national unity which had been established in December 1939. The value of such unity had been demonstrated in the recent crisis over the Finnish question. It was enhanced by the misfortunes which fell upon neighbouring countries in subsequent months. The danger that internal disunity could lead to surrender to strong German pressure was manifest. In the background were warning memories of the 1914–18 war years, when Germans and British were able to exploit for their own advantage the occasionally open and bitter dissension in Sweden's internal politics.

But even though in 1939–45 internal harmony existed in Sweden and discouraged outside interference, this alone would not have prevented a Great Power from attacking her, if that Great Power really wished to do so. Then what of the assumption that Sweden's armed forces would restrain a possible attack?

Cautious judgements are necessary here. No investigation of the Great Powers' appreciation of the strength of the Swedish armed forces and their effectiveness has yet been made. Sweden's prospects of holding out against a German attack – and this in fact was the crucial question – were not rated high in either Berlin or London: a few weeks in the first year of the war, somewhat longer subsequently. But all the same, even weeks and months can have been of considerable importance in Hitler's calculations; his time and resources were often limited. It is also obvious that the Swedish government, and particularly Günther, attached great weight to increasing, at appropriate times, the armed forces' readiness as a restraint to German desire to take action. However, the government, and Günther in particular, had no illusions about the weight of Sweden's military strength against a Great Power.

Cohesion and preparedness were indispensable elements in the efforts to keep Sweden out of the war. If one or other had been lacking, the prospects for these efforts would have sunk to zero. Yet the essential preconditions of ultimate success lay beyond Sweden's frontiers – with the belligerent Great Powers. Their interests, their demands on Sweden, and their estimates of the Swedish government's attitude to these interests and demands were decisive for the chances of Sweden's policies.

The strategic value of Sweden for the Great Powers was manifestly less than that of the neighbouring countries, Finland, Norway, and Denmark, all of which were drawn into the war. But was this due – as forecast in the Foreign Ministry's statement of principles in spring 1939 – to a common interest in leaving Sweden outside the war? Or is some uniform pattern otherwise to be found in their attitude to Sweden?

Hitler and his colleagues – so far as can be ascertained – assigned only slight importance to Sweden as a military and political factor in their struggle for the domination of Europe and the world. Her position and her military resources had only secondary importance for German strategy, at any rate so long as Germany's opponents left Sweden in peace. For Germany, Sweden was first a supplier of products such as iron-ore and ball-bearings, important or indispensable for her economy in wartime and, above all, for her manufacture of war materials. Even after the capture of the Lorraine mines in 1940 Swedish iron-ore could have been replaced only at the price of time-consuming and exceptionally costly modifications to German methods of steel production. The value Germany put on Swedish neutrality fluctuated with the fortunes of war. But so long as Sweden maintained normal exports to Germany and did not admit the forces of Germany's opponents into her territory or otherwise run their errands, Germany's main interests in Sweden were met.

The granting of transit facilities, over-flying rights, escorts, and mine-fields were more or less valuable services which facilitated Germany's conduct of the war. But for the Germans they were less important than deliveries of goods and the knowledge that their opponents could not avail themselves of Swedish territory. They were interpreted in Berlin pretty much as the self-evident consequences of Germany's enormous military strength in the North. Hitler's demands must be considered as comparatively modest, this overwhelming German strength considered. When German power declined, he allowed them to fade away without making any real difficulties for Sweden.

The political services rendered by Sweden were even more secondary. Here Hitler's government, and certainly most Germans, expected the Swedish government and public to be well disposed towards Germany's

225

New Order in Europe and her crusade against the Soviet Union. Memories of Sweden's sympathy for Germany during the First World War, the anticipation of Sweden's gratitude for Germany's decision to eliminate the communist menace once and for all, and the conviction that ties of common Northern stock would bring lasting support might have been behind German expectations, expectations which miscarried. Yet disappointment and bitterness at Sweden's failure to understand or appreciate Germany's efforts were not decisive for her Swedish policy. Once in 1940 the Germans had pressed the Swedish government to adopt a press policy which from the German point of view would show a reasonable respect for the state of affairs outside its own frontiers, no major demands were pushed hard.

But what can be established afterwards is not always what could be known for certain as events took their course. Hitler as a fallen dictator appears less formidable than the brutal and unscrupulous tyrant who was the Swedish government's nearest neighbour throughout the war. In dealing with him great caution was called for. Where the limits to concessions should be drawn was fiercely argued and certainly will continue to be argued. It can now be said that, on a number of occasions, for example when German proposals for transit facilities were rejected in May 1940 and July–August 1941, the Swedes took calculated risks. The same risks could presumably have been taken at other times as well: thus the transit of the Engelbrecht Division at midsummer 1941 could probably have been refused; compliance with the German navy's demands could have been kept within narrower limits than then permitted; the transit traffic could have been cut down, even ended, earlier than in fact happened. But at the time each of these decisions was actually taken, Sweden's situation appeared more precarious than in the light of what is now known. For most of the war Sweden was enclosed within Germany's sphere of power, with slight military strength of her own and no prospect of rapid and effective help from outside. Sweden's livelihood and economy were entirely dependent on the exchange of goods with Germany. Not to comply until after an ultimatum was to play with fire. Always to delay consent as long as possible and thereby fail to secure some reciprocal move or, at least, some gratitude in return was a poor policy. Certainly a concession could set Sweden on the downward path and put her in a worse negotiating position when faced with new German demands. But the government, foremost Hansson and Günther, had to deal with each case as it arose, in circumstances where fundamental values were irretrievably at stake and where merely to extricate oneself from a difficult situation and thereby gain time could represent a significant achievement. 'One does not struggle to keep out of war through a rigidity which provokes the conflict one wants to avoid', Per Albin Hansson said on the last day of the war, 8 May 1945, in justification of his government's wartime policy.

The Swedish government can hardly be blamed for assuming towards Hitler in certain cases an attitude which involved giving way, rather than taking in its opinion unwarranted risks for Sweden's continued existence as a free and independent state. It can perhaps be said that Swedish concessions contributed to what at one time seemed to be Germany's final victory, and a German New Order in Europe – by no means an implausible prospect in the period from the summer of 1940 to the autumn of 1942 – and that these concessions were thus in conflict with Sweden's long-term interests. But this contribution was in fact slight and of little consequence.

All in all Sweden, when her exceptionally exposed and weak position *vis-à-vis* Germany is taken into account, got off lightly. Thorough research into Germany's policy is necessary before it can be established to what extent this was due to long-term considerations on Germany's part, to German reverses in situations dangerous to Sweden, or to skilful Swedish tactics. Hitler's trust in the repeated Swedish assurances that Sweden would oppose by force of arms any Allied encroachment on Swedish soil should not be exaggerated. He was not the sort of man ever to allow such solemn assurances – from others as little as from himself – to limit his freedom of action. At the most critical periods for a German attack on Sweden, spring 1940 and winter 1942, the military shortcomings of the Allied expedition to Norway in the one case and the lack of available German troops in the other certainly carried greater weight than Swedish diplomacy or the preparedness of Sweden's forces. On the other hand, the significance of Sweden's foreign policy for the maintenance of peaceful and tolerable relations with Germany should not be underestimated.

For the Western Powers also Sweden was primarily of interest in the context of their war trade policy, but in an opposite sense. For Germany, Sweden was a supplier of valuable goods, for the Western Powers she was a correspondingly serious gap in their blockade. Their efforts to close this gap became more ruthless the longer the war lasted. When they were successfully concluded around the end of 1944, Sweden was *de facto* involved in the Western Powers' war on Germany to a greater extent than she had ever co-operated in Germany's war on her opponents. An early victory for the West was very much a Swedish

227

interest, and at this stage the Swedish government was dealing with those who not only wielded power for the moment, but who also would wield it in the rapidly approaching peace.

Strategically Sweden was not of greater importance to the Western Powers than to Germany. Plans to occupy the ore-fields in the north during the first winter of the war were in the first place aimed at Germany's ore imports. -Thoughts of opening a second front against Germany in the North, to reduce the pressure on France, were quite secondary in prevailing circumstances. For the rest, all these proposals were never properly developed. Later in the war Churchill proposed a landing in Norway, but the determined opposition of his military advisers shows how unrealistic they found plans for Allied operations in a Scandinavia occupied, or dominated, by Germany. The backdoor to Europe was to be opened not from the North, but from the South, in Greece, Yugoslavia, and Italy.

The Soviet Union's strategic interest in Sweden, particularly in the early years of the war, was to prevent her inclusion in Hitler's empire or her adherence to the German side in the war in the East. When it was judged that the risk of this had passed, and when the fortunes of war turned, Sweden became a much less important factor in Moscow's eyes. The Soviet Union in general showed much less eagerness than Britain or the United States for Swedish measures and steps against Germany. What it did ask, with an increasing display of displeasure, was that Sweden should not go on providing assistance to Germany. Even if this assistance was not unreasonable when Germany was militarily dominant, it could at a later date not be considered as corresponding to developments in the war. The Soviet Union's main requirement was that Sweden should acknowledge that Finland came within its sphere of interest. It showed appreciation when Sweden in 1940 and 1944 smoothed the way for the conclusion of the peace it sought with Finland.

As has been seen, the policies of the Great Powers towards Sweden during the war years had widely different points of departure. Yet it is possible to discern a similar pattern. For all of them Sweden had only a secondary strategic interest; none looked on the occupation of Sweden or her participation in the war as essential to victory. They were all content, even though they sometimes complained, with Sweden's declared aim of not being drawn into the war and of not joining any of the contestants. What they were all primarily concerned with — albeit from completely opposed standpoints — was Sweden's trade with, and concessions to, Germany. And this concern led them all to act in the same way. They demanded that Sweden should pay regard less to the rules of neutrality than to the facts of power. The rules of neutrality were judged and applied by them in accordance with the fluctuations of their political fortunes. When the tide of war was running against them, they demanded respect for the obligations of neutrality. When they were winning, they demanded respect for their power. But they all acknowledged *de facto* – they obviously could not do so expressly – that Sweden, in choosing to pay heed to one side or the other, was obliged to yield to the stronger at any given time. Swedish departures from the rules of neutrality were measured by the benefits, or the disadvantages, which any such departure involved for the interests of the Great Powers concerned. Swedish remonstrances concerning their own violations of Sweden's neutrality were answered by denials or rejections, acknowledgements or complaints, in accordance with whatever policy they were following at the time.

In the Great Powers' scheme of things – and it is worth underlining this again – respect for neutrality and the rules of neutrality carried far less weight than regard for their interests. A small country, which wished to live through a World War with its freedom and independence intact, was obliged to adopt in full measure a corresponding scale of values.

# Notes on sources and literature

The chapters are all mainly built upon the files in the archives of the Swedish Foreign Ministry. Detailed references are to be found in the original Swedish version of this work.

As no Cabinet Minutes were made, diaries and notes of various members of the government have often been drawn upon.

Prime Minister Per Albin Hansson's papers are in the main kept in Arbetarrörelsens arkiv. His diary entries for the years 1940–43 are short but very much to the point. In the Foreign Ministry Archives there is a collection of Hansson papers, containing some documents of interest about Swedish-Danish and Swedish-Norwegian discussions during the final war years.

The diaries of the Minister of Justice, K. G. Westman, cover the years April 1939–February 1943; owing to illness Westman left the government later in 1943. They are very well written and contain some shrewd observations on Swedish politics and politicians. Westman's papers are to be found in Uppsala Universitets Bibliotek.

The diaries of the Minister of Education, Gösta Bagge, are the most detailed, but have a certain bias. Bagge was leader of the Conservative party, the second largest party, but felt that he had not the corresponding position and influence in the government. The diaries contain much information about government discussions on foreign policy. Bagge's papers are kept in Riksarkivet.

The Minister for Commerce, from 1941 Minister without Portfolio, Frithiof Domö, often wrote notes of government discussions on the spot. They are useful, especially as they try to fix what really had been decided. Domö's papers are in Riksarkivet.

The Minister without Portfolio Nils Quensel has left some notes about government discussions during the later war years.

Notes from sessions of the Parliamentary Foreign Policy Committee

230

are kept in the Foreign Ministry. The notes were taken by the secretary of the committee, usually the Secretary-General in the Foreign Ministry. They were written for his and the Ministry's guidance, and are not to be compared with stenographic verbatim protocols.

The sources mentioned above are now almost all open to researchers upon request.

Some important sources are also printed.

In the years after the war the Swedish Foreign Ministry published some selections of documents, mainly concerning the events of 1940: *Förspelet till det tyska angreppet på Danmark och Norge den 9 april 1940; Transiteringsfrågor och därmed sammanhängande spörsmål april–juni 1940; Transiteringsfrågan juni–december 1940; Frågor i samband med norska regeringens vistelse utanför Norge 1940–1943*, Sthlm, Norstedts, 1947. The Foreign Minister's reports to the Parliamentary Foreign Policy Committee about Sweden's relations with Denmark and Norway are printed in *Sveriges förhållande till Danmark och Norge under krigsåren*, Sthlm, Norstedts, 1945. Special disputed questions are dealt with in some minor white papers: *Förbindelserna mellan chefen för lantförsvarets kommandoexpedition och tyske militärattachén i Stockholm 1939–1945; 1945 års svenska hjälpexpedition till Tyskland, Förspel och förhandlingar; Förhandlingarna 1945 om svensk intervention i Norge och Danmark*, Sthlm, Norstedts, 1946, 1956, 1957.

Speeches of the Prime Minister and the Foreign Minister during the war years are collected in Per Albin Hansson, *Svensk hållning och handling*, Sthlm, Tiden, 1945, and Christian Günther, *Tal i en tung tid*, Sthlm, Bonniers, 1945. Selected protocols from *Riksdag* debates, official communiqués, and ministerial speeches are printed in *Svensk utrikespolitik under det andra världskriget*, Sthlm, KF:s Bokförlag, 1946.

Essential information about Swedish foreign policy is also to be found in document collections of other countries. Especially should be mentioned *Norges forhold til Sverige under krigen 1940–1945*, I–III, Oslo, Gyldendal Norsk Forlag, 1947–50; *Akten zur deutschen auswärtigen Politik 1918–1945*, Series D VII–XII, E I–III, Kriegstagebuch des Oberkommandos der Wehrmacht (Wehrmachtführungsstab) 1940–1945, I–IV, Nachtrag zu IV/I, Frankfurt am Main, 1961–69; *Lagevorträge des Oberbefehlshabers der Kriegsmarine vor Hitler 1939–1945*, München, 1972; *Foreign Relations of the United States, 1939–1945*, Washington.

The most important memoirs about Swedish foreign policy during

231

the war years ar Erik Boheman, *Pa vakt. Kabinettssekreterare under andra världskriget,* Sthlm, Norstedts, 1964, and Gunnar Hägglöf, *Möte med Europa. Paris-London-Moskva-Genève-Berlin 1926–1940,* and *Samtida vittne 1940–1945,* Sthlm, Norstedts 1971, 1972. Valuable also are memoirs of some government ministers: Ernst Wigforss, *Minnen,* III, Sthlm, Tiden, 1954; Gustaf Andersson, *Från bondetåget till samlingsregeringen,* Sthlm, Bonniers, 1955; Axel Gjöres, *Vreda vindar,* Sthlm, Norstedts, 1967; Nils Quensel, *Minnesbilder,* Sthlm, Norstedts, 1973; Tage Erlander, *1940–1949,* Sthlm, Tiden, 1973; Bertil Ohlin, *Memoarer* I–II, Sthlm, Bonniers 1972, 1975.

Also Ivar Anderson, *Från det nära förflutna,* Sthlm, Norstedts, 1969; Vilhelm Assarsson, *I skuggan av Stalin,* Sthlm, Bonniers, 1963; Ragnar Casparsson, *Brinnande horisonter,* Sthlm, Tiden, 1963; Carl August Ehrensvärd, *I rikets tjänst,* Sthlm, Norstedts, 1965. Also some memoirs of Finnish principal actors should be mentioned: Gustaf Mannerheim, *Minnen,* II, Sthlm, Norstedts, 1952; J. K. Paasikivi, *Minnen,* II, Bonniers 1959; Georg Gripenberg, *London-Vatikanen-Stockholm, En beskickningschefs minnen,* II, Sthlm, Natur och Kultur, 1960; Edwin Linkomies, *I mitt lands tjänst. Minnen från statsministertiden 1943–1944,* Sthlm, Rabén & Sjögren, 1974; Väinö Tanner, *Finlands väg 1939–1940,* Sthlm, Bonniers, 1950; *Vägen till fred 1943–1944,* Sthlm, KF:s Bokförlag, 1952.

Only a few case studies about Swedish foreign policy during the Second World War have been published. To be mentioned are Krister Wahlbäck, *Finlandsfrågan i svensk politik 1937–1940,* Sthlm, Norstedts, 1964; Per G. Andreen, *De mörka åren. Perspektiv på svensk neutralitetspolitik våren 1940 – nyåret 1942,* Sthlm, Norstedts, 1971; Leif Björkman, *Sverige inför Operation Barbarossa. Svensk neutralitetspolitik 1940–1941,* Sthlm, Allmänna Förlaget, 1971; Åke Uhlin, *Februarikrisen 1942. Svensk säkerhetspolitik och militär planering 1941–1942,* Sthlm, Allmänna Förlaget, 1972; Rune Karlsson, *Så stoppades tysktågen. Den tyska transiteringstrafiken i svensk politik 1942–1943,* Sthlm, Allmänna Förlaget, 1974; and Ulf Torell, *Hjälp till Danmark. Militära och politiska förbindelser 1943–1945,* Sthlm, Allmänna Förlaget, 1973. Further, many interesting papers and reviews about war policy problems have been published in various volumes of the historical periodicals *Historisk Tidskrift* (Sthlm) and *Scandia* (Lund).

Sweden's wartime trade policy is very competently described by the then chief of the commercial department of the Foreign Ministry, Gunnar Hägglöf, in *Svensk krigshandelspolitik under andra världskriget,*

Sthlm, Norstedts, 1958. There are too some valuable works about especially important sectors of the Swedish economy during 1939—45: Ulf Olsson, *Upprustning och verkstadsindustri i Sverige under det andra världskriget;* Martin Fritz, *German Steel and Swedish Iron Ore 1939—1945;* Sven-Olof Olsson, *German Coal and Swedish Fuel 1939—1945.* (Publications of the Institute of Economic History of Gothenburg University 28, 29, 36, Kungsbacka, Elanders, 1973—75.) The export of ball-bearings to Germany is dealt with by Martin Fritz in 'Swedish Ball-bearings and the German War Economy' (the *Scandinavian Economic History Review* 1975:1). The safe-conduct shipping to and from Gothenburg is examined in a special study: Nicolaus Rockberger, *Göteborgstrafiken*, Sthlm, Allmänna Förlaget, 1973.

Sweden's wartime defence policy and military measures are to be described in a big work, edited by Militärhögskolans militärhistoriska avdelning (Department of Military History, Armed Forces Staff College). Two case studies are Erik Norberg, *Flyg i beredskap*, and Åke Holmquist, *Flottans beredskap 1938—1940,* Allmänna Förlaget 1971, 1972. Detailed information on military matters is contained in the above-mentioned works by Wahlbäck, Björkman, Uhlin, Torell, and Karlsson. Minor papers on special problems are to be found in various volumes of *Aktuellt och historiskt*, the yearly publication of the Militärhistoriska avdelningen.

Case studies of two leading Swedish newspapers are Jarl Torbacke, *Dagens Nyheter och demokratins kris 1937—1946*, Sthlm, Bonniers, 1972, and Torvald Höjer, *Svenska Dagbladet och det andra världskriget* (*Stockholm studies in History* 14), Sthlm, Almqvist & Wiksell, 1969. The legendary editor of the *Göteborgs Handels & Sjöfartstidning* is portrayed by his daughter, Ingrid Segerstedt Wiberg, *Torgny Segerstedt*, Sthlm, Bonniers, 1955, and the German view of him and his newspaper is discussed in Henrik Sandblad, *GHT och Hitlerregimen i belysning av tyska arkivdokument*, Göteborg, *G.H.T.*, 1960. Reviews of press and public opinion in certain phases of the war are given in Klas Åmark, *Makt eller moral. Svensk offentlig debatt om internationell politik och svensk utrikes- och försvarspolitik 1938—1939*, and Alf Johansson, *Finlands sak. Svensk politik och opinion under vinterkriget 1939—1940*, Sthlm, Allmänna Förlaget, 1973. German propaganda and Swedish reactions thereto are treated in Åke Thulstrup, *Med lock och pock. Tyska försök att påverka svensk opinion 1933—1945*, Sthlm, Bonniers, 1962.

It is impossible to list here foreign books of interest for wartime Swedish foreign policy. Only the most important can be mentioned here. Andreas Hillgruber, *Hitlers Strategie. Politik und Kriegführung 1940–1941*, Frankfurt am Main, Bernard & Graefe, 1965; Walther Hubatsch, *'Weserübung'. Die Deutsche Besetzung von Dänemark und Norwegen 1940*, Göttingen, Musterschmidt, 1960; Michael Salewski, *Die deutsche Seekriegsleitung 1935–1945*, I–II, Frankfurt am Main, Bernard & Graefe, 1970–75; Earl F. Ziemke, *The German Northern Theatre of Operations 1940–1945* (Department of the Army pamphlet No. 20–271), Washington, 1959; Llewellyn Woodward, *British Foreign Policy in the Second World War*, I–V, London, HMSO, 1970–76; W. N. Medlicott, *The Economic Blockade* 1–2, London, HMSO, 1952–59; J. R. N. Butler and others, *Grand Strategy* II–VI, London, HMSO, 1957–72; Tuomo Polvinen, *Finland i stormaktspolitiken 1941–1944*, Sthlm, Norstedts, 1969; Max Jakobson, *Vinterkrigets diplomati 1937–1940*, Sthlm, Norstedts, 1967; Arvi Korhonen, *Barbarossaplanen och Finland*, Sthlm, Norstedts, 1963; Peter Krosby, *Finland, Germany and the Soviet Union 1940–41, The Petsamo Dispute*, Madison, Wisc., University of Wisconsin Press, 1968; Anthony F. Upton, *Finland in crisis 1940–1941*, London, Faber and Faber, 1964; Stig Jägerskiöld, *Fältmarskalken, Gustaf Mannerheim 1939–1941*, Helsingfors, Schildts, 1975; A. S. Kan, *Vnesjnaja politika skandinavskich stran v gody vtoroj mirovoj vojny*, Moscow, Nauka, 1967; Magne Skodvin and others, *Norge og den 2. verdenskrig. Mellem nøytral og allierte* and *1940 Fra nøytral til okkupert*, Oslo, Universitetsforlaget, 1968–69); Viggo Sjøquist, *Danmarks udenrigspolitik 1933–1940*, Khvn, Gyldendal, 1966; Nils Svenningsen. *Tidsrummet 1919–1961 in Den Danske Udenrigstjeneste 1770–1970*, II, Khvn, Gyldendal, 1970.

# June 1940

**Swedish troops**

⬗ Division

⬗ Cavalry Brigade

⬗ Regiment

⬗ Battalion

1.ak 1st Army Corps

ÖN Upper Norrland's Group

J Jämtland's Group (division)

Ö Eastern Military District

G Gotland's Defence

**German troops from the Swedish Defence Staff's estimate**

■ Division

ÖN

J

2.ak

Ö

1.ak

G

# June 1941

*Swedish troops*

⊠ Division

⊠ Regiment

⊠ Battalion (7 = numbers)

2.ak 2nd Army Corps (Staff)

ÖN Upper Norrland's Military District

N Northern Military District

Ö Eastern Military District

G Gotland's Military District

S Southern Military District

*German troops from the*
*Swedish Defence Staff's estimate*

◼ Division

# March 1942

*Swedish troops*

⊠ (Division symbol)   Division

⊠ (Regiment symbol)   Regiment

⊠ (Battalion symbol)   Battalion

2.ak   2nd Army Corps (Staff)

ÖN   Upper Norrland's Military District

N   Northern Military District

Ö   Eastern Military District

*German troops from the Swedish Defence Staff's estimate*

■ (Division symbol)   Division

237

# July/August 1943

Swedish troops

XXX  Army Corps (Staff)

XX  Division

X  Infantry Brigade

Armoured Brigade

III  Regiment

II  Battalion (5 = numbers)

II    2nd Military District
III   3rd Military District
IV    4th Military District
VI    6th Military District
VII   7th Military District

German troops from the
Swedish Defence Staff's estimate

XX  Division

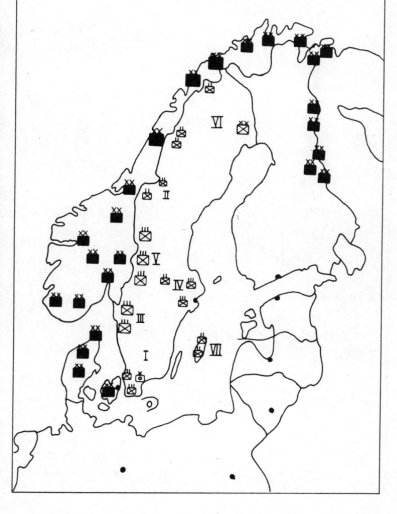

# September 1944

*Swedish troops*

⊠ Division
▭ Armoured Brigade
⊠ Regiment
⊠ Battalion
I-VII 1st-7th Military District

*German troops from the Swedish Defence Staff's estimate*

■ Division

SCALE

0   100   200   300

MILES

N

Arctic Circle

LOFOT
ISLAN

Trondheim

N
O
R
W
A
Y

Bergen

OSLO

Ka

Kristiansand

Skagerrak

North
Sea

Gothenburg

Kattegat

GT.
BRITAIN

Halsingborg

DENMARK

Malm

COPENHAGEN

Falster

G E R

240

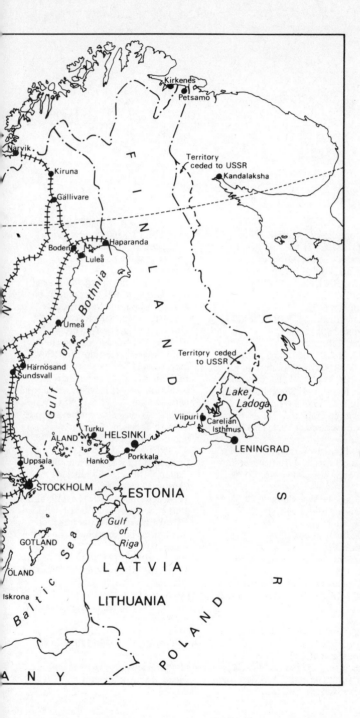

241

# Index

Kuusinen, Otto, Finnish-Soviet
politician, 23, 29, 44, 47

Ladoga, Lake, 169
Lapland, 32ff., 38, 55
Latvia, 15, 23, 70
lead, 20
League of Nations, 4, 9ff., 11, 14, 27, 35
leave traffic, of German troops through
Sweden, 96ff., 125ff.; *see also* transit
Legation: *British*: in Helsinki, 69; in
Stockholm, 104, 131, 153 (*see also*
Mallet): *Finnish*: in Moscow, 55;
in Stockholm, 41, 179; in Washing-
ton, 110, 173 (*see also* Erkko;
Gripenberg; Kivimäki; Paasikivi;
Wasastjerna): *German*: in
Stockholm, 49, 67, 70, 85, 96, 106ff.,
129, 141ff., 153ff., 187, 211, 221
(*see also* Thomsen; Wied):
*Norwegian*: in Moscow, 55; in
Stockholm, 94, 160ff., 212, 220
(*see also* Bull; Esmarch): *Soviet*:
in Stockholm, 188, 221 (*see also*
Kollontay): *Swedish*: in Berlin, 62,
65ff., 95ff., 120, 122, 127, 139, 166ff.,
186, 206 (*see also* Richert; Post):
in Copenhagen, 218ff.; in Helsinki,
51, 55, 78, 102, 105, 170, 172, 186,
194ff. (*see also* Beck-Friis;
Westman); in London, 45, 69, 131,
135, 148 (*see also* Prytz); in Moscow,
55, 103, 109, 123, 178 (*see also*
Assarsson; Söderblom); in Paris,
38, 44ff.; in Washington, 151 (*see
also* Boström): *U.S.*: in Helsinki,
172, 179; *see also* Johnson
Leningrad, 180, 183
Leopold III, King of the Belgians, 65
liaison, military: Allied, with Sweden,
219; British: with Finland, 46; with
Sweden, 45ff.: French: with Finland,
46; with Sweden, 45: German, with
Finland, 102; Swedish: with Finland,
77, 92, 102, 191; with Germany, 84,
121; with Norway, 214
Liberal Party, 25
liberation: of Denmark, 204, 210; of
Norway, 204, 210; *see under
non-Nordic countries by name*
Libya, 93
Lie, Trygve, Norwegian Foreign
Minister, 210ff., 217
Linkomies, Edwin, Finnish Prime
Minister, 176ff.

*Lionel*, 131, 140, 145, 154; *see also*
Norwegian ships; sequestration
Lithuania, 22ff., 70, 119
Lofoten Islands, 95
Lorraine, 225
Lozovskij, Salomon, Soviet Deputy
Commissar for Foreign Affairs, 34,
80
Luleå, 10, 32, 55ff., 64, 83, 125, 163,
165, 187
lumber, 203
Luxembourg, 67, 73

machinery, 19, 164
machine-tools, 205
mail, German, through Sweden, 165;
*see also* courier; transit
Mallet, Sir Victor, British Minister in
Stockholm, 145, 177; British
compromise peace, 74; German
surrender, 221; and *Norway*:
Anglo-French campaign, 45ff.;
sequestrated Norwegian ships,
123ff., 141ff.: and *Sweden*: German
transit traffic, 156; puts pressure on,
199ff.; reports on Swedish situation,
93, 108ff., 130, 207; Swedish trade,
163ff., 199ff.; and Swedish-Finnish
relations, 190ff.
Malmö, 112, 165, 205
Mannerheim, Gustaf, Marshal and
President of Finland: and Åland, 77;
halts Finnish advance, 171; peace
negotiations, 174, 191ff.; becomes
President, 90, 184, 189, 193; and
*Germany*: arms supplies, 81: and
*Sweden*: military liaison, 92
maps, German smuggling of, 165ff.
Maugras, Roger, French Minister in
Stockholm, 46ff.
mediation: for Britain, 73ff.; for
Finland, 30ff., 45ff., 73ff., 181ff.,
190ff.; for Germany, 144, 216ff.;
U.S. for Finland, 174
Mers-el-Kebir, 76
metal products, 93, 197
meteorological reports, 208
Military Attaché: German: in Helsinki,
102, 106; in Stockholm, 110;
Swedish: in Helsinki, 102; in
Moscow, 183
mines: iron, 56, 81, 124, 225; nickel,
78, 100, 128
mining, naval: British, 56, 58; German,
19, 21, 84, 110, 119, 150; Swedish,